The
KING'S
TRAITOR

The KING'S TRAITOR

Reginald Pole and the Tudors

HELEN HYDE

AMBERLEY

First published 2025

Amberley Publishing
The Hill, Stroud
Gloucestershire, GL5 4EP

www.amberley-books.com

The right of Helen Hyde to be identified as the Author of this work has been asserted in accordance with the Copyright, Designs and Patents Act 1988.

ISBN 978 1 3981 1148 6 (hardback)
ISBN 978 1 3981 1149 3 (ebook)

British Library Cataloguing in Publication Data.
A catalogue record for this book is available from the British Library.

1 2 3 4 5 6 7 8 9 10

Typesetting by SJmagic DESIGN SERVICES, India.
Printed in the UK.

Appointed GPSR EU Representative:
Easy Access System Europe Oü, 16879218
Address: Mustamäe tee 50, 10621,
Tallinn, Estonia
Contact Details: gpsr.requests@easproject.com,
+358 40 500 3575

CONTENTS

Preface   7

Acknowledgements   9

Family Tree   11

1 The Pole Family and Early Family Fortunes   13

2 The King's Cousin and the King's Scholar   24

3 The King's Great Matter: Reginald Pole and the Divorce   32

4 Fireworks from Rome: Cardinal Pole and the
Events of 1532–37   43

5 'Pity it is…'   59

6 Danger for Pole from within the Church   71

7 Danger from Henry VIII and England Waxes and Wanes   86

8 Mary Tudor and 'my good cousin' Reginald Pole   95

9 'I am come not to destroy, but to build; to reconcile,
not to condemn'   108

10 Reginald Pole and Thomas Cranmer: Poles Apart? 124

11 Philip I of England and Cardinal Pole:
    Another King and Another Conflict? 140

12 Cardinal Pole and the Women in His Life 158

13 Cardinal Pole as Governor and Patron of
    Town and Household 176

14 Cardinal Pole's Artistic Patronage 194

15 The Death of Cardinal Pole, His Legacy
    and His Reputation 207

Notes and Abbreviations 216

Chronology 256

Bibliography 262

Index 276

PREFACE

To many Tudor enthusiasts Reginald Pole (1500–58) is simply a name or, at best, a character in *The Tudors* or Hilary Mantel's *Wolf Hall* trilogy. The aim of this book is to make him better known and to try to understand his complex character and the events of his life. It is a popular history book but nonetheless relies on academic studies and archival research to throw some light on his overlooked role in the period.

This is also a book about patronage: that of Henry VIII, that of the Pope and, in turn, that of Pole himself. It is about the rules of patronage and what happens when the recipient goes against the demands of his patron and abuses that patronage, with sometimes disastrous results – not just for himself, but also for his family. It is also the story of a man of noble lineage and royal blood and what that meant in Tudor times.

Inevitably, this work also covers the area which has arguably led to Pole's neglect in popular history: his role as a cardinal of the Catholic Church. Most popular historians blanch at the thought of setting forth into Church history, but it is impossible to understand Pole without examining his religious beliefs in the tumultuous years of the Reformation and how these affected his actions and thus his life. I have therefore brought to bear my experience researching and writing about another Renaissance cardinal. The pivotal question in Pole's life was, inevitably, whom was he to choose: the king or the Church?

This book covers Pole from his early life until his death and looks at his relations with Henry VIII, Mary Tudor, Thomas Cranmer, Philip of Spain and the popes of the period. In a book of this limited scope and size, certain things have had to fall by the wayside – his relations with the English Hospice in Rome; his literary patronage and some of his writings – but hopefully with no detrimental effect on our understanding of this enigmatic man. Who was Reginald Pole? By the end of this book, I hope that we will be able to answer that question.

Helen Hyde
Battle, 2025

ACKNOWLEDGEMENTS

Anyone who is interested in Reginald Pole must acknowledge a huge debt of gratitude to the life's work of the late Thomas F. Mayer (1951–2014). His biography *Reginald Pole, Prince and Prophet* is complex but necessary reading and his work on Pole's published correspondence is essential to our understanding of this man. Only through reading the synopses of the letters that Pole wrote and received (thousands in number, and they are far from complete due to the vicissitudes of time) and exploring them in further detail can we form a picture of Pole and the years in which he flourished. Equal praise must go to the late John Edwards for his biography *Archbishop Pole* and to Eamon Duffy for his studies on the cardinal.

I first came across Pole during my research for a biography of Cardinal Bendinello Sauli (d. 1518) and he has stayed with me, in the back of my mind, since then. Lockdown saw that thought come to fruition when I realised that there was simply no modern accessible biography of this cardinal for those interested in Tudor history. I am most grateful to Professor Steven Gunn for his initial support of this idea (and indeed for his reading of the first draft of the manuscript), to Sarah Hall for casting her eagle eye over both drafts, and of course to Connor Stait at Amberley for commissioning the work and for his patience. My editor, Alex Bennett, was kindness itself in the final stages of production. The years since lockdown have seen me dedicated to Pole outside of my normal work while also having to recover from a traumatic head-on car crash. Dr Stewart Blake played a major part in my recovery: thank you.

This book would not have been possible without the help of archivists and librarians. Special mention must be made of the staff at the London Library, Battle Library, the Archivio Apostolico Vaticano and the Public Records Office in Kew. Thank you all. Galo Garcés Avalos was kind enough to furnish me with some useful bibliographical references. Maria Forcellino and the owner of the Michelangelo *Pietà* were generous with their time. Dr Piers Baker-Bates was extremely helpful and made me smile: thank you. Those who were happy to read and comment on the manuscript possessed varying degrees of historical knowledge as I felt it important to get a layman's view of Pole, and especial thanks should go to Brian Parker.

Writing is a lonely process, and I am one of those people who needs a lot of space and, above all, quiet: both were very helpfully provided by Mari Mason and Stephen Shakeshaft; Ian and Lotta Rosam; and Sheila and Stan Wendon – and, of course, their cats; I cannot write without a cat in the house, so thank you also to Poppy and Seren, the inimitable Maisie, and Mister and Mishka. And of course, to my own cats: Timmy, Rosie and Jess.

My biggest debt of gratitude is to my husband, Roy Hyde, who patiently supported me through the trauma of the car crash and has read and digested Pole in more detail than he would probably wish (but is too kind to say so). Thank you, Roy. You really are No. 1 husband, and this book is dedicated to you.

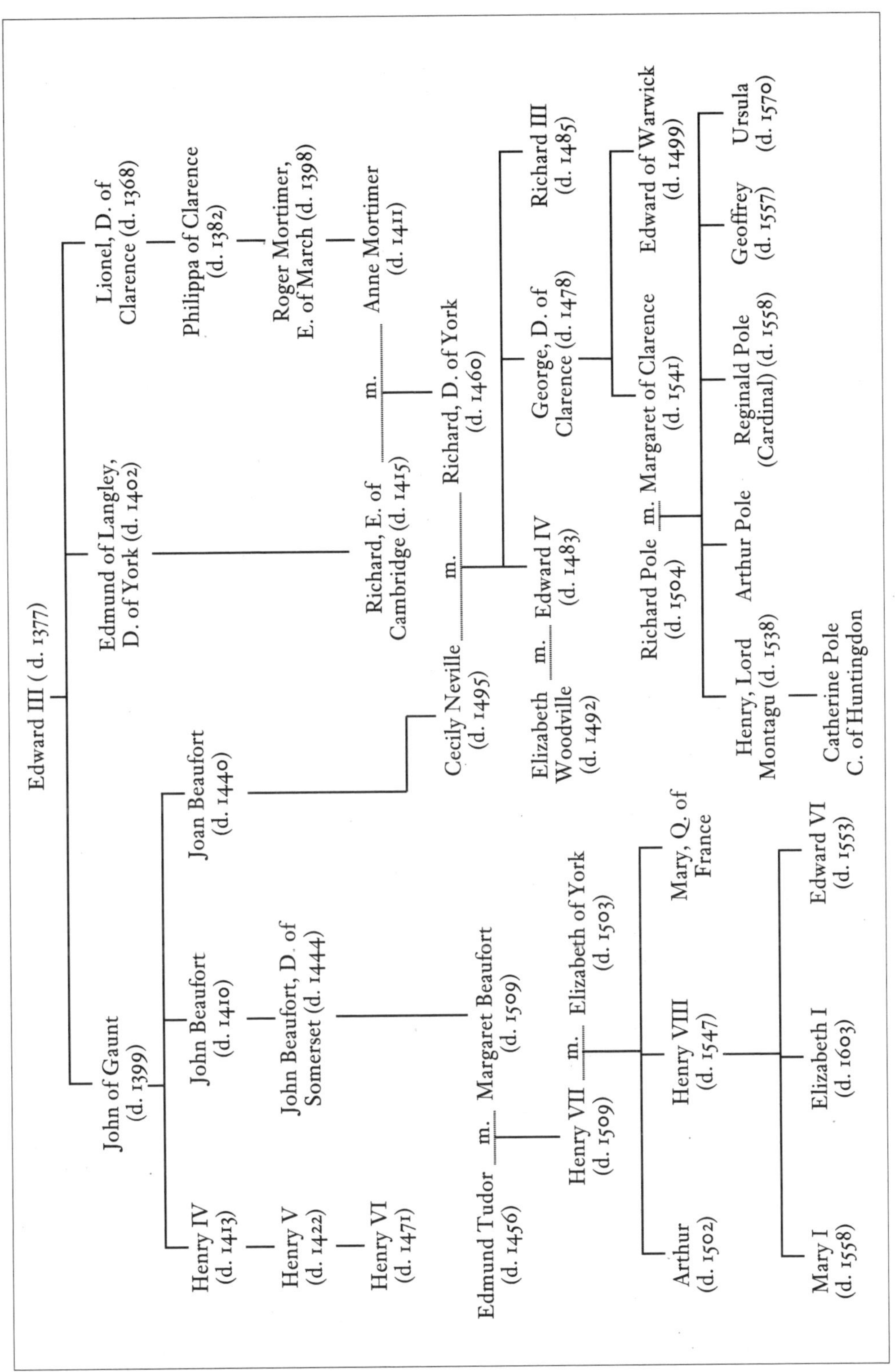

Fig. 1. A simplified family tree of the houses of Tudor and York.

I

THE POLE FAMILY AND EARLY FAMILY FORTUNES

When Reginald Pole (fig. 2) was born in March 1500, the future Henry VIII was almost nine years old. He was still Duke of York and of secondary importance within the royal family to his brother, Prince Arthur, the heir to the Tudor throne. The destinies of both princes were to be closely entwined with those of the Pole family.

Henry and Arthur were the sons of Henry VII (r. 1485–1509), the man who had set the Tudors on the throne by his victory over the unpopular Richard III (r. 1483–5) at the Battle of Bosworth on 22 August 1485. Through his marriage in 1486 to Elizabeth of York, the eldest daughter of Edward IV (r. 1461–70, 71–83), Henry had united the factions of Lancaster and York, whose strife in the mid-fifteenth century has come to be known as the Wars of the Roses. Perhaps he might have felt entitled to lower his guard after his years spent in exile and his unexpected victory on the battlefield, yet his claim to the throne was essentially weak: it came from his mother, the indomitable Margaret Beaufort (1443–1509), a great-granddaughter of John of Gaunt, the third son of Edward III, but a member of the illegitimate Beaufort line. There were others with far stronger claims – including the mother of Reginald Pole and her younger brother, Edward of Warwick.

Various attempts were made to usurp Henry during his reign and much effort was expended on defeating or neutralising their threats. And indeed, at various times during the reigns of both Henry VII and his son, Henry VIII, the Pole family came to be viewed as just such a threat. Who, then, were the Poles? Margaret Pole (1473–1541) (fig. 3), Reginald's mother, was the daughter of George, Duke of Clarence, the disgraced brother of Edward IV who was, according to Shakespeare, drowned in a butt of malmsey for his treason in 1478. She was thus a Plantagenet (namely of the House of York) and was a mere four years old when her father was executed. Her brother, Edward of Warwick, was born in 1475.

With the death of Edward IV in 1483 and the disqualification by Richard III of Edward's own children – Edward V and Richard, Duke of York – on the grounds of their 'illegitimacy', the value of Warwick was potentially immense, providing the attainder (a sentence passed by Parliament without a trial) against his father and heirs was ignored: as the son of Clarence his claim to the throne was stronger than that of Richard III. He was also the only surviving and 'legitimate male descendant of Edward III, through his fourth son, Edmund, duke of York, and also by a female line from that king's third son, John of Gaunt ... [he] thus represented the claim which the Tudors would later make for themselves, to combine the Yorkist and Lancastrian inheritances' (fig. 1).[1] He was therefore of great interest to Richard III and later to Henry VII. Richard ensured that he was kept under close watch in the household of Anne Neville, Warwick's aunt and Richard's wife, and he was present at Richard's coronation and knighted in the same year. Margaret also then became a ward of Richard.[2]

Henry VII was not slow to appreciate Warwick's value: after his victory at Bosworth one of his first actions was to have Warwick brought to London. While both he and Margaret were sent initially to live with Margaret Beaufort, Warwick was then transferred to the Tower of London, a secure prison where he was kept out of the public eye. He remained there, except for a brief, organised, excursion in February 1487 to show that he was very much alive (despite a certain Lambert Simnel claiming his identity), which remained the case until 1499.[3]

As a girl, Margaret of Clarence posed a much weaker threat. She could not, in practice, ascend the throne, but it might still be possible for malcontents to rally around her. She stayed close to the court and was present in 1486 at the christening of Prince Arthur. Following the Lambert Simnel conspiracy, it seems that she was married off quite quickly to Richard Pole, a half-cousin of the king, in 1487.[4] This was not quite the drab and unworthy marriage that some historians make it out to be: Richard, born around 1458, although not a member of the titled aristocracy, came from a Lancastrian family strictly loyal to Henry VI (r. 1422–61, 1470–1) in the mid-fifteenth century and could thus be trusted by Henry Tudor. Furthermore, Richard's own mother, Edith St John of Bletsoe, was the older half-sister of Margaret Beaufort. Hence any children of this union of Richard, cousin of Henry VII, and Margaret, daughter of the Duke of Clarence, would be very closely related to Henry VII and his heirs. As Schenk notes, 'it was the inescapable destiny of Reginald Pole to be either the friend or foe of Henry VIII'.[5]

In 1487 Richard Pole was knighted immediately after the Battle of Stoke Field, which ended the claim of the pretender Lambert Simnel. Richard was to become a powerful figure in north Wales after his marriage to Margaret later in the same year, holding various Welsh castles and becoming chamberlain of North Wales for life in 1490. He continued to receive positions of responsibility throughout the decade, the high point of which was surely his appointment as chamberlain to Arthur, Prince of Wales, in 1493 at the latest. His post in Arthur's household was of the highest importance as he was to prepare the prince to rule and it 'moved Pole to the heart of the Tudor establishment'.[6] He was then made a member of the elite Knights of the Garter in 1499.[7] Margaret Pole's future thus looked settled and prosperous, and she became the mother of five surviving children: Henry, later Lord Montagu, born in 1492; Arthur, who was to become a sophisticated courtier under Henry VIII; Ursula, who was to marry the son of the Duke of Buckingham; Reginald; and lastly Geoffrey (*c.* 1504).

Yet tragedy was to strike, not once but thrice. The 1490s had seen the emergence of yet another pretender to the throne, Perkin Warbeck, who claimed to be Richard, Duke of York, the younger son of the late Edward IV and allegedly still very much alive.[8] Warbeck attempted to invade England, was eventually captured, spent some time at court, fled and was then imprisoned in the Tower. Once there, a plot, seemingly real, emerged involving both Warbeck and Warwick, with the latter to be made king. Warbeck was hanged on 23 November 1499 and Warwick was beheaded on the 28th.[9] With his death the legitimate male line of the House of Plantagenet came to an end. Warwick had been imprisoned from the age of eleven until the age of twenty-four, seemingly with few or no attempts to educate him in the Tower: the chronicler Edward Hall described him as 'without all company of men and sight of beasts, in so much that he could not discern a goose from a capon'.[10] He is now generally believed to have been unworldly rather than simple, and naïve and innocent of any wrongdoing. We do not know Margaret's thoughts on hearing of her brother's execution, but she had been pregnant with Reginald Pole at the time and the tragedy of Warwick's death was to reverberate down the family, and through Reginald, for years to come.

Yet brighter times had seemed to beckon: in May 1499 Richard Pole officiated at the proxy wedding of Prince Arthur and Katharine of Aragon. This prestigious match and alliance to the daughter of Ferdinand of Aragon and Isabella of Castille was to signal, in the king's mind, that Henry VII and England were now worthy of serious consideration on the international stage. Upon Katharine's arrival in England the couple were married in person on 14 November 1501 and Margaret Pole, as the wife of the prince's chamberlain, entered her household and she and Katharine became friends. Margaret 'was to be the greatest of all Katharine's friends' and it was a friendship which endured for the rest of Katharine's life.[11]

After a short illness, Prince Arthur died on 2 April 1502 and Henry, his younger brother, became heir to the throne. Katharine then endured seven years of relative penury and neglect at the hands of Henry VII, but during this time she and Margaret Pole seemingly remained close. Their bond may well have been strengthened by a third tragedy: in October 1504 Richard Pole died. Both were now widows and both faced straitened circumstances. The loss of the income from Richard Pole's posts was considerable; most of his lands were in the hands of Henry Pole, his eldest son, yet he was still a minor and indeed a royal ward. Furthermore, the attainder on Warwick meant that there was no financial resource to be gained from his lands lost through his 'treason'. Margaret Pole went to Syon Abbey with her youngest children and while there received financial help from Margaret Beaufort, the king's mother and her earlier guardian, from at least 1505 to 1509.[12]

All was to change completely when Henry VII died and his son ascended the throne as Henry VIII (fig. 4) on 22 April 1509, initially, as he was a minor, under the guidance of his father's surviving councillors and Margaret Beaufort until his birthday on 28 June of that year. He very much knew his own mind and was determined to set a different tone from that of his father. After the death of Prince Arthur, Katharine of Aragon had been betrothed to Henry when Prince of Wales, and a papal dispensation had been granted to allow the match despite the fact that she was his brother's widow. She was then thrown over, on the instructions of Henry VII, so she must have been delighted when, on 11 June 1509, Henry chose to marry her and thus began a brief period of intense happiness for both.

Margaret Pole became one of Katharine's ladies-in-waiting, and both she and Henry Pole were present at the royal couple's coronation. She was 'summoned to London, lodged at the king's expense and given livery clothing as if she had been a countess'.[13] Royal favours continued to follow: in 1509 she was given an annuity of £100 by Henry VIII; Henry Pole began to receive gifts of clothing and by 1512 had become one of Henry's sewers (servers).[14] Henry VIII was, indeed, continuing to show that he was not like his father: in 1512 he elevated Margaret to her ancestral status as Countess of Salisbury and restored her rights as heiress to the same. She thus became 'potentially one of the most influential and powerful women in England'. She was the first woman 'to hold a peerage title in her own right' – and, as Pierce notes, with the later exception of Anne Boleyn, the only one.[15]

Although she was not alone in being shown favour – Henry was also generous in that period to other of his Yorkist relatives – the elevation of Margaret was particularly significant and several reasons may have lain behind it. Reginald Pole later said that it was the deathbed wish of Henry VII because of his guilt over the execution of Warwick: in fact the reversal of the latter's attainder states that Margaret's younger brother acted out of innocence, and she thus then received all the lands that he had held at the time of his death; it may also have been due to the friendship between the two women and also, of course, because Henry simply wanted to do it and was fond of this relative whom he seemingly regarded as a second mother.[16]

Other members of the family also benefitted from the royal couple's approval and affection: Henry Pole accompanied the king on his Tournai expedition and returned knighted in 1513, and from 1514 was known by his courtesy title Lord Montagu. Arthur Pole, the second Pole son, was part of the entourage which accompanied the king's sister Mary to France to marry Louis XII. Arthur was athletic and, like the king, keen on jousting: it can be hardly coincidental that in 1516, the same year that he made his debut as a jouster, he was appointed a squire of the king's body, a sign of Henry's favour. By 1518 he had become a gentleman of the Privy Chamber, 'a prized position, as such men were hand-picked by the king and enjoyed his trust and friendship'.[17] In 1520 both he and Montagu accompanied Henry to France for the meeting at the Field of the Cloth of Gold. Still in favour later in the decade, in 1526 he was once again a squire of the body.[18] On the other hand, very little is known about Geoffrey Pole's early years: he seems to have been neither as skilful a courtier as Montagu nor as athletic as Arthur. Indeed, with Reginald, he was to prove the undoing of his family.

Ambitious marriages were arranged for the Pole children: Montagu to Jane Neville, the daughter of Lord Bergavenny; Arthur to Jane Pickering, the daughter of Sir Roger Lewknor; Geoffrey to Constance Packenham; but the jewel in the crown was the marriage of Ursula Pole to Henry Stafford, son and heir to the Duke of Buckingham. As Hazel Pierce notes, that marriage 'united two very respectable claims to the throne'.[19] The reason behind such favours was clearly the good will and patronage of the king. As we will see, while the family remained in his good graces, financial and social success were guaranteed. It was of course also always necessary to recognise and befriend those men who were close to the king and had his ear: Margaret Pole at various points in her life gave annuities to Cardinal Wolsey, to Thomas Cromwell and to Charles Brandon (the Duke of Suffolk and the king's brother-in-law).[20] Certainly, relations with Wolsey were cordial to say the least: she seemed to expect him to advise her; some of her staff at different times came on Wolsey's recommendation and Wolsey may well have been behind the fecund marriage of Ursula to Henry Stafford.[21]

Meanwhile, that of Henry VIII to Katharine of Aragon was marred by four miscarriages, one stillbirth and the death of an infant prince.[22] There must have been a huge sigh of relief when a healthy child was born, and indeed lived, in 1516. That child was Mary Tudor (fig. 5), and she was to play a significant role in the lives of the Pole family, even before she finally ascended the throne. Margaret Pole was present at her christening on 20 February (she in fact sponsored her confirmation, which took place at the same time), remaining as part of the queen's household and then becoming Mary's governess.[23] As noted by Beccadelli, Reginald Pole's earliest biographer, her accession to this post was not just because of the affection of the royal consorts but also because the Countess of Salisbury was 'of distinguished prudence and discretion, and of most exemplary piety, besides her royal birth and near relationship to the king'.[24] Such was the status that she brought to the role of governess that Mary's household was substantially increased.[25]

But just as royal favour could be won, it could also be lost, both temporarily and permanently, and not necessarily through one's own fault. Mere association or friendship with someone who had offended or plotted against the king was sufficient to ensure disgrace. There can be little doubt that Edward Stafford (1478–1521), Duke of Buckingham and the father-in-law of Ursula Pole, was the foremost peer of the land at this time. He was the 'single largest private landowner in the kingdom' and renowned for his sartorial extravagance at court functions and festivities. He was the son of the second Duke of Buckingham, who had rebelled against Richard III and paid with his life; he had grown up a royal ward, entrusted to the care of Margaret Beaufort, and he eventually regained possession of his father's inheritance, albeit with large financial penalties due to the pecuniary machinations of Henry VII. Under both father and son the Duke of Buckingham was a marginal figure at court, with little political weight.

Yet Buckingham had a strong claim to the throne through his descent from the youngest son of Edward III and as Davies notes, 'Buckingham's royal blood was dangerous'.[26] Henry regarded with suspicion the fact that on the marriage of Henry Stafford to Ursula the duke had agreed to pay Margaret Pole the huge and curious sum of £2,000. It may have been a loan, but 'Henry believed he had detected the beginnings of a menacing dynastic conspiracy of the sort that scarred his father's reign'.[27] There had been talk during the reign of Henry VII about who would take the throne in the event of his death, and Buckingham's name had been mentioned (but, significantly, the name of Henry had not featured). Such dangerous speculation continued: Buckingham had not planned to usurp Henry VIII or to kill him but talk about the future after a king's death and ill-concealed criticisms of current policies, even if reported to the authorities by disgruntled ex-servants, was enough for Buckingham to be summoned to London on 8 April 1521, indicted for high treason and then executed on 17 May of that year. The aftershocks of his fall did not fail to reach others.

Buckingham had been close to the Poles, not just because of his affection for Ursula but through his friendship with the family. He gambled regularly with Henry Pole, and the Venetian ambassador even mistook the Pole brothers for Buckingham's nephews. Indeed, when Buckingham was arrested 'no family came in for a greater share of the king's displeasure than the Poles'.[28] Henry Pole was arrested and placed in the Tower of London, as was Lord Bergavenny, another of Buckingham's sons-in-law (and father-in-law to Montagu); Arthur was expelled from court and Margaret Pole was removed from her position in Mary Tudor's household.[29] These were serious, but only temporary, lapses in royal favour: Margaret Pole received New Year gifts from the queen in 1522 and was fully reinstated as Mary's governess by 1525 (and may well have regained some influence before then), and in May 1522 Montagu attended the king's meeting with Charles V at Canterbury, while Arthur joined Henry's French campaign in 1523 and was certainly fully restored to royal favour by 1526.[30]

As his family rose, so, of course, did Reginald Pole. His was a childhood and adolescence far removed from the royal court. Probably educated at home in his early years, from 1507 he attended the Carthusians' grammar school at Sheen and probably Christ Church Priory in Canterbury.[31] He was quite possibly destined for the Church from an early age (perhaps due to the poverty in which the Poles found themselves after the death of Richard Pole, perhaps because aristocratic families always found it useful to have a major churchman on the team): he certainly felt so and berated his mother for this in 1536, saying, 'You had given me utterly unto God … you never took any care to provide for my living nor otherwise, as you did for other, but committed all to God, to whom you had given me.'[32]

Reginald was given an exhibition of £12 in 1511 and in the following year went to Magdalen College, Oxford, residing there until 1519.[33] This is further confirmation that he was destined for the Church: Magdalen was 'a centre for arts teaching with a humanistic bent, and for the preparation of priests for the Church'.[34] The king provided further for him: in 1513 Henry instructed the prior of St Frideswide in Oxford to pay Reginald a pension and eventually to find him a suitable benefice.[35]

In 1515 Reginald received his BA, and in 1517 the king appointed him to the prebend of Roscombe in Salisbury Cathedral; the following year Henry gave him the deanery of Wimborne Minster and then a year later he was nominated to Gatcombe (Yatcombe) Secunda, also in Salisbury Cathedral.[36] A life dedicated to study, the Church and the furtherance of Henry's interests seemed to beckon.

2

THE KING'S COUSIN AND
THE KING'S SCHOLAR

Although he may not have seemed very grateful later in his life, Reginald Pole was well aware of what he owed the king. Henry VIII did not limit himself to providing Pole with a series of benefices: it was with the king's blessing and financial help that Pole left for Padua, where he was to study at the university, arriving there by the end of April 1521 at the very latest.[1] Padua was the place to be for an aspirant Englishman who wanted to become *au fait* with the latest scholarship.

The fact that he was the king's cousin and a member of the nobility was, inevitably, to be important throughout Pole's life. It was something he, and later those who supported him against Henry, were to emphasise and play on again and again. His nobility made him an attractive figure both to governments and to individuals: to know Pole was to get closer to the king. As early as 1515 he was allowed to enter the university library at Oxford in lay dress because of his royal rank, and in May 1521 at Padua he was granted a licence by the Venetian government (under whose patronage the university stood) to export plate and clothes because of his social position; in 1523 his servants were allowed to carry arms. He had an easy entry into Venetian patrician society, and in February 1525 he was invited to a gathering at the prestigious Ca' Dandolo while on the feast of Corpus Christi he was at mass with the Doge of Venice in St Mark's.[2]

Pole was much fêted and honoured when he arrived first in Venice and then Padua, and, as a close relation of the king, he was expected to live magnificently, as befitted one of his status. To do so was expensive, and although Henry had provided him with £100 per annum, Pole was obliged to write to the king on 27 April 1521 saying that in order to live up to the expectations of the local magistrates and *podestà*, who had provided him with a huge and magnificent palace, he would need more money or would have to move elsewhere.[3] Indeed he 'set an excellent table with luxurious wine' and his palace was large enough to house not only his own household but also that of the English ambassador to Venice when the latter was in Padua.[4]

In short, it simply was not possible for Pole to live the life of a normal, private student: England had close relations with Venice and in addition to pursuing his studies, Pole was expected to strengthen these relations where possible. Others were flattered by the chance to know such an august person: both Pietro Bembo (1470–1547), a poet, historian and later a cardinal, and Desiderius Erasmus (1466–1536), probably the foremost scholar of the age, mention his noble birth in their first letters to him.[5] Indeed, Henry himself was quick to underline their blood relationship when it suited him: the Venetian ambassador reported from England on 1 April that Henry 'recommended his "nephew" Reginald, who is coming to study at Padua'.[6] But blood, like milk, could curdle and after the treachery of the Duke of Buckingham and the subsequent temporary disgrace of the Poles, when the Venetian ambassador described how Venice had greatly honoured Pole 'for love of your majesty' Henry replied that 'it was best not to overdo it, in case he got ideas like the others had'.[7] Thankfully, Henry's rancour soon passed on this occasion.

Pole was, so to speak, the 'king's scholar' and was one of only a few who benefitted from this great favour. They included John Mason (1503–66), king's scholar at Paris, and John Clement (1500–72), at Padua from 1522, both studying medicine.[8] Both had higher academic profiles than Pole, and Clement had been tutor to the children of Thomas More. But why did Pole wish to go to Padua rather than remain in England? The university in Padua was a major centre of Renaissance Humanism and Pole's tutors at Oxford had included Thomas Linacre and William Latimer, both of whom had studied at the Italian university. The latter supplied him with an introduction to his old tutor, Nicolò Leonico Tomeo (1456–1531). Pole's time at Padua has been described as 'essentially a continuation and completion of Oxford'.[9] At this stage in his life, Pole was not overly interested in religion and he went to Padua to study classical authors in their original language (Latin or Greek) – a field in which Corpus Christi (where he had earlier lodged in the residence of the president of the college and was later elected a fellow *in absentia*) had excelled.[10] He could have had no better private tutor than Leonico, who lived in his palace. He was the foremost interpreter of Aristotle and Plato in the original Greek.[11] Together, he, Pole and Thomas Lupset (*c.* 1495–1530), who joined Pole in Padua in 1523, read from these classical authors exhaustively.

Patronage was very much a part of sixteenth-century society. Pole was given the opportunity to study abroad because of the king's patronage, but also because of his closeness to Wolsey: his time at Padua has been described as 'under Cardinal Wolsey's personal direction' and in October 1520 Pole wrote to Wolsey saying that 'you are like a mother to me, providing immortal benefits'. Once in Padua he again writes to the cardinal thanking him for all his help, which he will never forget.[12] Pole is described as particularly favoured by Wolsey, as shown by the prebends he awarded him, and in 1525 he writes to Wolsey again, saying that he hoped he would not be thought ungrateful or be forgotten: indeed, he was awarded a prebend in York Minster in the year that he returned to England.[13] Thomas Lupset, described by Beccadelli as 'an Englishman, in eloquence, learning and piety equal to the first of his countrymen', was also a beneficiary of Wolsey's good will and at some point became tutor to his illegitimate son, Thomas Winter. Wolsey clearly trusted Pole as Winter was seemingly in Padua with him in 1522 and possibly later.[14]

Pole was not just a recipient of patronage, but also a patron: he provided food, board and presumably wages to Leonico and in return Leonico tutored him in the unexpurgated versions of classical texts and also dedicated his *Dialogi* to him in 1524. Another tutor, Battista Leoni, who probably also taught philosophy and Aristotle to Pole, so esteemed him that he presented him with a marble panel of the *Judgement of Solomon* by the Italian sculptor Giovanni Maria Mosca (active 1515–73).[15] The tentacles of patronage were far reaching: Pole's closeness to Cardinal Wolsey meant that the man who had originally been Wolsey's patron, Bishop Richard Fox, but who now sought his favour, nominated Pole to be a fellow of Corpus Christi on 14 February 1524, thus giving him additional financial support.[16] Pole was clearly a generous patron: Lupset offered Germain de Brie, a canon of Notre

Dame, 'an honourable place in the friendship of his Maecenas, Reginald Pole' and it is likely that the benefice that Lupset received in 1526 was through Pole's patronage.[17]

Pole had much to offer members of his household: the kudos of knowing the cousin of the king; a magnificent lifestyle; and an educated and, indeed, kind patron. One of the first to benefit from his hospitality and support was Christophe de Longueil (1488–1522), also known as Cristoforo Longolio. He was a worthy person to benefit from the patronage of a relative of the king: the illegitimate son of a bishop, he had held an interesting and prestigious series of posts before encountering Pole. These had included personal secretary to Philip the Handsome (later to become Philip I of Castile) and tutor to the future King of France, Francis I (r. 1515–47).[18] Embroiled in controversy during his time in Rome, he had fled Italy and gone to England where he met Linacre (one of Pole's tutors), who was later to pen an introduction for Pole to Longolio. On his return to Italy he was with his friend Pietro Bembo at Padua, joined the household of Stefano Sauli, brother of the disgraced but prestigious cardinal Bendinello Sauli (d. 1518), and then became part of Pole's household in July 1521 by the latest, i.e. shortly after Pole's arrival at Padua.[19] He was to be Pole's tutor in the imitation of the style of Cicero, although it should be noted that just before his death his interests had changed to the refutation of Lutheranism.[20]

We gain some insight into Pole's character from Longolio's letters: he describes Pole as learned, modest, taciturn, shy and not fond of disputation.[21] Theirs was not to be a long relationship: Longolio, whose health had never been strong, fell seriously ill, dying on 11 September 1522. While ill, he wrote to Pole, bequeathing him his reputation and his library (some of his books are now, through Pole, at Oxford). In 1524 it was probably Pole who wrote and published a life of Longolio, together with his letters.[22] In turn, Longolio introduced Pole not only to Bembo but also to Marc'antonio Flaminio (1498–1550), who was to become so important to Pole later in his life. Flaminio was enrolled at the university at the same time as Pole and, like Longolio, had been a member of the household of Stefano Sauli.[23]

Pole had known More, Linacre and Latimer and undoubtedly other scholars in England and at Padua he was thrust into a new circle of men of letters. For instance, his friendship with Longolio meant that he could not but be friends with Pietro Bembo. The latter's career was as varied as it was long: a successful courtier, poet and scholar, he had also been papal secretary to Leo X and when Pole met him he was in semi-retirement from the Roman curia in his villa in the Paduan countryside. If Leonico and Longolio were dedicated to the study of Latin and Greek, Bembo favoured the Italian vernacular. Membership of Bembo's own circle in turn introduced Pole to Jacopo Sadoleto (1477–1547) and Gian Matteo Giberti (1495–1543), both of whom were to be lifelong friends, influencing Pole's later religious studies and his attitude to Church reform.

As Wade notes, 'Bembo was in many ways a convincing model for Pole: a nobleman and patron of scholars who had tried to balance the demands of public life with a desire for scholarly retreat'.[24] Inevitably a new English circle of scholars sprang up in Padua around Pole. Thomas Lupset was an intimate of Erasmus, having helped the famous scholar with his *New Testament* when he was at Cambridge; he wrote a letter to Erasmus, introducing Pole and praising him as having exceeded all expectations and being highly esteemed by his cousin the king.[25] Thomas Starkey (*c.* 1498–1538) had known Pole at Oxford and was certainly in Padua in 1525, if not earlier. Although it is not known whether he became part of Pole's household at Padua, he had certainly become his secretary by early 1529 and features greatly in the tumultuous events of the following years.[26] John Clement, who had been reader in Greek at Corpus and probably knew Pole there, visited in the summer of 1524 when he brought a copy of Thomas More's *Utopia* to Leonico; Richard Pace (*c.* 1482–1536), previously the king's secretary and now envoy to the Venetian government, had studied with Leonico and was a personal friend of Pole.

Thus Pole's life was spent in study, corresponding with and visiting other scholars and travelling to Venice. An event occurred in 1525 which was to have a lasting effect on him: he visited Rome on a flying visit to mark the Jubilee (a year in which all sins were forgiven) and was horrified by what he saw. Richard Morison (*c.* 1513–66), a member of Pole's household a few years later, reported that Reginald fled the city quickly precisely because of this.[27] Pole was later to become a member of the Catholic Reform movement and this visit must have been the initial spur for this. He was accompanied on his visit by Lazzaro Buonamico (1477/8–1552), who had been the tutor of Longolio and Flaminio in the household of Stefano Sauli and was to be part of Pole's household in the 1530s.[28] Henry VIII wanted Pole to return to England and only granted him permission to visit Rome on condition that he went incognito and did not visit the curia or Pope Clement VII.[29] This was perhaps a sign that the relationship between Henry and the Pope was becoming strained and that all was not well at the Henrician court. However, Reginald was greeted with honours and acclaim in Florence and especially in Rome thanks to his friend Gian Matteo Giberti, a man with reformist inclinations and numerous contacts in the curia through his proximity to Clement VII.[30]

Indeed, Pole left Italy in early 1526, arriving back in England by November at the latest.[31] Why did Henry want him to return? Why had he spent a goodly sum of money on Pole's education abroad at all? Schenk notes:

> The king's main desire was probably to use his kinsman's gifts in the service of the state, or the church, or both ... [He] expected, not altogether unreasonably, that men of outstanding abilities, who had enjoyed the best education of their age, should eventually render some practical service to their country.[32]

Like all patrons, Henry sought something in return for his patronage. Exactly what he required of Pole was to be revealed in the long term as both difficult and troubling to Pole's conscience.

3

THE KING'S GREAT MATTER: REGINALD POLE AND THE DIVORCE

In 1526 Reginald Pole arrived back to a different country from that which he had left in 1521. On the surface much remained unchanged – his mother, Margaret Pole, was once again governess to Mary Tudor; Katharine of Aragon was still queen; his brother Arthur was again squire of the body to the king; Wolsey was still the king's right-hand man and England was still very much a Catholic country. Yet the ground was shifting beneath Pole's feet.

The divorce of Henry VIII from Katharine of Aragon (although Henry sought an annulment, it was always referred to in contemporary documents as a divorce) is an event of which few people are unaware. What most people do not realise, however, is the complexity of the divorce process; how it involved not just passion, but international politics, religion and a sense of dynastic destiny. It saw the downfall of the second most powerful man in England after the king and changed, over the years, from a request for a divorce into something that would indelibly shape England's future.

Henry and Katharine of Aragon

Why did Henry choose Katharine of Aragon? It may, of course, have been mutual attraction: at the age of twenty-three, Katharine was 'the most beautiful creature in the world', of childbearing age and the object of Henry's admiration. He justified marrying her by saying that it was his father's dying wish, but there is also some evidence that he was in two minds about any future marriage, 'claiming (according to a report of one of his councillors) that it would burden his conscience to marry his brother's widow'.[1] It is clear from contemporary sources that, certainly in the early years, both were in love and happy; shortly after the wedding, Henry wrote to his father-in-law, Ferdinand of Aragon, that 'if I were still free I would choose her for life above all others'.[2] But above all 'he wanted the support of Katharine's father … his obvious ally in a war against France'.[3]

In a royal marriage there was enormous pressure to produce an heir, especially for a dynasty so recently, and shakily, established as the Tudors. The lack of an heir could plunge England back into the slaughter of the so-called 'Wars of the Roses'. After one miscarriage in the first year of marriage, Katharine gave birth to a son, Henry, on 1 January 1511. He died on 22 February of that year, a mere seven weeks later. As Starkey notes, while the younger Henry lived, the older Henry had never 'been so in love with Catharine (*sic*) as at that moment; never would he be so fully again'.[4]

Despite several other pregnancies, Henry remained without an heir. There were rumblings in Rome in 1514 that 'the king of England meant to repudiate his present wife … because he is unable to have children with her'.[5] Politics had also started to play a more important role in the marriage, as the actions of Katharine's father inevitably affected the atmosphere both at court and between husband and wife. Ferdinand's contemptuous treatment of Henry in his French campaign of 1512 certainly did little to foster domestic bliss, but any discontent on Henry's part temporarily receded with the birth and survival of Princess Mary in 1516. But another miscarriage and a stillbirth followed, the latter, in 1518, being Katharine's last pregnancy.

The international political situation changed rapidly during these years: in 1515 Louis XII of France died, and he was succeeded to the French throne by his cousin Francis I (a dashing rival to Henry and one who fathered children at remarkably, and annoyingly, regular intervals). The following year Ferdinand of Aragon died and was succeeded on the Spanish throne by Archduke Charles, who, in 1519, was elected Holy Roman Emperor as Charles V. Europe was divided between these two powers – France and the Habsburg Empire – and their main battleground was the Italian peninsula and, if possible, control of the papacy. Where did England figure in this? It was useful and important but not essential: alliances could be formed without England but were often stronger with its presence. And, of course, England needed to protect itself from invasion and Henry VIII still hankered after re-conquering France and reliving the glory days of Henry V (r. 1413–22).

When Reginald left for Padua in 1521 England was still very much a Catholic country, despite the stirrings of Lutheranism in Germany and elsewhere. The papacy was not just a spiritual power but also a temporal power, and one in need of support and aid against the attacks of Martin Luther. In that same year, Henry (with some help from others) wrote the *Assertio Septem Sacramentorum* (Defence of the Seven Sacraments) in defence of the papacy against Luther. He argued – ironically, given later events – that 'papal power was historically rooted, necessary for the unity of the Church and the ultimate guarantor of uniformity of faith'.[6] In return, in October 1521 Leo X invested him with the title of 'Defender of the Faith', one that our present monarch still uses.

So, what had changed by 1526? Certainly by 1525, when Princess Mary was sent with her own household to Ludlow Castle to rule in the Marches, it was known that the queen would have no more children. Sending Mary to rule as Prince Arthur had done was a sign that she might succeed her father, but equally the elevation, also in 1525, of Henry Fitzroy, the king's illegitimate son born in 1519 from his liaison with Bessie Blount, to the dukedoms of Richmond and Sussex and his posting to govern the north, was a sign that he might well accede to his father's throne if made legitimate. Henry VIII had been left with no clear-cut, legitimate, male heir and once again international politics was changing. In 1522 Charles V had been betrothed to the infant Princess Mary, and Williams believes that this was a sign that Henry was resigned to there being no heir and was 'looking to resolving his difficulties by anticipating the birth of a male heir in the next generation – to his daughter'.[7] But in 1525 Charles threw her over for Isabella of Portugal. He also failed to help Henry invade France. Was this the start of Henry loosening his ties with Spain and with his Spanish wife? The fact that he had no heir from Katharine and had been rebuffed by Charles V became of critical importance when Henry suddenly and violently fell in love.[8]

Henry and Anne Boleyn

Politics also played its part in the presence of Anne Boleyn at the Tudor court. Born around 1501, her mother a Howard and her father Thomas Boleyn, a skilled diplomat, courtier and landowner, she was sent to the court of Margaret of Austria, the aunt of Archduke Charles (later Charles V), at Mechelen in 1513 and became a maid of honour to Margaret at what has been described as 'Europe's premier finishing school'.[9] She was there only a year when, again through her father's connections, she was sent to the French royal court. There she spent seven years, mostly in the household of Queen Claude, the wife of Francis I, and perfected her knowledge of the French language and assumed many French airs and customs. She was recalled to England in late 1521 by Cardinal Wolsey, partly to marry her off to an Irish nobleman and settle a dispute over an earldom and partly because the English court was in a 'time of flux': relations between Henry VIII and Charles V were becoming increasingly cordial, including a proposed attack on France, and the marriage negotiations between Charles V and Princess Mary were flourishing, while relations between England and France were deteriorating.[10]

And indeed, Anne's first recorded appearance at court was 4 March 1522 when she took part in a pageant to welcome the Imperial ambassadors to court. She represented the virtue Perseverance, a quality she was to illustrate in abundant quantity over the coming years. Yet she did not immediately catch Henry's eye. It is more likely that at the time he was enjoying an affair with her sister, Mary Boleyn (*c.* 1499–1543), and there is little or no mention of Anne in surviving records of this period. It was not until 1525 or 1526 that what had probably been a dalliance based on the tenets of courtly love 'had begun to grow into something deeper and more dangerous'.[11] By early 1527 Henry and Anne were believed to have 'secretly exchanged vows and pledged themselves to one another'.[12] Divorce was in the air and eventually came out into the open.

Inevitably, Henry turned to his most competent and trusted minister, Cardinal Wolsey, to obtain the divorce. In May 1527 Wolsey, as papal legate, set up a secret tribunal and cited Henry VIII for living unlawfully with his brother's widow. This marked the start of legal proceedings, and the tribunal met several times. It was the first time that the king had 'publicly explored the possibility of an annulment'.[13] Henry believed, whether sincerely or for his own benefit, that the Bible expressly prohibited the marriage to a brother's widow, citing Leviticus 18:16 and 20:21: 'Thou shalt not uncover the nakedness of thy brother's wife: it is thy brother's nakedness' and 'If a man shall take his brother's wife, it is an impurity: he hath uncovered his brother's nakedness; they shall be childless.' For Henry, not having a son was the equivalent of being childless. Henry being Henry, he also chose to ignore a conflicting passage in Deuteronomy.

He maintained that his marriage had been against God's law and that 'not even the Pope had any right to dispense anyone from their duty to obey that law, and therefore that his marriage, although originally sanctioned by a papal bull, was invalid'.[14] However, once again politics intervened: Katharine of Aragon was the aunt of Charles V and in May 1527 Imperial troops entered the papal city and the brutal Sack of Rome began, with Pope Clement VII prisoner for many months in the Castel Sant'Angelo. It was obvious that the Pope, who was effectively the prisoner of Charles V, would not do anything to further to upset the Emperor and the tribunal ended without a conclusion.

Henry's 'Great Matter' became a 'public international issue' in June 1527 when Henry told Katharine of his plans to divorce her as they had been living 'in sin for eighteen years'.[15] An attempt by Wolsey to circumvent the Pope and assume papal authority failed, and Wolsey and Henry then turned to Rome again. In December there then began a series of embassies from both cardinal and king which continued for the following three years, all thwarted by 'the remarkable mixture of hesitancy, furtiveness, intelligence and inscrutable obstinacy that was Clement'.[16] The embassies pleaded that the marriage was invalid not on biblical grounds but because the bull allowing the marriage to go ahead – a papal dispensation issued by Julius II in 1504 – was defective. Henry was seeking a commission led by two cardinals which would give a definitive sentence on the marriage. The waters became even murkier when a second dispensation was discovered in Spain in 1528. This was a papal brief which differed in some details from the papal bull of the same date, most importantly by suggesting that Katharine's marriage to Arthur had perhaps been consummated.[17] This was, and remains today, a contentious issue, but the likelihood is that Katharine had indeed remained a virgin before her marriage to Henry.[18]

Two cardinals were appointed by Clement to hear the case, Wolsey and Cardinal Lorenzo Campeggio (1474–1539), but the latter's gout and the dragging of feet in the Vatican meant that the Legatine Court did not open at Blackfriars until the end of May 1529 with an emotional Katharine of Aragon appearing in person and throwing herself at Henry's feet. Katharine's side referred the case to Rome, allowing the wily Campeggio to terminate proceedings in London in late July of that year. Henry was furious and Wolsey was in disgrace. Charles Brandon, the Duke of Suffolk and Henry's brother-in-law, slapped the table and shouted, 'By the Mass, now I see that the old said saw is true, that there never was legate nor cardinal that did good in England.'[19]

Once again, Henry had been outwitted by politics: the Treaty of Barcelona, signed between Clement and Charles in July of that year, meant Clement was always going to accede to Charles' wishes. Where was Henry to turn? In early August 1529 a little-known cleric named Thomas Cranmer (1489–1556) (fig. 6) began his meteoric rise to ecclesiastical prominence by suggesting that the major universities should be consulted as to the legality and validity of the papal dispensations.[20] It was at this point that Reginald Pole became involved.

Pole and Paris

Reginald's early biographers have him as retiring quietly to Sheen, a place he knew well, on his return from Italy.[21] It is generally assumed that he was recalled to England by the king, who was now looking to secure his learning and his services in pursuit of his divorce. He was still clearly in royal favour: the king sponsored his appointment as dean and then canon in Exeter Cathedral in 1527 and there is a suggestion that he may have begun to learn Hebrew: a sure sign 'that the king was grooming him to play a role in the Great Matter'.[22] Reginald applied to the king to continue his studies, but this time in Paris. Whether this was linked to the disgrace of his patron, Cardinal Wolsey, is unclear, but clearly the king was happy: on 16 October 1529 he gave Reginald a pension of £100.[23] A letter of 12 October of that year seems to hint at his imminent arrival in Paris, and once he was established there Henry was quick to take advantage, appointing him as his agent and ordering him to get opinions favourable to the divorce from the Paris theologians, perhaps informally at first but certainly formally as of 1 May 1530.[24] There can be little doubt, as Edwards notes, that Henry 'regarded him as an ideal man for the job, both well-qualified and loyal' for this important position.[25]

He was not alone in Paris but was accompanied by Lupset, Starkey and Edward Foxe.[26] Yet it was Pole who had the central role in dealings with the theologians, and once again the fact that he was Henry's 'dearest relative' can only have been of help.[27] He reported directly to the king and also the Earl of Wiltshire, Thomas Boleyn, and there is no doubt whatsoever about Reginald's commitment to Henry's cause at this time.[28] He was even given an extra £70 in April 1530 and congratulated in July in a letter from the Duke of Norfolk on his enthusiasm and loyalty; he was told that Henry was now singing his praises after he had successfully secured the judgement of the theologians that the Pope did not have the power to dispense from divine law, i.e. that Henry's first marriage was invalid.[29]

On his return from Paris in late July 1530 Reginald retired to Sheen again and there, slowly, his opinion changed (and over the coming years he rewrote the Parisian episode both for his own mind and for others').[30] He had returned to an England shortly to be without Wolsey who died on 29 November 1530 en route to London, having been arrested for treason on 4 November – the day before the so-called 'Reformation Parliament' had opened. The parliament lasted for seven years and the bills that it passed were to change England forever.

Relations at court between Henry and Katharine of Aragon deteriorated and Anne Boleyn forbade courtiers to visit Katharine and pass information to her regarding the divorce proceedings.[31] It was clear that at some point Reginald would have to come to a decision as to whether or not to offer his public support to the divorce, and it would not be easy for him. Henry was opposed to any compromise that might acknowledge papal authority to determine the divorce: to thwart any disagreement he had fourteen clerics charged with *praemunire* ('the offence of introducing foreign – in practise, papal – authority into England in preference to royal authority'), including John Clerk (d. 1541), Bishop of Bath and Wells, and John Fisher, Bishop of Rochester (1469–1535), who had been much loved by his late grandmother Margaret Beaufort and was a fierce defender of Katharine of Aragon.[32] Henry refused to go to Rome to defend his divorce in front of the Pope and the curia and his approach hardened: 'Henry now became something more than an importunate subject knocking aggressively at the door of the curia; he began to deny that he was even a subject.'[33] He urged his ambassadors in Rome to ask the Pope to send the case back to England and if this failed then to threaten the Pope with a General Council.

At home in January 1531 Henry issued a writ of *praemunire* against the whole clergy for having recognised Wolsey as papal legate. Once the clergy had paid the (large) fine he then demanded to be recognised as Supreme Head of the Church of England, a title approved by the convocation of bishops (with a caveat) in March of that year. In May 1531 Pole was not one of the members of the Canterbury convocation who protested against the king's measures against the English Church and 'the implication is that, at this stage, he probably went along. at least externally, even with the royal headship of the English Church'.[34] But Reginald's relations with his patron and cousin became turbulent: at some point in late 1530 Henry had offered him the archbishopric of York (the second most important in the country) or the bishopric of Winchester if he would publicly support the divorce, presumably in the hope that he would prove as efficient and devoted as Wolsey. A meeting of uncertain date (but probably late spring/early summer 1531) took place between Reginald and the king. He had planned to offer a compromise view on the divorce but instead said the opposite. Henry was allegedly so angry that he put his hand on his dagger and stormed out. According to Thomas Cranmer, writing to the Earl of Wiltshire, Reginald then wrote a (lost) book against the divorce, in which he stated that 'he had never wanted to be involved in this cause'. The succession and the risk of further civil conflict worried him and he wanted Henry to submit to the Pope's eventual judgement.[35] There can be no doubt that the book existed: Thomas Starkey referred to it in a letter to Pole in 1535, as did Pole himself in May 1536.[36] His elder brother, Montagu, who had been created a baron with a seat in the House of Lords in December 1529 and was thus expected to toe the royal line, also had an audience with Henry in which the king said that he understood Reginald's reasons and nobody would be dearer to him if he would only accept the grounds for the divorce.[37]

Reginald was still at court in July 1531 and according to the Imperial ambassador, Eustace Chapuys, he told the king that if he stayed in England he would use his position as dean of Exeter to speak his mind on the divorce.[38] Is this why, in early 1532, Reginald left England, not to return for more than twenty years? Was he avoiding the issue or planning a campaign from abroad? Or did he leave, as Smith suggests, because of 'the precarity of [his] political position'? Did he feel that, as someone with a claim to the throne, life would be quieter and safer abroad?[39] Whatever the reason, he clearly left with Henry's good will and approval: he kept his previous allowance of 400 ducats and was also allowed to retain his ecclesiastical benefices.[40] However, things were very soon to change.

4

FIREWORKS FROM ROME: CARDINAL POLE AND THE EVENTS OF 1532–37

In early 1532, Reginald travelled through France, first to Avignon and then to Carpentras, the episcopal seat of his friend and fellow scholar Jacopo Sadoleto (1477–1547). He then slowly wound his way down to Padua once again. As during his previous stay, he regularly visited Venice, and this time became intimate there with men who were to influence his religious beliefs.

Meanwhile in England, the pace quickened at court: Anne Boleyn had moved into Katharine's old lodgings and was thus positioning herself as queen. There was also the first sign that Henry might consider himself as separate from Rome and eventually as Supreme Head of the English Church. This came in August 1530 when he insisted that nobody could be summoned out of their homeland to a foreign jurisdiction, by which he meant that the divorce should not be heard in Rome.[1] Anticlerical measures started to proliferate: in March 1532 Parliament, under Henry's direction, passed the Act in Conditional Restraint of Annates, which slashed fees paid to

Rome by English bishops, and then in May the Submission of the Clergy was passed which 'in effect gave the king the right to pass upon all legislation of the Church'.[2] This was a momentous move and occasioned the resignation of Sir Thomas More as Chancellor. More was to prove to be a thorn in Henry's side.

Anne's patience and perseverance finally reaped their reward: in September 1532 she was made Marchioness of Pembroke with adequate financial provision to maintain a suitable lifestyle and in October she accompanied Henry to France to meet Francis I and strengthen the current *entente cordiale* between the two countries with a view to helping Henry obtain a divorce. But Clement VII insisted that Henry leave Anne and return to Katharine within a month or face excommunication. This fell on deaf ears. Indeed, it is likely that it was during the French trip, or on the return from France, that Anne finally surrendered herself to Henry: certainly, by late January 1533 she was pregnant. Conveniently, the Archbishop of Canterbury, William Warham (a supporter of Katharine of Aragon), had died in August 1532. Thomas Cranmer, who shared the evangelical leanings of Anne and was chaplain to her family, was nominated to the archbishopric by Henry in January 1533 and approved by Clement in the following months.

Henry very much needed Cranmer and his support and, of course, needed the Machiavellian Thomas Cromwell (c. 1485–1540), a former member of Wolsey's household and a man whose ingenious ideas were to propel him to prominence in Henry's court. While still married to Katharine, and with the divorce nowhere in sight, Henry secretly married the pregnant Anne. Further anti-clerical measures were passed by Henry and his Parliament: the Act in Restraint of Appeals meant that Church matters would no longer be sent to Rome for adjudication on appeal, and in April the Southern Convocation of bishops voted that the marriage of Katharine and Henry 'was impeded by divine law, which no Pope could dispense' and was declared null and void by Cranmer.[3]

The speed of events accelerated even further, pushed on by Anne's pregnancy and the need for the child to be legitimate. On 6 April John Fisher, the aged Bishop of Rochester and a stern and prolific critic of the divorce, was briefly arrested. Anne appeared officially as queen on 13 April and less than a month later she and Henry were publicly married.

And what of the Pole family during this period? They had been allies and friends of Katharine of Aragon but, in order to survive, their loyalties had had to adapt and indeed, they were seemingly not openly suspect at this stage as leaders, or even as members, of a conservative faction against Henry and his reforms. In 1530 Montagu (Henry Pole) had signed the petition to the Pope asking for a divorce; on 30 May 1533 Francis, Lord Hastings, the husband of Montagu's daughter, was made a Knight of the Bath; at the banquet following the coronation of Anne Boleyn on 1 June, Geoffrey was a server and Montagu had been intended to be her carver but was unable to attend due to serious illness.[4] Both Katharine and Mary were powerless in the face of the drama which was unfolding. We can only imagine Mary's reaction to the usurpation of her beloved mother and their enforced separation. Inevitably she would not take it well, and it is noteworthy that she was not abandoned by the Poles: the family remained loyal to the mother and daughter. Only four days after the coronation Montagu, Geoffrey and Hastings dined with Mary, and Montagu again dined with her on 24 June.[5]

The Pope was far from idle: on 11 July Clement excommunicated Cranmer and threatened Henry with the same, urging the king to return to Katharine. This was at best wishful thinking: Henry was awaiting the birth of his son and heir. Elizabeth Tudor was born to Anne and Henry on 7 September 1533 and Henry, while disappointed, feigned jubilation. Though Mary may have heaved a sigh of relief at the birth of a daughter, she was in fact mistaken: orders promptly arrived to break up her household and the following month she was instructed to join Elizabeth's household. Her position had greatly diminished in importance.

On 27 September, shortly after the birth of Elizabeth, Chapuys, the resident Imperial ambassador in England, suggested to Charles V that he should intervene with military force and retrieve Reginald from Padua as he and Montagu would have strong claims to the throne. Reginald could then marry Mary. It would be a marriage wished for by the queen, and Mary would not be averse to the idea.[6] This all came to nothing, but the idea of military intervention and of such a union was not new and would resurface again in coming years.

The drama did not abate: in 1534 the influence of Thomas Cromwell became ever more manifest. Parliament confirmed the Act in Restraint of Annates of the previous year, and the Submission of the Clergy rendered Convocation powerless. The Act of Succession of March in that year placed any children of Anne and Henry as heirs to the throne. Mary was in fact disinherited and all male subjects had to take an oath to uphold the Act.[7] After various writings against the divorce (including his publication of *De Causa Matrimonii Serenissimi Regis Angliae* in 1530) and his involvement with the 'Maid of Kent', a Benedictine nun who claimed that visions told her, among other things, how Henry and the country would suffer if he persevered with his divorce, it was the refusal to take this 'oath to the succession' which once again saw John Fisher sent to the Tower and his livings revert to the king on 17 April 1534.

That same day Sir Thomas More was also sent to the Tower. The Act of Succession and its oath were the undoing of both. In May Convocation declared that the authority of the Pope was the same as that of any other foreign bishop – that is, nil – and in documents of the period he is henceforth referred to as the 'Bishop of Rome'. In November and December the Act of Supremacy and the High Treasons Act were passed. Parliament formally recognised Henry as head of the English Church and death awaited anybody guilty of 'maliciously denying the royal supremacy' or speaking against the king. It was also treason to deny that Anne Boleyn was queen or either deny or fail to acknowledge Henry as head of the Church, a move perhaps deliberately aimed at More and Fisher.[8]

Reginald, in the meantime, had become progressively more immersed in theology and religion. This may seem inevitable to us – he was, after all, a holder of ecclesiastical benefices – but it was not a given by any means in the sixteenth century, when benefices were held for personal advantage and a less-than-holy life was often the norm. In late October 1532 he wrote to Sadoleto that 'divine things [are] so much better than human ... [I] have not read so much Latin for four years as I write now, since [I have] been concentrating only on theology'.[9] He sought a life of prayer and study of the Scriptures and became friends with some of the Catholic reformers of the period: men who believed in doing their duty to the Church and to their flock and that the Church could be reformed from within. Gian Matteo Giberti was previously secretary to Clement VII, a reforming bishop and generally regarded as a holy man; Gian Pietro Carafa (1476–1559) co-founded the order of the Theatines and was an austere traditionalist, and Gasparo Contarini (1483–1542) later led efforts to reconcile the Lutherans and the Catholic Church.[10]

This seemingly did not stop Reginald from plotting against Henry, possibly as early as 1534.[11] In that year, Martin de Zormosa, the Spanish consul in Venice, reported to the Emperor that Pole had confided his political aspirations to him. He 'entertained a very intimate correspondence with the discontented English subjects in North Wales, Berwick and Somersetshire and other parts of the kingdom. If the Emperor would only give him a little help, he would easily dethrone king Henry, and place England at the disposal of the Emperor.'[12]

Reginald's claim to the throne, like that of Montagu, as a great-nephew of Edward IV, was a strong one and while he may not have wanted the throne for himself, he most certainly wanted England to return to the fold of the Church. His brother Geoffrey clearly shared this view: in the same period he wanted to enter the Emperor's service in Spain and was only deterred by Chapuys' warning that it would bring much danger to his friends.[13] As Scarisbrick notes, in this period there was 'a serious threat of an aristocratic attempt (backed, if not initiated, by John Fisher), to unseat Henry'.[14]

The death of Clement VII in September 1534 and the election of Alessandro Farnese as Pope Paul III in the following October did little to change relations between England and Rome. On 17 June 1535 Pole wrote to Charles V with a plan of his own which advocated peaceful means first, possibly his return to England to plead and if necessary to be a martyr. Many details of his plan are lost and Charles, despite Contarini's enthusiastic endorsement of Pole and his altruistic aims, was not convinced.[15] This was, of course, high treason but Pole was determined to bring England back into the Catholic fold. And what of the relations between Henry and Reginald at this stage? In short, they were amicable: Henry had allowed him to go abroad once more to study and also funded the trip by allowing him to keep his benefices. He knew that Reginald's views were not his own but seems to have thought that he would come round and was anxious to have his opinion in writing. Reginald agreed, even when, or perhaps because, the request was made by Thomas Starkey, a previous intimate of his at Magdalen, and his secretary at Padua, Paris and the Charterhouse at Sheen. On his return to England, probably in the autumn of 1534, Starkey was appointed chaplain to Reginald's mother, Margaret Pole. Cromwell spotted his use as a link to Reginald and he became a royal chaplain (and indeed champion).[16]

In February 1535, Starkey wrote twice to Pole to ask for his views on the divorce and the supreme headship of the Church in England. He claimed that the king would be happy to have him home even if they disagreed, and:

Henry told me that he would rather you were dead than that you should dissemble in hopes of advancement. No need to fear that people will accuse you of changing your mind, since you were not arrogant in your first opinion, at least as far as I can remember, since I saw your book only once.

This was a reference to the lost book by Pole on the divorce written before he left for Italy and when he was doing his best, but failing, to adapt to Henry's point of view.[17] Further pressure was applied by Cromwell himself. As we shall see, Pole took this advice literally. He replied on 12 April and said he would get to work straight away and make the king happy. He was chivvied again by Starkey in June, who assumed that Pole would be sincere. He expected to hear within two months and that Pole would 'temper your style as your prudence, learning, and judgement' dictate.[18] This was a change from earlier and may reflect Henry's growing insecurity: in the same month bishops were ordered to preach on the royal supremacy each Sunday.[19] Certainly Reginald's attitude changed, almost certainly as a result of learning of the executions of several Carthusian monks who were hanged, drawn and quartered in early May, the beheading of John Fisher (who had been awarded a cardinalate in prison on 21 May) on 22 June, and the execution on 6 July of Sir Thomas More for failing to take the oath of succession.

As Marshall notes, Chapuys was not overstating the case in his descriptions of Fisher and More as 'persons of unequalled reputation in this kingdom'.[20] More and Pole had known each other for some time as well, and it is clear that they shared mutual esteem. From around 1518 Pole was close friends with John Clement, the tutor of More's children and an eminent humanist and physician who married More's ward, Margaret Giggs.[21] At about the same time More wrote to Pole thanking him for his recommendation of a physician and for his mother making up the prescription, and in 1524 Leonico wrote to More that Pole 'constantly speaks about you not less plainly than with truth, and he declares that you may truly and rightly be accounted one of the most learned men alive, deeply versed in the study of all the true arts'.[22]

Many years later, when he was in a position to honour his old acquaintance, Pole was in the vanguard of those pressing for More's recognition as a Catholic martyr and got his own protégé to write More's biography. Montagu was also seemingly sympathetic to More: he had been appointed to the commission to try him, but did not attend the trial.[23]

Pole was perhaps less than honest regarding his intentions. Moving between Venice and Padua, he had already started working on his letter (which was to become a book) by 24 September 1535 (and he finished it by 30 March 1536). At the end of October, he wrote to Cromwell that he was 'certain I always deserved and shall continue to merit his [the king's] favour ... Tell the king I am ready to serve him. Anything I do is his as a payment for my education.'

The king's patronage of Pole was to be repaid. Yet the combination of the deaths of More and Fisher and the forthright defence of Henry's position, together with the denigration of the papacy to be found in works by Richard Sampson (d. 1554) (his *Oratio*) and Stephen Gardiner (1483–1555) (*De vera obedientia*), which reached Pole at the end of 1535, provoked in Pole such a response that Henry must have marvelled at this kind of 'payment' from his cousin. As Pole himself wrote to Contarini: 'These books do not allow me to remain silent.'[24] And indeed, the first two parts of his work *Pro ecclesiasticae Unitatis Defensione*, generally known as *De Unitate Ecclesiastica* (*Defence of the Unity of the Church*), deal mostly with the refutation of these two works.

De Unitate has been described as 'the most significant individual act of resistance to Henry's Reformation'.[25] Reginald's aim was to persuade Henry to return to the Church, but as we will see, this was not the way to do it. *De Unitate* is not an easy read, but certain themes emerge. Perhaps most surprising is his insistence on his gratitude to Henry, 'one who has been so generous to me, one whose many favours I so gratefully acknowledge'. The king 'bestowed exceedingly great benefits upon me', but Reginald must defend the Church. He earnestly believes that he is writing this book for Henry's good.[26] What also stands out his love for Fisher and More, 'my dearest friends', who

suffered gravely at the hand of a Christian king ... They suffered because they did not want to abandon the Church, the spouse of

Christ, while its members were being torn asunder. These men preferred to have their own bodies dismembered rather than have the unity of the body of the Church destroyed.

This was dramatic stuff and more was to follow. Henry had them killed because 'they refused to defer to your opinion'.[27] He criticises Henry for allowing an already frail Fisher to be imprisoned in filthy conditions in the Tower and calls their deaths 'murders' which left him 'speechless and stunned for about a month, shattered as I was by the wonder and novelty of such unheard of cruelty'.[28] He does not hesitate to attack Henry, accusing him of having no scruples in discarding a wife of twenty years because he was 'miserably burning with passion for the love of a girl. She, indeed, has said that she will make herself available to you on one condition alone. You must reject your wife whose place she desires to hold…'[29] Pole believes that Satan influenced Henry to declare himself Supreme Head of the Church, and if he died now then he would not have the right to lawful burial.[30] Pole's hatred of Anne Boleyn is also evident: he states that any marriage to her is as illicit as that to Katharine given that Anne's sister (Mary Boleyn) was the king's lover for a long period. To Reginald, Anne is a 'harlot' and Elizabeth 'the daughter of a prostitute'.[31] Katharine was, in his opinion, and as she herself stated (and seemingly as Henry himself had once told the Emperor), a virgin when she married Henry. Pole may perhaps have learnt from his mother that Arthur, who died aged fifteen, was physically frail and probably unlikely to be able to consummate the marriage.[32]

Reginald appears to be politically naïve, calling on Charles V 'to act on behalf of the Catholic Church, so that England may return to the fold'. He then goes so far as to claim that there was a 'fifth column of Catholic supporters in England, who could rise against their king, if he did not change his ways, and there was also the suggestion of an economic blockade'.[33] This, like his earlier (albeit peaceful) plea to Charles V in June 1535, was treason.[34] Yet *De Unitate* 'is derived from my love for you. As the saying goes, my love for you knows no bounds.' He is aware that plots and assassination attempts may well follow, although 'how could my death be of profit to you?'[35] This was heady stuff, and Thomas Starkey, who had begged Pole to give his opinion to the king, was so aghast at the violence of the treatise that he wrote to the king to express his shock.[36]

Pole sent the work to England in the hands of his servant Michael Throckmorton in May 1536. It was for the king's eyes only, but obviously did not remain so. He had waited until after the death of Anne Boleyn to send it, in the (erroneous) belief that this meant a greater chance of reconciliation between England and Rome. Aware of the incendiary nature of his work, he had tried to ensure that the Pope should not see it (although he almost certainly had heard of its contents). Throckmorton was to tell Henry that his master's only goal was the truth and, given the length of the work, that an abstract would be helpful for the king.[37]

The work arrived in an England that was still far from calm. Anne Boleyn had been executed on seemingly trumped-up charges of adultery and incest on 19 May and eleven days later Henry had married Jane Seymour (*c.* 1508–37), a timid antithesis to the strident Anne. Mary Tudor was refusing to accept the second Act of Succession, which placed any heirs from the marriage of Henry and Jane as first in line to the throne and meant that her parents' marriage was invalid. On 18 July 1536 the Act Extinguishing the Authority of the Bishop of Rome was also passed by Parliament, severing 'England's final links to the papacy. Any expression of support for the Pope's authority became an offence punishable by loss of property under *praemunire*. To refuse another round of oath taking was treason.'[38] And Henry insisted that the devout Mary take the oath. Eventually, and after much agonising, she did so, confirming her father was Supreme Head of the Church and that she was illegitimate on 22 June. Four days later, Margaret Pole returned to court and declared that her son Reginald was a traitor. She had no choice: as if it wasn't enough that they had a claim to the throne, one of the Poles was now throwing insults at the king from Italy. What else could she do? Others wrote to Reginald in despair. Tunstall begged him:

> Remember your country, which you now oppose. The king brought you up. Your support of papal monarchy will discomfit your family and all your friends. Keep searching and you shall find the truth. If you do, the king will have you back.[39]

And, surprisingly, this was seemingly true. *De Unitate* was not the *coup de grâce* for Henry's relationship with Pole. He wrote, via Throckmorton, to invite Reginald back to England to discuss the work as 'their opinions differ in many points, or rather in everything'.[40] As was obvious, Reginald could not return while the oath meant that he would have to say that Henry was head of the English Church.[41] Temptingly, the Pope wished him and other learned, reform-orientated men, including Giberti, Sadoleto and Carafa, to go to Rome to discuss summoning a council of the Church, issuing a formal summons to Pole on 19 July and saying that he would lodge him in the papal palace – a mark of signal favour. Reginald was to represent the English nation.[42] The summoning, and eventual proclamations, of this group was an unsuccessful precursor of the later Council of Trent. Was the Pope intent on a fight with Henry for Pole's 'soul', so to speak? It rather looked like it.

In mid-August Starkey wrote to Reginald complaining that, in addition to the lack of respect for the king shown in *De Unitate*, if he went to Rome at the Pope's bidding 'wise men will think you foolish for following a foreign bishop instead of your "natural sovereign lord"'.[43] There is mention in other correspondence of lost letters from Pole to the king and others which were clearly of a more conciliatory nature, but the call of Rome and the Catholic Church and the possibility of serving on a reforming council were too strong. He ignored the letter from his brother Montagu, in which 'gentle Reginald' was told, 'Let no scrupulosity so embrace your stomach but that we, which be so knit in nature and so happily born under so noble a prince, may so join together to serve him, as our bounden duties require.' If he obeyed a summons from the Bishop of Rome, then 'farewell all bonds of nature, not only of me, but of all mine, or else instead of my blessing they shall have my curse'.[44]

Worse was to follow in a missive from Margaret Pole, perhaps at the king's insistence, but perhaps from her heart: she had never been so upset, even after the death of her husband or of a child, as she had been by the king's anger.[45] Reginald was torn: should he return home? Giberti and Carafa persuaded him not to, and he set off for Rome, arriving in November 1536.

The events of 1536 had been momentous in every sense of the word for Henry VIII: Katharine of Aragon died; Anne Boleyn miscarried a son and was subsequently (and consequently perhaps) executed, as were her brother and five other courtiers accused of adultery and incest with her; Henry fell in love with and married Jane Seymour; England finally separated from the Bishop of Rome (the new name for the Pope); his cousin Pole sent him *De Unitate* with its searing insults and calls for penance; and then, to round off the year, the Pilgrimage of Grace, potentially a revolt which could dethrone a king, sprang into life. Here is not the place for an in-depth exploration of the Pilgrimage. In short, it began in October 1536 in Lincolnshire, and after that was suppressed it spread to other areas of the north and lasted, in sporadic outbursts, until February 1537. Its causes were many: discontent at the break with Rome; religious change as prescribed by the Crown in the Ten Articles of 1536 and elsewhere; the divorce from Katharine of Aragon and the removal of Mary from the line of succession; the dissolution of the smaller monasteries (whose role as a support system in the countryside was often essential); the enclosures of common land and their concomitant economic effect; and the behaviour and policies of Henry's advisors, especially Cromwell. It ended in disaster for the organisers and some of the participants. They had chosen to trust the promises made by the Duke of Norfolk, who had been sent by Henry to quell the rebellion, but execution was the inevitable outcome.[46]

Unrest in England could only seem good news to Reginald and the Pope and, to show his esteem for Reginald (as Pole himself believed) and to give him a position of authority (and thus more able to influence events in England), on 22 December 1536 Paul III made him a cardinal. In the short period he had spent in Rome he had also previously been made an apostolic protonotary, a clerical post in the Vatican administration and a sign of papal approval. Protonotaries were often elevated to the cardinalate, and so it proved with Reginald.[47] He was then given a pension of 200 *scudi* per month on the titular church of Santi Nereo e Achilleo (fig. 7); pointedly, this was the church of which John Fisher had briefly been titular cardinal. Pole did not hold it for long: on 15 January 1537 he was transferred to the more prestigious Santi Vito e Modesto (fig. 8) and on 31 May 1540 to Santa Maria in Cosmedin (fig. 9).[48]

Pole was aware of the dangers that accepting a cardinal's hat would involve. Beccadelli writes:

> Reginald himself was the only objector to this promotion, which he opposed with great modesty and plainness; representing to his holiness that such a dignity would at this juncture be very unseasonable, as it would destroy all his influence in England, where every body [*sic*] would be ready to suspect he would be much too biassed [*sic*] to the interest of the papal see; besides the manifest ruin it would bring his own family.

When ordered to prepare himself for the tonsure, he 'as a sheep before his shearer, &c he resigned himself'.[49]

Whether Henry and his court heard of Reginald's reservations or not, they were horrified. Starkey wrote to him urging him not to accept and Tunstall asked him to give up his red hat, but the deed had been done. To become a cardinal would be declaring himself Henry's 'open enemy'.[50] And Pole's resistance to Henry was important and unprecedented: he became, in the eyes of dissident Catholics, their leader and his resistance was unprecedented. He was not only a man of pious and learned reputation, but an aristocrat and a Yorkist.[51]

Communications were not as swift as today. Although letters could take weeks to arrive, that is no explanation for why both Paul III and Reginald were so slow to take advantage of the Pilgrimage of Grace. Chapuys knew as early as 14 November 1536 that Paul III was thinking of sending Reginald to England and it had already been suggested to the Pope that

Pole should be made a cardinal in early November.[52] Pole wrote to the Pope with a series of demands and suggestions and was appointed papal legate in a secret consistory on 7 February 1537, ostensibly to 'attempt to help forward a general pacification, to inquire into the spread of heresy, and to announce a general council', but he also hoped that he could persuade Francis I and Charles V to support the revolt. Yet this was only approved on 14 February 1537. In fact, Reginald was to issue 'an ultimatum to the king of England, and if that failed, to implement his excommunication by force of arms', but by this time only the last embers of the revolt were flickering.[53] He urged the Pope for a wide-ranging brief and adequate funds, and he finally set out on 18 February. As Pastor notes, 'this delay, and still more the indecision and blind assurance of the "Pilgrims", gave Henry VIII time to subdue the northern districts. The whole movement was a demonstration rather than an actual phase of war, and this Rome [and Pole] did not understand.'[54]

But now, reconciliation between Rome and England was no longer possible (if it ever had been in Henry's eyes). From this point onwards, anybody who communicated with Pole, in any form, was a traitor. The situation was certainly not helped by the Pope offering an indulgence to anyone who committed to returning Henry to the Catholic Church.[55]

Reginald's mission proved to be pointless: neither Francis I or Charles V were eager to offend Henry at this point by entertaining Pole, and he was made to leave France. He hovered around the Low Countries trying to enter the Emperor's territory before finally returning to Rome and renouncing his legation on 19 October 1537.[56] This was one of the most dangerous periods of Pole's life, not only for him but for his family as well: Henry was unforgiving of this 'double dyed traitor'.[57]

5

'PITY IT IS…'

'Pity it is, that the folly of one brainsick Poole, or to say better,
of one witless foole, should be the ruin of so great a family.'[1]

The danger to Reginald's life was quick to manifest itself after
he sent Henry *De Unitate*, accepted a cardinal's hat and then
set off on legation to Francis I and Charles V. The papacy's
aim was to unite these two Catholic rulers against Henry,
the schismatic, and thus abate their mutual enmity and most
importantly stop further disastrous incursions into the Italian
peninsula. For Henry, Pole's legation was the icing on the cake
of his betrayal and if there had been threats but unspecified
danger before (and a refusal to entertain any of Pole's more
accommodating overtures), with this the danger became ever
more open.[2] In April 1537 Sir Francis Bryan (d. 1550), also
known as the Vicar of Hell, a member of the Privy Chamber
and often an intimate of the king, and Sir Peter Mewtas
(d. 1562), also a member of the Privy Chamber, were sent
to France to either kidnap Pole or kill him with a handgun.

Cardinal Ridolfo Pio da Carpi, noting that Bryan was 'as desperate and as unhappy as you can imagine' when he didn't succeed and used 'evil language which showed clearly the state of Henry's soul', urged the Pope to protect Pole at all costs.[3] Yet this was not all-out war against Pole: Bryan's official mission was to stop Pole being received as papal legate by Francis I; killing him was an add-on.[4] And not all were unsympathetic: Bishop Stephen Gardiner was ambassador in France and had been ordered to arrest Pole as a traitor, but he refused and made sure that Francis I simply expelled Pole from France instead. Ambassador Sir Thomas Wyatt (1503–42) was also ambivalent at this point, corresponding with Pole but not meeting him.[5]

As the legation progressed, the situation became openly more serious: while Reginald was kicking his heels in Cambrai in spring 1537 and waiting for positive developments in his legation, he was told that '100,000 pieces of English gold would be given to any man who brought him back to England alive or dead'. The modern equivalent is £15.3 million.[6] Cardinal Érard de la Marck (1472–1538), the Bishop of Liège, was among the rulers offered ten thousand foot soldiers with ten months' pay in a war against France if they would deliver Pole to Henry.[7] It was believed that Henry would have liked to burn Reginald, suspended in chains over a fire.[8] There can be no doubt that this must have been an agonising time for his family and it is difficult not to agree with Soberton that in private the Poles sided with Reginald. Certainly Geoffrey Pole sent Hugh Holland to warn him about the plots and allegedly said that if Mewtas had succeeded in killing Reginald, then he in turn would have killed Mewtas, even if he was in the king's presence.[9]

Pole was not always as cowardly as he is sometimes portrayed: he refused to travel to Liège, a safe haven, in disguise, and only accepted an escort. Attempts were made to infiltrate his household and in this period a William Vaughan tried to join Pole as a servant, only to find that Pole in turn tried to 'turn' him to gather news for himself. The cardinal was very cognisant of the fact that he had lost everything he most valued – country, family and friends – for what he saw as truth and justice, but he was ready to do anything 'for the honour of the head of the Church and the utility of his Church' and if need be he would give up his life for the same. The Pope persisted in summoning him back to Rome from his legation, but even this was dangerous, with the need to find a safe route which would avoid potential ambushes.[10] He was eventually welcomed back by the Pope and cardinals in Rome on 18 October 1537.

If Henry could not punish him abroad, then he would do so at home. Pole was stripped of his benefice at Wimborne in June 1537 and worse was to follow. Prince Edward was born on 12 October of that year, but any hopes that the arrival of a son might have assuaged what Pole called Henry's 'insatiable hatred' were misplaced, and certainly after the death of Jane Seymour in the weeks following Edward's birth Henry was grief stricken. A gradual chill towards other members of the Pole family began to be felt: although Montagu was present at the christening of Edward, Geoffrey Pole was not admitted to court and the brother of Michael Throckmorton (Pole's servant who had delivered *De Unitate* and who had double-crossed Cromwell) was sent to the Tower.[11]

Pole, meanwhile, was occupied on Church business, although, as ever, this was often linked to politics. In January 1538 he was part of the group of cardinals preparing for a general council and in April he accompanied the Pope and other members of the curia on the long journey to a peace conference at Nice where the Emperor 'embraced him with the cordiality of a brother, and honoured him with his conversation for a considerable space of time', although Sir Thomas Wyatt was now trying to 'do something' about Pole.[12] The outcome of the Nice conference was not to Henry's advantage: the Treaty of Toledo of January 1539 saw a ten-year truce between the Emperor and Francis I. Henry was essentially sidelined in the power play of Europe, and, as the frantic fortification of 1539 shows, frightened that they would join forces against him.[13] He and Cromwell decided to flex their muscles at home.

Cuthbert Tunstall's warning that Reginald's family would suffer proved to be prescient.[14] On 29 August 1538 Geoffrey Pole was arrested and sent to the Tower. He was held for two months before being interrogated and what he then said had disastrous consequences for the surviving members of the Pole family. This has come to be known as the 'Exeter Conspiracy', and in essence it involved the uprooting and destruction of the remaining legitimate offshoots of the Plantagenets, namely those descended from Edward IV who had a claim to the throne. On 26 October, under huge psychological pressure and having attempted suicide, and perhaps under the threat of torture, Geoffrey began to talk. He ignored Montagu's earlier warning that he should 'never open anything if he should be examined, for if he opened one all must needs come out'.[15] Soon Lord Montagu and his son Henry Pole were arrested and sent to the Tower, as were his cousin Henry Courtenay, Marquess of Exeter, and Sir Edward Neville.

Yet there were robust reasons for the arrest of Geoffrey: he had corresponded with Reginald without showing these letters to the king and had sent Hugh Holland to meet Reginald and warn him of the danger to his person and that 'the world in

England waxes all crooked'.[16] There were less robust reasons for the arrest of the others, including Courtenay's wife Gertrude and their son Edward. Much was hearsay based on the evidence of their servants about remarks made about the king, but it must be said that these remarks were indeed treasonous by the strict letter of the recent and draconian legislation. It had also been agreed among them that if the king were to die, then Mary would accede to the throne and marry Reginald (who was only a cardinal deacon and could be dispensed from his orders). It was no longer possible for a person to wish the cardinal well – 'Reynold [Reginald] should do good one day' – or to speculate on, or allude to, the king's death. Montagu had made a series of incriminating remarks in the hearing of his brother and a servant named Jerome Ragland, including that 'the king is not dead, but he will one day die suddenly; his leg will kill him and then we shall have jolly stirring' and that 'the king has a sort of knaves in his privy chamber about him'.[17]

Indeed, both Montagu and Courtenay had 'form': Montagu had been imprisoned briefly when the Duke of Buckingham was tried for treason and the Marquess of Exeter was removed from the Privy Chamber in 1531 and accused of 'assembling' the locals of Cornwall.[18] Montagu was not really one of Henry's inner circle: he was never a member of the Privy Chamber and was never appointed to the Order of the Garter. His role at court was ceremonial.[19] Neville was guilty by association: he was the brother of George, Baron Abergavenny, and his niece Jane was married to Montagu. They were charged with 'desiring the king's death and seeking to deprive him of his title as Supreme Head of the Church ... and with abetting Cardinal Reginald Pole'.[20] If, ostensibly, the evidence was far from concrete, there were in fact signs of collusion which are not mentioned in the interrogations and were thus presumably not known to Cromwell or the king but which support the thesis that those arrested had been unhappy: in late March 1536 Montagu had dined with Eustace Chapuys, the Emperor's ambassador, to update him on a possible new marriage for the king; Gertrude Courtenay was also in regular contact with Chapuys and the latter had to warn Geoffrey Pole to be more discreet in his dealings: he had seemingly regularly asked Chapuys to urge the Emperor to invade.[21]

At this point it would seem that Castillon, the French ambassador, was correct when he wrote on 5 November 1538:

> The king told me a long time ago he wants to exterminate the House of Montague that belongs to the White Rose, the Pole family, of which the cardinal is a member … So far I don't know what he means to do about the Marquess … It looks as if he is searching for any excuse he can find to destroy them.[22]

Those arrested paid the price. In early December Montagu and Exeter were tried in separate trials. On 9 December their servants and associates mentioned in the interrogations were hanged, drawn and quartered at Tyburn, and Montagu and Exeter and Neville were then beheaded on Tower Green. That same month Paul III was finally ready to promulgate the bull of excommunication against Henry which in theory would depose him and absolve his subjects from obedience. He was ostensibly moved by the dissolution of the monasteries which had begun in 1536, Henry's negotiations with Lutherans and the destructions of shrines, above all that of Thomas Becket.[23] Geoffrey, ashamed and bewildered, was pardoned, released and eventually fled to Flanders and later joined Reginald in Rome.[24] Sir Nicholas Carew (1496–1539), Henry's master of the horse, was also implicated in the Exeter Conspiracy and executed the following year. Gertrude Courtenay was eventually pardoned and released but the young Henry Pole and Edward Courtenay remained in the Tower. Henry was never seen again, although there were hopes that he would be released, and Edward was to play a significant role in later events.[25]

The executions were not well received in other countries and a campaign was begun by Cromwell to further blacken the conspirators' names by claiming that Reginald had planned to return to England and that they would together have driven out Henry and married Edward Courtenay (the son of the marquis) to Mary Tudor and even replaced Henry with the Marquess of Exeter. Henry himself told Sir Thomas Wyatt to inform the Emperor that Montagu and Exeter had planned to murder the whole royal family.[26] This was set down in writing by Richard Morison (who had ironically benefitted from Pole's patronage when abroad) in his *An Invective against the Great and Detestable Vice, Treason*, as will be discussed in a later chapter. Although all of this was seemingly shutting the stable door after the horse had bolted, it was clearly felt that action needed to be taken.

Did the plot exist? Was it, as has been claimed, 'probably nothing more than a fiction'?[27] Were they just muttering aloud what many people thought or had they secretly formulated plans which simply had not come to light? It is difficult not to agree with the Dodds sisters who note, 'They were less a political party than a group of friends, who loved the old Faith, hated Cromwell, and longed for a change of policy ... They did not trouble themselves about anything so strenuous and intellectual as a plot.'[28] Certainly, they were guilty of treason within its legal definition, but it is difficult to say that they formed a real threat to Henry, despite his paranoia about the alliance of Francis and Charles. If Charles or Francis had invaded then Exeter's lands in Devon and Cornwall would have been a threat to Henry, but neither was actively contemplating invasion.[29] Yet it is also difficult to disagree with Pierce that 'they possessed the inclination [to plot against the crown] and a real potential to do so'.[30] England was fraught with anxiety following the Treaty of Toledo: the French ambassador, de Marillac, wrote to Francis I on 2 April 1539 of the fear of war and how 'the coast has been fortified and one hundred and fifty vessels had been armed and made ready'.[31] The Act of Six Articles, almost reactionary in some of its affirmations of traditional Roman Catholic teaching, was rushed through Parliament to appease Charles V and the Pope. Henry, faced with the political alliance of France and the Holy Roman Emperor and Reginald's behaviour, could not have acted otherwise: 'The families had both the propensity and the capability to threaten the security of his throne, and it is not surprising that they died for it.'[32]

An innocent victim of all this was Reginald's mother, Margaret Pole. Once a favourite of Henry VIII, the fact that the royal progress of the summer of 1538 passed close to her main residence of Warblington Castle but did not stop there was a sign of her impending fall from grace. She was implicated by no one in the interrogations of Geoffrey and the others, but again had lands in Wiltshire and Hampshire which would have proved useful in an invasion. She was also the mother of one executed traitor and another who lived abroad lambasting Henry with anathemas, in addition to Geoffrey, who had to live with the guilt of the 'evidence' he had revealed. Hers is not a happy story (if there ever is such a thing in the Henrician age). In early 1539 she was closely questioned at her own home and that of the Earl of Southampton but gave nothing away, most probably because she had nothing to give away. She was simply an ardent Catholic who had favoured Katharine of Aragon and was still loyal to her daughter, Mary Tudor. Margaret was clearly a formidable figure: the earl and the Bishop of Ely, her interrogators, wrote to Cromwell that 'we may call her rather a strong and constant man, than a woman. For in all behaviour, how so ever we have used her, she has showed herself so earnest, vehement and precise, that more could not be.'[33]

An attainder was passed against all members of the conspiracy, including Margaret and Reginald, in May 1539: Margaret's possessions and lands, which might have proved so useful to an invading army, were taken by the Crown. She was sent to the Tower by 20 November of that year at the latest.[34] The only evidence ever produced against her was a tunic conveniently found in her home which had on it the king's coat of arms and pansies and marigolds, the flowers representing a possible union between Reginald and Mary, a supposition which, as we shall see, recurred in Reginald's life.[35] She languished in the cold and damp Tower for eighteen months and her request for warm clothes was actioned by the council in March 1541, so she was clearly to be made comfortable at that point. It is unknown if she was able to see and comfort her young grandson Henry Pole or Edward Courtenay. Reginald was thunderstruck by her arrest and imprisonment: in September 1539 he wrote to Contarini:

You have heard that my mother has been condemned, to eternal life. This septuagenarian [*sic*] woman has no close relative except her daughter [Ursula Pole], and my house has only my nephew left. The tyranny began with the priests, spread to the nobles, to women, and to innocent children...[36]

All, including Margaret, were surprised when she was executed on 29 May 1541. De Marillac, the French ambassador, describes her death and execution as 'a case worthy of ... great compassion'.[37] She was taken out of her prison at seven in the morning and executed with few witnesses. She died, aged sixty-seven, at the hands of an inexpert executioner: it took several attempts to decapitate her and it was a sorrowful end. In the eyes of de Marillac, her 'long imprisonment, her noble birth, her age ... and the fact that she had lost one son, seen another banished and the total ruin of her house should have exempted her from such a death given that a natural death could not have been so far away'.[38]

There are various possible explanations for this sudden decision by Henry. For instance, the French ambassador had heard that the Tower was to be cleared before Henry started his royal progress in the north of the country and there had also been further unrest in the north earlier that year: Henry presumably feared that she might become a figure head for a new uprising. Henry still hated Reginald and knew that the death of his mother would cut him to the quick. There is also the possibility that Reginald was, or had been, intent upon rescuing her.[39] There is a memorial to her, but not on the site of the execution, and she is buried inside the church of St Peter ad Vincula within the Tower.

The life of Henry Pole, Montagu's son, still hung in the balance: despite being 'so young and innocent' it was rumoured in June 1541 that he would be one of the next to lose his life as it would be difficult for the king to forgive him, most probably because of who he was: Pole's nephew. In July Courtenay was allowed to exercise more and had been appointed a tutor, while Henry was 'badly and strictly confined' and was not allowed the same.[40] He then disappeared from sight – his fate is one of the great Tudor mysteries.

Reginald himself believed that his family's downfall was linked to their devotion to the Church, and they were thus martyrs. In reply to the letter of condolence from Francis I he replied that the 'calamities … are connected with those of the Church, and of the [Catholic] religion'.[41] And he had again been asked by the Pope to act as legate for the Church, this time setting off on legation on 27 December 1538, with a view to papal promulgation of the excommunication of Henry VIII. Scarisbrick believes that 'officially Pole's purpose was to call upon Charles and Francis to withdraw ambassadors from England and impose a commercial embargo, but there can be no doubt that he thought in terms of military action and had set out for Spain to preside, as he hoped, over an invasion of his motherland'.[42]

He was to be disappointed. Pole went to see the Emperor in Toledo but to no avail: despite an audience of over an hour, Charles would not move without Francis and wanted to concentrate on defeating the Turks and tackling the Lutherans; Francis I meanwhile did not receive the legate and refused to act without Charles V. Furthermore, Pole's life was, once again, repeatedly under threat: Wyatt, now ambassador to the Emperor, requested that Pole's diplomatic immunity be removed and pledged his own money as a reward for Pole's death; the cardinal had to stay longer in Gerona because of an assassination plot.[43] If Henry believed Reginald's relatives were guilty of treason, then the cardinal himself was even further tainted by this legation. It was treachery of the highest degree.

On his return from legation, Reginald stopped at Carpentras to see Sadoleto and then at Verona to spend time with his friend Gian Matteo Giberti, having received permission from Paul III to absent himself from Rome till Christmas. He stayed in monasteries and was greatly saddened and wrote to Contarini that he needed 'solitude for my sick soul'.[44] He spent the year of 1540 in Rome and the threat level was still sufficiently high (and would remain so while Henry was still alive) for the Pope to give him a bodyguard.[45] For the next few years, religion, learning and reform were hopefully to provide a quieter life for Cardinal Pole.

6

DANGER FOR POLE FROM WITHIN THE CHURCH

By the 1540s Cardinal Pole had two sets of enemies: those in England and those within the Church. But how did he become, in the eyes of some, an enemy of the Catholic Church?

During his first stay at Padua, Reginald had studied philosophy and the classical authors; his second stay in the 1530s saw a very different emphasis. As can be seen from the company he kept, his acceptance of the cardinal's hat and, of course, from *De Unitate*, his thoughts had turned to religion. In December 1535, at the very time that Pole was writing his book, John Friar wrote to Starkey from Padua that 'Pole is studying divinity ... despising things merely human and terrestrial. He is undergoing a great change, exchanging man for God.'[1]

Pole himself believed that his mother had destined him for a Church career. It can be of little surprise to us, with hindsight, that a boy/man who ostensibly showed little interest in religion *per se* should have been gifted to the Church: we only have to think of the notorious Borgia cardinals or, closer to home,

Cardinal Wolsey, who viewed an ecclesiastical career not just as a route to God (and he was, in some ways, a reformer) but also as a path to power. However, Reginald was a little different: yes, the cardinalate would help him influence English affairs, but he had also become a devout and pious man. Reginald's 'conversion' had been fermenting for some time and was to become absolute. It was his commitment to the Catholic Church and the Pope which saw him held in esteem by popes and many cardinals for much of his career – and, of course, hated by Henry VIII. He was a reformer, but still a Catholic.[2]

Reginald had met Gian Matteo Giberti, who was soon to become an important reforming bishop, during his first stay in Italy. He had been horrified by the stench of corruption he encountered during a brief (and supposedly anonymous) visit to Rome in 1525 and had withdrawn to a retreat at Syon after his return from the canvassing of the theologians of Paris. Surely all of this must have contributed to a sense of religious purpose. On his return to Italy, Reginald visited the reformer Jacopo Sadoleto at Carpentras and then moved to Venice in 1534/5, living in a house on the Grand Canal and enjoying the company of reformers such as the influential Benedictine abbot Gregorio Cortese in the gardens of the abbey of San Giorgio Maggiore, where he argued that 'virtue alone could conquer fortune and make man immortal'.[3] Pole's closeness to the Benedictines would continue throughout his career and he eventually became Cardinal Protector of the order.

It was thus perhaps inevitable that Reginald was drawn to Catholic reform. But what exactly was this? It had begun some time before Martin Luther nailed his ninety-five theses against Church practices to the church door in Wittenberg and was thus not a movement which began in opposition to Protestantism (a label later given to those of the Lutheran persuasion): its purpose was 'to correct ills in the Church and reinvigorate its life and mission'.[4] New religious orders sprang up and there was an emphasis on charity and a holy way of life, as witnessed by the *Compagnia del Divino Amore*, which spread to Rome early in the sixteenth century and is now seen by some as 'marking the beginning of effective Catholic reform'.[5] Gian Pietro Carafa, who was at first Pole's friend and then later his enemy, especially when he reigned as Pope Paul IV (fig. 10), was a member. The point is that it was *Catholic* reform: it abhorred the idea of schism. The movement gathered momentum with the election of the aged (and previously corrupt) Pope Paul III in 1534. Paul was surprisingly very receptive to the idea of the reform of the Church and had favoured the idea of a general council from the beginning of his papacy. This was to come to life with the Council of Trent in the 1540s, in which Pole was to play his part.

It was Reginald's friend, Gaspare Contarini, who was to provide the stimulus for many of Paul's initiatives. He suggested the formation of a reform council in 1536. As we saw in the previous chapter, Paul invited a number of reformers to Rome – Carafa, Cortese, Giberti, Sadoleto and Pole, among others – and they had arrived in Rome by November of that year. Pole was given rooms in the Vatican above the Pope's and began to wear ecclesiastical dress.[6] Of note is the fact that Pole was the only layman in this group, indicating the esteem in which he was held by both the Pope and Contarini. It is simply not enough to say that on hearing news of the contents of *De Unitate* the Pope 'subsequently summoned him to Rome to make him a cardinal'.[7] He was summoned to Rome also for his personal qualities, learning and piety, all of which could be brought to bear on Church reform.

The council conferred for three months and in March 1537 submitted the report of the *Consilium delectorum cardinalium et aliorum prelatorum de emendanda ecclesia* (Council of selected cardinals and other prelates concerning correcting the Church). Although the report, which advocated an overhaul of the curial system and an emphasis on the pastoral responsibilities of priests, lingered on some dusty Vatican shelf it was, in Olin's opinion, 'preparing for the future' and papal support for the idea of reform was confirmed by the elevation to the cardinalate of three members of the commission – Carafa, Sadoleto and Pole – in December of 1536. Reginald was clearly viewed as a reforming force: in 1537 he was chosen as one of four cardinals to reform the Datary (the office responsible for the collation of certain benefices to suitable candidates) and in January 1538 he was one of the cardinals chosen to prepare for a general council of the Church.[8] As Ryrie notes, in Italy in the 1520s and 1530s 'reformation seemed like a real possibility'. The aim was not to banish Lutherans and other dissidents from the loving arms of the Church, but to 'absorb, co-opt, and house train his [Luther's] insights, views which pushed Catholic orthodoxy in a particular direction but did not, yet, contradict it'.[9]

Reform was in the air not only in Rome. In Naples there was a group who followed the preachings of Juan de Valdés (*c.* 1490–1541). He had fled Spain to avoid the Inquisition which was investigating his views, among which, perhaps most significantly, was the 'priority of faith over works to secure salvation' or justification by faith alone (*sola fide*), as it came to be known. This was a concept shared by Luther and other Protestants, but stood in contradiction to the Catholic belief of the importance of good works for salvation.[10] Valdés had arrived in Naples by 1535 and published many influential works. Among his followers were four people who were to become important to Reginald in the following years: poets Marc'Antonio Flaminio and Vittoria Colonna (1492–1547) (fig. 11), and Giulia Gonzaga (1513–66) and Pietro Carnesecchi (1508–67).

Pole found his beliefs to be in line with the group of reformers known as the *spirituali* (the spirituals) and was eventually to be viewed as their leader. He was for inclusion, not exclusion, and was 'both "reformer" and "Catholic"'.[11] At this point the *spirituali* were still united with another group of Italian reformers, the *zelanti* (the zealous or hardliners), who included Carafa in their ranks. Both worked together until the Colloquy of Regensburg in early 1541 (an attempt to bring religious unity to Europe) and these years saw the *spirituali* at their apogee: it was a 'time of confidence and hope, when it seemed that the schism [between Catholics and Lutherans] might be healed'.[12] But Regensburg was a disaster: Cardinal Contarini developed a thesis on justification by faith which the Lutherans accepted only to find that in Rome the Pope and consistory rejected it. For reasons which remain unclear to this day, Pole, a close friend and supporter of Contarini, left Rome and did not give it as much support as a baffled Contarini expected. Pole made excuses about his departure, which may have been caused by some doubts about Contarini's solution, and claimed he had tried to return to Rome but did not make it in time. Pietro Bembo blamed Pole's absence from Rome for its rejection by the Vatican.[13]

After the collapse of Regensburg, relations between the *spirituali* and the *zelanti* worsened. Pole was appointed as legate to the Patrimony of St Peter in August 1541 and was based at Viterbo where he gathered around him a like-minded group of reformers in what has come to be known as the *ecclesia Viterbiensis* (the church of Viterbo).[14] Schenk describes the time at Viterbo as the start of 'the second stage of his spiritual maturity'. Pole had previously leant on Contarini and now others leant on him.[15] The reformist preachers Bernardino Ochino (1487–1564), vice general of the Capuchins and a favourite of Vittoria Colonna, and Pietro Martire Vermigli/Peter Martyr (1499–1562), an old friend of Pole, were commissioned to preach and Pole had previously pushed for papal approval of Vermigli.[16]

Flaminio, who had been with Valdés in Naples, joined Pole at Viterbo in October 1541 – not, as some believed, to convert Pole to more extreme views, but because Pole, as he himself stated, recognised that Flaminio's soul was in danger and wished to lead him again onto the path of moderation. As Apollonio Merenda later testified, however, Flaminio had preached Valdesian ideas to the group (and would help in the publication of some of Valdés' works after his death).[17] Vittoria Colonna resided in a nearby convent during these years and sought Pole's spiritual advice. William Peto (1483–1559), an Observant Franciscan friar who had spoken out against Henry's divorce, been imprisoned and cited in the same attainder as Reginald, also joined the group and was to figure again during Pole's time in England.[18] There even seemed to be papal approval of the views of the *spirituali*: a consistory of 2 June 1542 saw the elevation to the cardinalate of Giovanni Morone, Tommaso Badia and Gregorio Cortese, all of whom are generally viewed as supporting the beliefs of the *ecclesia viterbiensis*. Morone was certainly close to Pole in the coming years.

The days of the Viterbo group were spent in idyllic theological leisure. The administration of the Patrimony was light work and Pole wrote to Contarini that he studied in the morning, saw to official business in the afternoon and 'the rest of the day I pass with this whole and useful company of Carnesecchi and our Marc'antonio Flaminio ... Marc'antonio feeds me, and the better part of our household, with "food which does not die" in such a manner that I do not know when I have felt greater consolation, nor greater edification.' He worried that this idyll would be interrupted, and this proved to be the case.[19]

The death of Contarini in August 1542 devastated Pole but did not endanger him or the Viterbo group. In the same period the flight to Protestant countries of Vermigli (who had informed Pole of his decision to flee) and Ochino (who had been summoned to Rome by the Inquisition and consulted Contarini, Pole and Vittoria Colonna, among others, as to whether he should obey the summons) was far more dangerous. He even continued to write to Colonna from abroad, sending her a new sermon in December of that year. After seeking advice from Pole, she forwarded his letter and sermon to the Inquisition. Her letter to Cardinal Cervini, her friendly contact in the Inquisition, makes clear her awareness of the danger in which the *spirituali* found themselves:

> It pains me much that the more he thinks to excuse himself the more he condemns himself and the more he thinks to save others from the shipwreck the more he exposes them to the floods.[20]

Even worse, Emanuele Tremelli, a Jewish scholar whom Pole had converted to the Catholic faith in 1540, also absconded to the Protestants.[21] The impact of these separate flights from Italy and the Church took a while to sink in but it soon overturned earlier opinions such as that of an agent of Cardinal Gonzaga who had previously reported that 'the Inquisition may examine the writings of Valdés through and through, but concerning Pole and his companions, the best opinion prevails'.[22] There now seemed to be a 'new and unlooked for coalescence between the concerns of the *spirituali* and those of the Protestant reformers'.[23] Although Ochino and Vermigli had escaped the Inquisition, the latter then turned its beady eye towards the Viterbo group with Pole at its head. Indeed, this has been viewed as the point at which 'a far more repressive and intransigent attitude began to dominate the Catholic scene'.[24]

The publication in Venice in 1543 of the anonymous *Trattato utilissimo del beneficio di Gesu Cristo crocifisso verso I christiani* (*The Benefit of Christ Crucified*) sharpened Inquisitorial knives. It was to prove very popular, allegedly selling over forty thousand copies over the coming years, but enjoying less popularity with the Inquisition, being banned in Venice in 1549 and burnt in Naples.[25] Questions over its authorship still remain, but it is now generally accepted that Pietro Carnesecchi was correct in later asserting that it was initially written by a Benedictine monk associated with Valdés' followers, Benedetto da Mantova, and then rewritten at the monk's request by Flaminio (seemingly with Pole's help) at Viterbo.[26] There is little doubt that Pole was closely linked to a book whose 'central theme is the remission of sins, as a gift received by the believer as a result of Christ's Passion and death on the Cross. It has no place for works in the process of achieving salvation.'[27] Once again the concept of justification by faith alone was seemingly central to Pole's beliefs, although, as will be seen, what he was able to condone in an anonymous publication was more than he was able to later condone in public. There was to be a clash between his personal views and those that he had to propound as a cardinal prince of the Church.

And it was as a prince of the Church and as a papal legate *a latere* (representing the Pope) that he was sent to Trent where the general council was to be held. Murphy believes that the 'culmination of Pole's role as a "reformer" came in his service as legate at Trent'.[28] The council was convoked in October 1542 for November of that year and Pole was appointed a legate with full powers to make decisions along with Cardinals Parisi and Morone. The appointment of Pole and Morone, another cardinal whose orthodoxy was suspect and who had associations with the Viterbo group, perhaps indicated tacit papal approval for the Viterbo 'church'. Few of those summoned arrived at Trent and Pole stayed in the city until May 1543. This false dawn was followed by the council proper, which met in December 1545 and continued, in three sessions, until December 1563. Pole's attendance, this time with Cardinals Cervini and del Monte as legates (notably only Pole's appointment was unchanged), was not long lived 'despite the great distinction paid to Pole by all present' as witnessed by Beccadelli.[29] What exactly was the purpose of the council? It had the opposite aim of Regensburg (and indeed of Pole's own beliefs) and was not aimed at bringing people together, but it 'systematically clarified, and hardened, nearly every position in Catholic theology'.[30] It was schism made flesh.

He left for Trent in early April 1545. In the gap between the two councils he had written a book, *De Concilio liber Reginaldi Poli*, on the council and its purpose. Overell believes that 'Pole's main interventions at the council were attempts to slow down proceedings so that Protestant delegates might arrive in time to give their views'.[31] On 7 January 1546 an opening address written by Pole, the *Admonitio ad Patres*, was read to the council by Angelo Massarelli, who was a far more orthodox figure and thus able to lend it more credence. Pole wrote that the council's three main tasks were 'the uprooting of heresies, the reformation of ecclesiastical discipline and of morals, and lastly the external peace of the whole Church'.[32] He believed that of the evils of the Church 'we are in great part the cause'. They were all to examine their collective conscience for 'our ambition, our avarice, our cupidity have wrought all these evils on the people of God'. Ever wary of the role of rulers in religion, he was adamant that those at the council 'must serve their princes with all loyalty and zeal; but as becomes bishops. They must serve them as the servants of God and not as servants of men.'[33] Their allegiance was to be to the Church, and not to their country. They were, in effect, to follow Pole's own example. Such was its success that it was read again at subsequent opening sessions of the council.

Pole fell ill in early 1546 and gave his last speech to the council on 21 June, asking for delegates to follow the *via media*, the middle way, by reading all works (and thus also implying Lutheran works) 'with an open mind, retaining whatever was worthy of approval, and rejecting what was not ... Impartiality must be their guiding spirit.'[34] This was undoubtedly based on his personal experience: at Viterbo the group had openly read 'a great quantity of Lutheran books' as Bernardo de Bartoli, previously a Viterbo intimate, testified in 1555.[35] On 28 June, with papal licence, he left Trent for Padua as his health had all but collapsed. This, happily for later critics of Pole, coincided with the council's debate on justification by faith. Yet Pole had been dogged by ill health throughout his life: he suffered from what was probably the sweating sickness in 1519, was ill again in 1525 and 1532, and in 1537 had a 'catarrh' and fever; he was ill again in 1538; was delayed in arriving at Toledo due to ill health and was once again ill in November 1547 and again in April 1555.[36] The problems at Trent with his left arm and then his eye were seemingly severe and could potentially have resulted in paralysis. They were also commented on by contemporaries – Beccadelli described them as a 'rheumatic disorder' – and are thus unlikely to be a fiction. He then spent the next two months sick and recovering at Priuli's villa at Treviso.[37]

Reginald contributed to the discussion on justification through his nominee Girolamo Seripando and via letters. Ostensibly because of his ill health, the Pope did not force him to return to Trent. Although he was to give his opinion on a draft decree on justification, he excused himself on the grounds of his illness. Instead, he sent a memorandum, *De Iustificatione annotatio*, on 9 October in which he 'showed himself to favour a view of justification which was in essentials Lutheran'.[38] Yet the council passed a definition of justification as a mixture of good works and faith. Pole had failed. He was still quietly rebelling, which would remain very rare for Pole: when it came to Church matters he was normally nothing if not obedient. He did not sign the first decree on justification of early 1547 and did not attach his seal to two printed versions of the decree of 1548 and 1549.[39] He returned to Rome on the Pope's orders but still flourished in the Vatican, taking a 'leading role in consistory, and was identified with Morone as spearheading reform efforts'.[40] Ironically, given all the future problems that his stance on justification would cause him, Fenlon believes that by 1554 Pole, having studied the epistle of St James, had accepted the decree promulgated by the council.[41]

The Inquisition continued to circle members of the Viterbo group. In 1546 Pietro Carnesecchi was summoned to Rome. This was 'intended to be an exemplary demonstration of

Cardinal Carafa's intention to move against "the enemy within"'.[42] Pole wrote to Paul III pleading for Carnsesecchi's release as he knew his 'singular probity' and piety.[43] He succeeded, but Carnesecchi was arrested three more times over the coming years, culminating in his execution for heresy in 1567. The Inquisition rarely gave up its pursuit of those in its sights. In 1550 Pole was appointed to a commission to supervise the Inquisition but was unable to stand up for others of his supporters who fell into the Inquisitorial net, such as his chaplain Apollonio Merenda and Vittore Soranzo (1500–58). Indeed, by 1551 he had withdrawn from the commission.[44]

Thus the late 1540s saw Pole still held in high esteem by many in the church, albeit under the watchful gaze of the distant *zelanti*. More drama was to follow. In 1549 Paul III died. A conclave of the cardinals and their attendants began in November of that year and it was to last a long time. Each cardinal cast a vote in each ballot and a two-thirds majority was required to accede to the throne of St Peter. There is an Italian saying, *'chi entra papa, esce sempre cardinale'* (who enters the conclave as Pope, always comes out a cardinal), and this was to prove true in the case of Cardinal Pole. At play in a conclave were both religious and political forces. Paul III had seemingly left instructions for his grandson Cardinal Alessandro Farnese, and described Pole as 'superior to all others, in his birth, his character, and his learning'.[45] Although many fellow cardinals shared this view, the support of the Emperor and his own youth, his reforming zeal, his passivity towards becoming Pope and his English nationality were to work against him. For some he would be 'too holy to be elected' and for others not conventionally holy enough.[46]

Yet as Murphy notes, he was eminently suitable for the highest post in the Catholic Church: he had defended the papacy to the last in *De Unitate* and was well known throughout Europe thanks to his legations and voluminous correspondence.[47] In fact he was very much the early favourite to succeed Paul: the bankers' odd were 80 to 1, then rising as high as 95: and at one point he came within one vote of the two-thirds majority needed. The French cardinals had yet to arrive and the Imperialists, fearing that their arrival would mean the election of a Pope unfavourable towards the Emperor, tried to have Pole elected by acclamation, i.e. a 'general rendering of homage' by the cardinals. The upright Reginald 'caused his friends to be informed that he desired to ascend to the Supreme Pontificate through the door, but not through the window'.[48]

By 5 December it was assumed that he would be the next pontiff: 'The papal vestments had already been laid out for Pole, and he had himself composed an address of thanks which he had shown to several persons. Outside, in front of the Vatican, the people assembled in great crowds, while the troops were standing with flying colours, ready to salute the new Pope.'[49] They were so sure that Pole would be made Pope that the conclave itself, with its separate cardinalitial cells, was being dismantled by the conclavists.[50] It was not to be: Carafa, a *zelante* to his back teeth, attacked Pole's orthodoxy, especially in the matter of justification, before the vote of 5 December and accused him not only of being a heretic but of sheltering a 'platoon of heretics' at Viterbo. Pole treated him as if he was mad, yet Carafa's intervention may well have proved to be the deciding factor. It was certainly seen as such in the *Pasquinate* (the anonymous satirical verses attached to an allegedly talking Roman statue in Rome, and a good barometer of contemporary opinion). In one Carafa was berated:

> You should be ashamed ...
> to have treated the English Cardinal so badly
> He wanted the papacy
> And you, in front of all the cardinals
> As a rotten Imperial heretic
> you canonized him with a thousand proofs.[51]

Pole was not elected pontiff and the conclave dragged on until the election of Giovanni del Monte as Julius III on 8 February 1550.[52] As Ryrie notes, the failure to elect Pole 'is another tantalizing might-have-been: a young, idealistic and energetically reforming pontiff, determined to hold both the centre and also to widen the circle in an effort to bring home as many of the sundered Protestant brethren as possible'.[53] Pole had behaved nobly, but also passively, with regards to becoming Pope. He wrote to the nephew of Jacopo Sadoleto that he was conscious of having put God ahead of himself in the conclave and his attitude is reflected in a letter by Marc'antonio Flaminio to Ulisse Bassiano of 14 December 1549: 'As far as regards becoming Pope, you can be absolutely sure that our cardinal [Pole] will come out of the conclave as equally happy if he is a cardinal as if he is a Pope, but no one will believe this, not knowing him as well as I do.'[54]

Was it God or love for his country which had stopped Reginald accepting the papacy? Nicholas Harpsfield (1519–75), a Catholic exile and later a close collaborator with Pole in England, believed that he had refused through love of England and the hope that someday he would personally be able to reunite the country to Rome.[55] Or did he simply not want the responsibility? Beccadelli wrote that Reginald saw being Pope as 'an object of dread, not of ambition, and he should pity the man who looked on it in any other light'.[56]

Although not Pope, Reginald was still a highly esteemed cardinal and the year after the election of Julius saw him appointed to commissions supervising the Inquisition, the reformation of the Datary and the workings of the reconvened General Council at Trent. The following three years would see him busy on papal business.[57] However, he now had a declared enemy, Cardinal Carafa, whose view was that 'heretics must be treated as heretics'.[58] Carafa forgave little, and he was to be the bane of Pole's life in his last years.

7

DANGER FROM HENRY VIII AND ENGLAND WAXES AND WANES

If there was danger to Pole from within the Church, that emanating from England did not simply fade away. Reginald had become 'the English government's favourite bogey man, an icon of treachery'.[1] In April 1537, Henry wanted him 'trussed up and conveyed' to Calais; his designs on Pole were to become ever more sinister.[2]

Pole was well aware of the threats against him: on his legation of 1537 he wrote to Cardinal Érard de la Marck from Cambrai that he was worried about English spies and assassins; he later told the Pope's secretary that he was conscious of the 'insatiable hatred that the king shows me, trying to persecute me in every way', that Henry had put a price on his head and then confirmed to the Pope that it was only thanks to de la Marck's help that he had escaped ambushes.[3] Ross Williamson lists the would-be kidnappers and/or murderers of the cardinal in this period as Sir Thomas Palmer, Sir Peter Mewtas, John Wingfield, Francis Hall, the aforementioned Sir Francis Bryan and the English ambassador himself, John Hulton.[4]

Yet Reginald was determined to carry on and not to hide away: he would accept the danger 'for the honour of the head of the Church and the utility of his Church'.[5] On his second legation the Pope insisted that he leave Rome in secret and travel incognito and Henry charged his ambassador in Spain, Sir Thomas Wyatt, to help the assassin he had sent to kill Pole. Wyatt failed to ensure Rudston's success because Pole changed his return route to Rome. The ambassador was recalled.[6] Henry was relentless: he had also written to Francis I demanding the arrest of Pole once he was on French territory.[7] Although others appreciated his bravery and how he suffered in the defence of the Church, Pole himself was extremely grateful for the three months spent in a monastery near Carpentras as a balm for his soul in the face of such unwelcome celebrity. He spent the year of 1540 in Rome and the Pope, as previously noted, gave him a bodyguard.[8] Yet despite the danger to himself, Reginald followed the tenets of the Church and was merciful when he came across those who wished to act against him. He was lenient with Alessandro da Bologna and two other young men who were exposed as couriers for Henry while trying to pass as Flemings. On hearing they had been imprisoned, Pole freed them.[9]

His life was a continual attempt to evade the ambushes that lurked around every corner. Plots against him were everywhere, with sympathetic rulers trying to track down would-be assassins.[10] Pole was resigned, trusting in God's providence that 'He, for whose cause I am persecuted, is greater and more powerful than he who persecutes me'.[11] Yet if Pole was plotted against, he was not beyond involving himself in some murky plotting. Mayer believes that in late 1544 and early 1545 'he had intrigued with both English Franciscans in the Low Countries and with Cardinal Beaton in Scotland'. There was seemingly a network of Franciscan spies feeding information to Pole and Beaton, and passing correspondence between them.[12] Prior to this was his involvement with the intriguingly named Gregory 'Sweet Lips' Botolph. He was a chaplain to the governor of Calais, Viscount Lisle (an illegitimate son of Edward IV and thus a relative of Henry VIII). Calais was still an English possession and Botolph was very much a Catholic, but one worried by the spread of Lutheran views. In early 1540, on learning that the Emperor's train was passing near Calais on its way to Spain, he put a proposal to the papal legates who were also in the train: if the Pope would provide mercenaries, Botolph would help them capture Calais, from where they could travel to England, 'seek out the by-then excommunicated king and capture or kill him if he resisted arrest … They could also rescue Pole's mother.'[13] Cardinal Cervini, one of the papal legates, believed him and sent him to Rome. On reaching Rome he sought out Cardinal Pole who then took him to the Pope, leaving Botolph impressed that 'he was able to come and go in the papal apartments as he pleased'.[14]

It was agreed that Cardinal Cervini would travel to England as an envoy of Francis I to offer Henry a seemingly unattractive deal: he could enjoy a full pardon of his sins against the Church and keep the lands and possessions of the monasteries that he had suppressed in exchange for rejoining the Catholic Church and renouncing the supremacy of the English Church. On refusing this offer (as he almost certainly would), Henry would be excommunicated and deposed. This was all proposed for September 1540.[15] On returning to Calais, Botolph disobeyed Pole's instruction to go to Louvain and wait for events to unfold while posing as a student. Pole's intuition that Botolph would reveal the plot came true: Henry arrested

Viscount Lisle and the other conspirators and resumed trying to assassinate Pole. Botolph, under Imperial protection and with the help of Pole, was never caught, instead being briefly imprisoned for his own protection and then released.[16] This may also explain the execution of Margaret Pole (for which there was no justification): the plan to rescue her is alluded to in a letter from Pole after her execution in which he writes, 'As to what you write of my affairs, both what was lovingly planned for my mother's release and about that friend of yours who procured this ... Afterwards ... he was kept in custody, although he has since been liberated.'[17]

Yet the situation Reginald found himself in was becoming ever more serious, for Henry had tired of bungling amateurs and was happy to spend money. He eventually hired an Italian mercenary, the ruinously expensive Ludovico dall'Armi. The affair of dall'Armi is well documented.[18] Henry hired him to, in turn, hire mercenaries and 'to murder Pole or anyone else in southern Europe who had fallen into the king's bad books'.[19] He has been described as 'Henry VIII's gangster ... the perfect criminal type: vain, violent, plausible and impudent'.[20] Dall'Armi emerged on to the scene in Italy in 1545 and was initially regarded with suspicion both by the English and papal representatives, but won over the former by his alleged devotion to the king and by the troops that he seemingly had available. The Pope even organized an abortive plot to have him killed and tried to persuade the Venetians to expel him from their territory, to little avail. He was allowed to live in Venice provided he remained a private and upstanding citizen.[21] This proved a difficult task for dall'Armi: he was directly involved in one murder in Venice and had been behind an attempted murder in Venetian territory.[22] He then fled to England, convinced

Henry that he was a wronged man and returned to Venice in 1546 with the guarantee of a safe conduct from the Venetian government for a man who was now Henry's 'noble and beloved familiar' and seemingly even negotiating treaties of alliance with France and Venice on Henry's behalf.[23]

This was all with the aim of killing Reginald Pole. The presence of dall'Armi and other hirers of mercenaries employed by the king's council caused great concern among Pole's fellow cardinals and the threat was very real.[24] Even before Pole's appointment as legate, Cardinal Morone, the papal legate in Bologna, tried to 'neutralize dall'Armi, cutting off his money and asking the duke of Ferrara to help apprehend him. Morone had no doubt that the troops dall'Armi was raising were meant to attack Pole.'[25] Cardinal Cervini, already en route for Trent with the other legate, del Monte, wrote to Pole on 5 March 1545 to alert him to the fact that dall'Armi was said to be in Venice and Pole did not leave Rome until April, with an escort of twenty-five horsemen and on a circuitous route, having sent one of his servants with the other two legates disguised as a cardinal.[26] Dall'Armi was certainly in Trent for some days in March 1545 and continued to be present in the area.[27] Pole himself was sufficiently concerned to take extra horsemen to Mantua and then had an escort from Verona to Trent.[28] He arrived in Trent on 4 May 1545.

All danger to Pole ended with two deaths in 1547. The first was that of dall'Armi, who was hanged in Venice for more gangster-like (but not Pole-related) behaviour, and the other, of course, was that of Henry VIII on 28 January. The accession of Edward VI, a boy-king, must have seemed a breath of fresh air to the cardinal after 'almost ten years [when] ... the threats had been as real as they had been serious'.[29] Religion in England was much changed and was to change still further. Henry has been described as believing he was 'a Catholic (but not a Roman one). But his Catholicism was self-deception, a disguise for his egoism.'[30] He chopped and changed his religious pronouncements as his inclination and political circumstances deemed fit. As Wabuda notes, he stood firm against many of the more Protestant innovations that Thomas Cranmer wished to introduce.[31] In contrast to this were the Six Articles of 1539: Catholic in tone and insistent on not allowing clerical marriage and confirming the real presence in the Eucharist, they were also a knee-jerk reaction to a possible foreign alliance and invasion against England. By 1540, with very few exceptions, all the monasteries had been dissolved, resulting in a huge transfer of land and its wealth, although, Henry being Henry, all monks – who were left more or less homeless – were to remain celibate for the rest of their lives.[32]

The last decade of Henry's life also saw what appeared to be contradictory attempts at reform: in May 1537 he ordered the defacing of all saints' relics belonging to suppressed religious houses and the following year 'saw the prohibition of candles in front of any statue except for the Holy Rood and the Easter Sepulchre'.[33] Yet seemingly intrinsically opposed to a simpler and purer religion à *la* Luther was the Act for the Advancement of True Religion and for the Abolishment of the Advancement of the Contrary of 1543, which did not allow the lower classes to read the Bible in English, despite the publication of the Bible in English only a few years earlier.[34] The so-called *King's Book* of 1543 was the last official doctrinal statement of his reign. It prohibited the use of the word 'purgatory', downgraded certain sacraments and praised the destruction of shrines and images, but never accepted justification by faith alone: good works were also necessary.[35] Doctrine still remained essentially conservative. So what was Henry: a 'Catholic without the Pope' or a monarch with Lutheran leanings? David Starkey disagrees with the first assessment and believes that his religious tendencies after leaving Rome were erratic. Perhaps even better is MacCulloch's aptly put description of his religious beliefs as 'a theological jackdaw's nest'.[36]

Edward VI (r. 1547–53) was to prove far more definite and evangelical (Protestant) in his views. He was surrounded by a council which, in Henry's last years, had become increasingly evangelical and had Edward Seymour, the newly appointed Duke of Somerset and the brother of the late Jane, as Lord Protector. This 'evangelical establishment ... [was] determined to join the religious revolution in the rest of Europe: to destroy the old world of devotion of the English Church'.[37] What would Pole's relations be with the new order? He was certainly not to receive any special treatment, especially not as a cardinal of Rome.

In October 1548 John Yonge wrote to Pole's servant Michael Throckmorton that Somerset 'would receive letters from Pole if he wrote as a private person'. They sent a mission to Pole and in return he sent two representatives to England. They were to tell Somerset 'of Pole's love, and then pass to the dangers threatening both him and the realm', namely a boy-king and possibly dangerous alliances. Pole was, as ever, naively outspoken and the council was not impressed. They refused to send him a pardon which would have enabled him to return to England, dismissed the dangers of which he wrote and 'had been forced to treat him as a foreign prince who preferred Rome to England "on the pretext of piety"'.[38] Harsh as this rejection may seem, however, it was neither threatening nor life endangering.

The religious climate was to change greatly under Edward. In July 1547 new Church Injunctions were issued and a general visitation of the whole Church was to occur.[39] In November of that year the Six Articles were cancelled and worshippers could receive the wine as well as the bread at communion; then all chantries (modified parts of the church where masses for the dead could be sung) were dissolved. The arrival of Vermigli and Occhino, who had fled the Italian Inquisition to find a safe haven in England, exemplifies how evangelical England had become.[40] In 1549 priests were allowed to marry and in June the New Book of Common Prayer came into use. This was all too much for some and the summer saw what has now been called the 'Prayer Book Rebellion' which began in Devon on 10 June. Further protests, fuelled by religious and economic grievances, spread to other areas of the country.[41] The demands of the Devonshire rebels were articulated in the 'Fifteen Articles' which they sent to London. They included ending the use of the new Prayer Book and 'we think it very meet, because the Lord Cardinal Pole is of the king's blood, [that he] should ... [be] sent for to Rome and promoted to be first or second of the king's council'.[42] The rebellions failed and 1550 saw the enforced use of the new Prayer Book and the destruction of any remaining religious statues. A leading focal point of Catholic dissent was of course Mary Tudor, the eldest daughter of Henry VIII. She remained a staunch, practising Catholic, and although at one point she considered fleeing England she failed to do so, only to find herself the following year under increasing pressure to stop hearing the mass from an ever more assertive Edward VI.

In 1552 Cranmer produced the second Book of Common Prayer and in early 1553 the Forty-Two Articles were issued:

much of the theological backbone of the English Church was now in place. Pole, meanwhile, was working on a new edition of *De Unitate* to include a preface addressed to Edward VI, but it is unclear if it was ever sent. He seemingly aimed to have his attainder of 1539 overturned – he had been excluded from a pardon that Edward had given to others – but was surely once again naively misjudging his prospective reader: the dogmatically evangelical Edward would have been as horrified as Henry at the attacks on his father and the defence of the Catholic Church.[43] In May 1553 Pole moved to Maguzzano to enjoy a quieter, more contemplative life. It was not to last: much was afoot in England.

8

MARY TUDOR AND 'MY GOOD COUSIN' REGINALD POLE[1]

Much has been written of Mary Tudor, the first English queen (r. 1553–58), and until the last century very little of it had been good. The soubriquet 'Bloody Mary' followed, inevitably, from the burnings of Protestants which coloured her reign from 1555 until her death in 1558. These will, of course, be discussed, but first it is necessary to trace how the paths taken by Mary, Margaret Pole and Reginald Pole intertwined.

When Reginald was born in 1500 his father, Richard Pole, was chamberlain to Prince Arthur and his mother, Margaret, was lady-in-waiting to his new bride, Katherine of Aragon. A strong friendship was formed between the two women and after the death of Arthur they seemingly remained friends and corresponded, even if they did not see each other. This all changed, as we know, with the accession of Henry VIII to the throne. As we have seen, Margaret was restored to court and her sons became members of the royal household, serving Henry in different capacities. Mary was born in 1516 and, as was the custom of the day, had a wet nurse who was in fact Margaret's granddaughter Catherine Pole.[2] This must surely have been a sign of trust and of intimacy with the Pole family. Indeed, Margaret was godmother at Mary's confirmation (which followed on immediately after her christening). In 1512 Henry created her Countess of Salisbury and restored many of the lands previously belonging to her late brother, Warwick, who had been so brutally killed by Henry VII.

Bonds were strengthened further in 1520 when Margaret Pole was appointed as governess to the only surviving child of Henry and Katharine, the young Mary. Margaret was 'a most pious and saint-like woman', as remembered later by one of Mary's ladies-in-waiting, her good friend Jane Dormer.[3] This appointment was a further sign of royal approval as Margaret was to 'play perhaps the most important role of any woman in Mary's early life … [she was] the main direct influence on the princess in the formative years of her life. It was a close and affectionate relationship that Mary never forgot.'[4] Mary's life changed dramatically when her father fell under the spell of Anne Boleyn and became disillusioned with the inability of the Pope to give him the annulment of his marriage that he so desperately sought. She was replaced as Henry's heir by the birth of Elizabeth and she was treated with contempt and disdain by both Anne and Henry. Her position and her father's affections were only reinstated when, under great duress and faced with imprisonment and worse, she acknowledged her own illegitimacy, Henry's position as head of the English Church and her revised place in the succession. Happier days were to arrive with the death of Anne Boleyn and Henry's later, more welcoming, wives.

Mary led a more private life away from court after Henry's death in 1547. He had appointed a Privy Council for the most part full of Protestants and which was eventually headed at first by Edward Seymour as Protector and then, after his usurpation, by John Dudley, later the Duke of Northumberland, as Lord President of the Privy Council. Inevitably there were to be clashes with her half-brother and his government. Mary had an 'intense, non-intellectual, and wholly uncompromising devotion to Catholicism' and she looked on in horror as the government stripped the churches of what they considered to be Catholic frippery, destroyed images and rewrote the church service.[5] She showed her dogmatic determination to not be swayed from her religious beliefs, and as Jane Dormer noted, 'she could not nor would not be persuaded in any entreaties or threats of the Protector, or any others, to shut her oratory or keep close her chapel which she had in her house, but openly to have mass said'.[6] She was at times deliberately provocative, ignoring the official use of the new Prayer Book for the first time on 9 June 1549 and instead celebrating a Latin mass in her chapel.[7]

Disagreements with Edward continued and although some of her household officers were later arrested, she remained at liberty but often in distress, even considering escape abroad under the protection of Charles V in 1550 but refusing at the last minute a very concrete offer of help when ships lay off the coast to transport her to safety. The fear of never ascending the throne kept her in England, and as the next in line to the throne there was little that the government could do to dissuade her from her beliefs. Edward and his council fixed on a more permanent solution: they would remove Mary from the succession and thus keep England a Protestant country. On 21 June 1553 Edward's 'Devise', which laid out his intentions, was approved. On 6 July Edward died and in Mary's place he had, eventually, chosen Lady Jane Grey to accede to the throne. On 25 May she had married Lord Guildford, the son of Dudley, and on Edward's death she was proclaimed queen. But Edward, unlike his father, had no legal right to leave the crown by will, and although Lady Jane carried much of the council, she did not carry the country. Within less than two weeks, and with no blood spilt (and despite turning a deaf ear to the advice of the imperial ambassador), the courageous and determined Mary Tudor was proclaimed queen.[8]

This would have enormous consequences for Reginald Pole. After the election of Julius III, he had been kept busy in Rome as a member of several commissions, discussing papal policy in various areas.[9] Probably exhausted rather than worried about the Inquisition's interest in the late Viterbo circle, he requested and received papal permission to leave Rome and in May 1553 took himself and his household to a Benedictine monastery at Maguzzano on Lake Garda.[10] It was there that he heard the miraculous news that Mary was the new – and, most importantly, Catholic – queen of England.

The Long Wait to Return Home

If Julius III had been so delighted at Mary's accession that he had cried and called a consistory, Reginald regarded it as 'such an important and clear victory for God's goodness against the malice of men, destroying in one moment all their great plans through a woman, one who had so unjustly suffered such great oppression for so many years'.[11] It was, for Pole, a 'happy and truly miraculous happening'.[12] He was, in his own opinion, the right person for the job of legate to Mary, 'being of that country and having previously been legate', and the Pope agreed.[13] Reginald was appointed, and later was also appointed legate for peace between Henri II of France (r. 1547–59) and Charles V, because of, as Julius wrote:

> ... your love for your fellow citizens; your knowledge of their language and customs; your high standing with them because of your family; your extraordinary prudence and eloquence ... your most ardent love and devotion toward God, and our lord Jesus Christ and His holy Catholic Church.[14]

Once again Pole's nobility was important, almost as important as his devotion to God. The cardinal was to absolve and reconcile all those who had sinned in schism in a wide range of ways – even by drinking milk and eating meat in Lent – and had truly repented. Perhaps most importantly for later developments, he was to punish any who resisted and turn them over to the secular arm (the courts who would pronounce sentences on heretics).[15]

On 13 August Reginald sent his first letter to Mary, rejoicing in the divine providence which had brought her to the throne and asking her opinion on his returning to England.[16] Her reaction may not have been what he had expected. She ignored this and following letters in which he stressed the need to renounce the supreme headship of the English Church (something which was not to happen until January 1555 when Parliament undid the acts which had created the title and position, although it should be noted that Mary never used the title). She was clearly acting under the influence of Charles V who, for reasons which were soon to become clear, thought that Pole was too hasty. She finally replied on 8 October, apologising for the fact that, at the moment, she could do nothing to expedite his arrival. Her tone had worsened by 28 October when, with the Emperor's approval, she described his legation as 'hateful to our subjects' because the English feared papal authority.[17]

The following months were to see a prolific exchange of letters between Charles, the Pope and Pole, despite Reginald's explaining to the emperor how his swift arrival in England could be so beneficial both to the Church and to England. He was not helped by the Pope changing his mind about his departure on a very regular basis: he left Maguzzano on 29 September 1553, but did not enter England until November 1554. Reginald was marooned in Europe, ostensibly trying to make peace between Henri and Charles, but in reality awaiting the Emperor's signal to proceed to England. His view of the Emperor at this time was less than complimentary: Beccadelli says that Pole compared himself 'to a person wrestling in a meadow of unmowed grass, who sees the surface waving by the motion of a snake underneath, though he cannot exactly distinguish the spot where he lurks', and he wrote to the Pope, 'The further I go on the way to England, the more clearly I perceive how I am travelling into a stormy sea.'[18] It was not going to be easy.

Matters continued apace in England: in August 1553 Catholic mass was publicly said in London and on 22 August John Dudley, the Duke of Northumberland who had led the scheme to install Lady Jane as queen, was executed. In a brilliant publicity coup for the Catholics, he had renounced his previous evangelical faith on the scaffold and returned to the Catholic fold and urged others to do so. Mary was crowned queen in Westminster Abbey on 1 October and opened her first parliament four days later. Parliament decreed that the marriage between Katharine of Aragon and Henry VIII had been valid and that Mary was thus legitimate. The statutes governing religion promulgated under Edward VI were repealed. But how secure did Mary feel? There can be no doubt that she was under pressure to marry, whatever her personal opinion of marriage and her sense of trepidation. She needed to marry to assuage the doubts of many that a woman could rule and also to secure an heir to the throne. If no heir was to be forthcoming then her ostensibly Catholic but inherently Protestant half-sister Elizabeth would be the next queen. Charles V was never one to miss an opportunity and in Mary's marriage he saw a way to increase his empire and his influence: she should marry his son, Philip of Spain.

Yet Philip was not the only option, and he certainly was not an attractive one to the English, who feared a Spanish takeover of their government, their habits and their country. Mary could, of course, marry an Englishman and the most touted candidate was Edward Courtenay. He had been imprisoned with his father, the Marquis of Exeter (who was executed as part of the reprisals against the Exeter Conspiracy), and remained in prison, at times in difficult conditions but with access to books and companionship, until Mary freed him on her accession. His mother, Gertrude Courtenay, became one of Mary's ladies-in-waiting and was not slow in promoting the idea of her son as the new queen's consort. On 14 September councillors broached the subject of Mary's marriage and suggested that Courtenay would be suitable. However, he had not helped his own cause with dissolute living (anathema to the pious queen) after so many years of imprisonment and by making his marital ambitions very plain. His hopes may have been raised by his elevation to the earldom of Devon on 3 September, but this was undoubtedly to repay the harm done to his family under Henry VIII rather than a sign of affection from Mary.[19]

There was also the (perhaps surprising) possibility of Mary marrying her cousin Reginald Pole. Although a cardinal, he had curiously been kept as a cardinal deacon since his elevation in 1536. Most cardinals were later raised to the rank of cardinal priest, or even higher to cardinal bishop, to show papal approval and as a reward for services rendered. Why was Pole still a cardinal deacon? He had been close to Paul III and was approved of by Julius III and there were no good grounds for such neglect other than the possibility that a far-sighted Pope might have envisaged an advantageous marriage to bring England back into the Catholic fold: only cardinal deacons could be absolved from their vows. And, in fact, the Emperor's ambassador in Rome reported 'on Pole's authority that Pope Paul had refused to ordain him precisely because he wanted to keep him as a possible marriage partner for Mary. "Things might proceed in such a way that [Pole] could marry the princess", ... and for this reason His Holiness has not wanted him to accept any dignity except a crown.'[20]

The idea of a match between Mary and Pole (and thus the rejoining of Lancaster and York once again) was not recent. As Schenk noted, 'Pole's name had often been mentioned in diplomatic correspondence as a potential husband for Mary, and it is possible that this match had at one time been envisaged by Mary's mother, Katherine of Aragon.'[21] Certainly in May 1537, when Pole was legate to foment support for the Pilgrimage of Grace, Juan de Silva, the Imperial agent in Rome, wrote to Charles V that Pole might marry Mary, which in turns gives further weight to his remaining a cardinal deacon. Hutchings also mentions, but gives no archival reference or date for, a letter in the Simancas state papers in which Pole 'actually proposed himself as a suitor for the Princess Mary'.[22] Imperial agent Eustace Chapuys mentions the idea of marriage between the two no fewer than three times, saying that it was a marriage of which Katharine of Aragon had approved and which Mary would have been happy to have seen realised.[23]

Yet, as the Dodds sisters note, Reginald 'never seems to have look upon the hypothetical marriage as anything but a disagreeable duty which he might be called upon to perform for the good of the Church'.[24] But the idea of such a marriage was clearly alive in the court of Henry VIII and this explains why in 1538 Cromwell produced as proof of her treachery what was allegedly a tunic embroidered by Margaret Pole with the symbols of the Pilgrimage of Grace and marigolds and pansies, the symbols of Mary and Reginald.[25] Even after Mary's accession Reginald was still mooted as a potential suitor: she is believed to have asked Gian Francesco Commendone, a papal envoy to northern Europe, if he could be released from his orders. It was not to be.[26]

Charles V had once been affianced to Mary when she was a child and had been almost a father figure to her during the following years, offering her mother and Mary support where and when it was possible. It was inevitable that she would rely on his opinion for a future husband. From the moment that he wrote to his ambassador – in his own hand no less – to make sure that Mary married Philip, the die was cast.[27] Mary, as she later told Reginald, wanted to marry 'so powerful and so Catholic a prince' that she would 'be able to re-establish and confirm religion in England'.[28] On 30 October she told Simon Renard (the emperor's right-hand man in this matter), under sacred oath, that she would marry only Philip. Parliament did not agree with her choice and addressed her to that effect on 17 November 1553, misjudging their woman: Mary had inherited her mother's obstinate nature and replied that, as queen, she would make up her own mind.[29] The marriage contract between Mary and Philip was signed on 14 January of the following year and later approved by Parliament. England's interests were in fact strictly protected: the country was to remain independent of Spain and although Philip could help Mary rule, all state offices were to be held by Englishmen. Philip would also have no right to succeed her in the event of her death.[30]

If news of the marriage was coolly received in England, it was greeted warmly in Rome. Reginald had written to Julius on 27 October and mentioned that he had refused to discuss whom the queen should marry; however, he had heard that Charles wanted her to marry Philip and that this explained the emperor's refusal to let him proceed to England. He was warned that he was not sufficiently enthusiastic about the marriage (he seems to have believed that Mary should have relied only on God, rather than on a husband) and was told by the Pope to show that he was favourable to the match.[31]

Indeed, some felt even more strongly and in January 1554 Thomas Wyatt (1521–54), an ex-soldier and the son of the late poet and ambassador of the same name, initiated a rebellion. Edward Courtenay was involved and Elizabeth Tudor was also implicated. The hatred of the Spanish marriage may well have been a cover: it is believed that Wyatt intended to depose Mary and replace her with either Lady Jane Grey (who was still in prison) or Elizabeth, and thus banish Catholicism.[32] Whatever its aim, the plot was doomed to failure: not all his co-conspirators rose to the challenge, tactical errors were made and on hearing that London was in danger an anxious Mary gave a rousing speech at the Guildhall to assembled Londoners in which she reassured onlookers that 'on the word of a queen … this marriage shall be for the benefit and commodity of the whole realm'. The city then sided with the queen and the rebellion failed. Wyatt was executed on 11 April.[33] Reginald regarded the quelling of the revolt as a sign of 'the particular protection that [God] has for the queen and her kingdom'.[34] The ever-suspicious Charles V had wondered if Pole was involved and secretly had his eye on the throne, but so pleased was he at the news of the rebellion's failure that he ordered fires to be lit and church bells to be rung, something he had apparently not done even for some of his own victories.[35]

Philip was to prove a considerate (if not enamoured) consort whose role was initially clearly defined. They were married on 25 July at Winchester Cathedral and one of the obstacles to Pole reaching England and reuniting her to the Church had been removed. As will be seen in a following chapter, the king, and by implication the Habsburgs, were as important as Pole in the dealings to deliver England back to Rome.

But there was a second stumbling block standing in the way of Reginald's return: with the dissolution of the monasteries, many courtiers and parliamentarians had benefitted from the gifting or purchase of Church lands under Henry VIII. Human greed meant that they were concerned that they would lose these lands, but in the eyes of the Church, and of Pole, these were still Church goods and papal approval was needed before any formal secession and absolution could be granted. At one point Reginald was calling for the complete restitution of Church property and stating that papal authority 'took precedence over all other law, so that he found it offensive for a parliament to endorse any papal decisions in English statute law'.[36] The thorny question dragged on. In June 1554 Julius III had issued a brief which gave Pole 'the fullest authority to leave all Church property ... in the hands of the present possessors'. He also had a secret brief from the Pope dated 5 August which said that he 'would always confirm and consider valid anything which his legate might do'.[37] This did the trick: in the same month, Pole showed signs of thawing when he said he could not give a dispensation for the holding of such lands without knowing what exactly they were, but he was sure that a solution could be reached.[38] He finally agreed not act on Church property without the approval of the king and queen who would 'find and propose a solution which in some way would be to the satisfaction of all parties'.[39] In other words, the matter was on hold but a solution looked likely.

On 3 November 1554 the council agreed to let Pole enter England. On 11 November he wrote to the Pope that Mary had written to the English ambassador in Brussels that he should tell Charles V (and Pole) that 'the right moment had come to summon me after such a long gap and to negotiate and conclude in this parliament the return of that country to the union and obedience of the Church'.[40] Events moved swiftly. Initially it was decided that he should not wear the regalia of a papal legate (but instead enter as ambassador) as that role would be announced later. He was also, at that point, not to discuss any details about Church property. Pole agreed.[41] Mary and Philip then issued letters patent allowing him to be legate in England and an escort was sent to Brussels to accompany him home. After he had arrived at Dover Parliament reversed his attainder, and Philip and Mary 'took the unaccustomed step of journeying to the Lords' Chamber to assent to that bill'.[42] He was finally in his homeland, after twenty-two years of absence and then exile.

On 24 November Reginald Pole disembarked near St Paul's, where a *Te Deum* was sung and a mass was heard in the church and he was greeted by the king and large crowds 'which showed great devotion and happiness at the sight of His Reverence, asking for his blessing'.[43] Still accompanied by large crowds, he proceeded to Westminster where he was then greeted by Mary and Philip. On 28 November he addressed Parliament as legate and movingly spoke of how he had been 'deprived of my homeland, deprived of my goods, deprived of my rank, nor could I see my relatives and was even forbidden to speak to them' and how grateful he was for the revocation of his attainder.[44] Two days later he absolved the country of schism and reconciled the country to Rome. All were kneeling as they agreed to submit to the authority of the Pope. It was a magnificent and moving occasion.[45]

Reginald was legate *a latere* and also the proctor of the Pope – as Mayer notes, he was 'virtually equivalent to the Pope in every way'.[46] Yet he was also aware of the needs of the Church's new subjects and on 24 December it was decreed that 'no possessor of Church property was liable to ecclesiastical censure, either then or afterwards'.[47] The See of Rome Act 1554 (also known as the Second Statute of Repeal) received royal assent on 16 January 1555. Cardinal Pole could now set to work on the reformation of the English Church and the conversion of English heretics.

9

'I AM COME NOT TO DESTROY, BUT TO BUILD; TO RECONCILE, NOT TO CONDEMN'[1]

Cardinal Pole arrived in England not only to reconcile the English Church to the Church of Rome but also to repair what he saw as the damage done by Edward VI to Church buildings, to the clergy and, in his eyes, to its people.

The Reform of the English Church

Pole was a conscientious churchman. The fabric of England's churches had been decimated by Edward's reforms, with some churches having little or no furnishings and decorations and many in a state of decay. On 25 October 1554, a Juan de Baraona wrote:

There are no richer nor more beautiful churches and temples in the world than those built on this land. However, they have suffered the worst ravaging that could be … Within them, saints and crucifixes have been carved up, some have had their noses cut off, others have been defaced and others stabbed. Many of the temples have been torn down.[2]

The clergy were both poor and uneducated. Much needed to be done, and Pole set about doing it. Within days of his arrival in England, 'it was decided that within two days all the bishops should come to His Reverence to consult with him about the needs of their dioceses'.[3] On 2 November 1555 a royal licence was issued authorising the convocation of a synod of bishops.[4] It opened shortly afterwards and continued for two months. The synod had been approved by the Pope, and Pole's friend, the Spanish theologian Bartolomé Carranza (1503–76), whom Pole had known at the Council of Trent and who had arrived in England in the train of Philip II, was present to advise Pole if needed.

The historical consensus on a period seems to run in cycles, depending on the opinions and beliefs of the historians involved and, at times, on new evidence. For many years the re-introduction of Catholicism under Mary and Pole was regarded as a sterile, and indeed failed, experiment.[5] Yet, the basis of a revitalised Catholicism emerged from the twelve decrees published on 8 February 1556. The decrees specified that mass was to be regularly celebrated; on 30 November each year there was to be a procession to celebrate the reconciliation to the Catholic Church; all papal decrees were to be revived; no heretical books were to be read without a licence; heresy was to be prohibited and all heretics to face censures and penalties; the seven sacraments were to return; the Sacrament of the Eucharist (the communion bread) was to be suitably housed; all clergy were to be resident in their benefice, non-residency having been 'the cause of almost all the evils in the Church'; clergy were not to hold more than one benefice (although ironically Pole, never a wealthy cardinal, had perforce been a pluralist); those clergy who had 'the cure of souls' were to preach and homilies (some of which were written by Pole himself) would be available to help those unable or not sufficiently educated to preach; clergy were to be of 'moral integrity and purity of life' and were to live unostentatiously, 'soberly, chastely, and piously' and not marry; high standards were to be set for admission to the clergy; there was to be no nepotism or simony and vacant benefices could only be passed to suitable candidates and following canon law; Church property could not be alienated and inventories were to be taken of the same; seminaries were to be established and were to recruit especially from the poor, with funding for this coming from beneficed clergy; and finally, there was to be a detailed visitation of churches every three years.[6] These were impressive and thorough decrees and the Council of Trent later took on board the foundation of a seminary in each diocese and the suitable housing of the sacrament.[7]

The bishops were to play a key role in the re-Catholicisation of England. Mary, and indeed Pole, did not choose men who would be good administrators but looked instead for men with an academic background, strong pastoral experience and the energy to carry through these reforms and the visitations needed to implement them.[8] As Duffy notes, 'the English Church under Cardinal Pole had a well-conceived and practical reforming agenda, and set about realising that agenda with notable effectiveness'. By the end of 1558 four seminaries were already active.[9] In the year following the promulgation of the decrees there were visitations to dioceses to garner local knowledge so that the decrees could work.[10] There was also to be a return to some of the 'glamour' of Catholicism:

banned liturgical ceremonies, such as Ash Wednesday and Palm Sunday, were to be reinstated. Churches were to be restored to their former glory; there was to be a new English Bible and a catechism for teaching, the latter commissioned from Bartolomé Carranza.[11] And although the time allowed for all this was cut short by the deaths of Mary and Pole and some of the decrees were not implemented, as a whole they sowed some healthy seeds: his episcopate was loyal and only one bishop accepted the return of Elizabeth I as head of the Church.[12] Indeed, as Jennifer Loach notes, 'there is now overwhelming evidence for the survival of Catholicism well into the reign of Elizabeth'.[13]

Much was thus happening both in England and in Rome. Mary believed herself to be pregnant at the time of Pole's arrival and the sad story of this and her later 'pregnancy' is well known.[14] She also had to deal with Philip's absences to resolve problems in the rest of his territorial possessions and missed him greatly. To recompense, Philip entrusted her to Pole and he was now 'chief advisor to the queen and council, virtual prime minister of England, [later] Archbishop of Canterbury, Cardinal and Papal Legate. To no one ... had so many positions been granted.'[15] He did not betray this trust: his letters to Philip show his concern for the queen, and his relationship with Philip is discussed in a later chapter.

Two New Popes

There were even more dramatic events in Rome. Pole had enjoyed cordial and respectful relations with Julius III, but the Pope died on 23 March 1555 and Pole made it quite clear that he did not want to attend the conclave or to be considered as a possible candidate for the papacy: he had much to do in England. Cardinal Marcello Cervini was duly elected on 9 April, taking the name Marcellus II, and Pole was overjoyed. They had been colleagues and friends for years and he wrote to Mary how he took 'great consolation and cheer [in his election] as I have both knowledge and experience of his goodness, learning and his other rare and excellent qualities, so we can hope for many good things and consolations for God's Church'.[16]

It was thus a great shock when Marcellus died just a few weeks later, on 1 May of that year, and in the ensuing conclave Gian Pietro Carafa was elected on 23 May and took the name of Paul IV. The seventy-nine-year-old Paul IV was a pious, irascible, pro-French heresy-hunter who made a very bad enemy. Reginald's relationship with Carafa had started well in the 1530s, and he even claimed to have asked Paul III to make Carafa a cardinal: he is mentioned as one of Pole's Italian circle in a letter from Padua of September 1534, when Pole clearly revered him, describing him as 'a most holy and learned man'.[17] Yet they became more distant as the years progressed and Pole became virtual head of the *spirituali* after the death of Cardinal Contarini. Carafa was a traditionalist who wanted nothing to do with Lutherans, and Pole's support for justification by faith led him to decry Pole's 'heretical' beliefs in the conclave following Paul III's death in an attempt to stop him becoming Pope. Relations had so far deteriorated that in early 1553 Julius III engineered a reconciliation between them at the monastery of San Paolo Fuori le Mura in Rome. Carafa was seemingly unable to forgive Pole's support of, and love for, Marc'antonio Flaminio, whom he considered an out-and-out heretic, yet this is curious as when Flaminio died in 1550 Carafa is believed to have been at his deathbed and saw that he died within the faith. Despite all this, Pole and Carafa were indeed reconciled, to the extent that Carafa proclaimed that in any future conclave 'he didn't want anybody else to be Pope other than Pole'.[18] Pole, in a letter of 9 August 1553, optimistically (and mistakenly) trusted in Carafa's good will and that they would disagree on nothing in the future, 'the scar having been removed from our friendship'.[19]

Things started promisingly. Paul IV wrote to Pole on 30 June 1555 that he had become Pope in his old age and in a difficult time and 'we especially need your advice and help and strongly wish you were here'.[20] But relations disintegrated over the coming years, certainly not helped by Paul's Neapolitan pride and his hatred of all things Spanish. To see Pole, as he believed, in cahoots with Philip of Spain, who was now king of England and, most importantly, the new ruler of the papal fief of Naples, did not improve his temper and he had once again become convinced that Reginald was an arch-heretic and an enemy of the Church. As Murphy notes, although Pole came to England as the Pope's legate he then became the *de facto* legate of Mary and Philip, using his legatine powers to support royal policy.[21]

Reginald found himself in the middle of a storm when war broke out between Philip and the papacy in September 1556. He did his level best to remain neutral by avoiding Philip as much as humanly possible and even wrote to him about the possibility of peace, offering to mediate with Philip if the Pope so desired.[22] It was to no avail: in April 1557 Paul revoked Pole's legatine powers (including those to encourage peace and as Archbishop of Canterbury) and this was confirmed in the following June.[23] This was in fact a setback for Catholicism in England, as without his legatine powers Pole could not summon a second synod to improve on and further implement the decrees of the first synod. Mary had been so aghast at the Pope's actions that she sent the papal documents back to Rome with a messenger, and when letters from her ambassador with instructions from Paul arrived, for some time Mary refused to let Pole see them. She also point-blank declined Pole's request to return to Rome to justify himself: she had been told by the English ambassador in Rome that he would be arrested for heresy on his return.

The idea that Pole might be tried for heresy in Rome brought out the Tudor in Mary: she was indeed her father's daughter and 'behaved as Queen of England first, and a Catholic ruler second … she ordered Pole, as her subject, not to leave England'. She told the English ambassador that if Pole was to be tried anywhere for heresy, it would be in England. There is a great irony in the fact that the 'man who had absolved England from heresy three and a half years earlier was now a fugitive heretic'.[24] For once, Pole too put his country and its needs before the Pope: even when deprived of his legatine powers he attempted to continue to function as legate up to and including 1558.

In the same month there was a failed conspiracy to depose Mary. It was led by Thomas Stafford (*c.* 1533–57), who was, awkwardly, the son of Ursula Pole and Henry Stafford. He had been supported by France and this led to England joining Spain and declaring war on France on 1 June 1557. After initial success there was a complete disaster: in early 1558 the French regained Calais and its pale, the last remaining English territory in France which England had held since the days of Edward III. This was a personal and public relations disaster for Mary, who took it very hard – much to Pole's concern, as can be seen in a letter to Philip – and seemingly felt the pain of the loss until the end of her days.[25] Despite an eventual peace being made between the papacy and Spain, Paul was relentless: he sent his nephew Cardinal Carlo Carafa to Flanders in October 1557 to demand Pole's extradition.[26] This hostile situation was to continue for what remained of Pole's life.

In letters to the Pope and his nephew, Pole restated his loyalty to the Apostolic See and said that Mary and her councillors believed (and rightly) that the Pope was badly informed about the situation in England. [27] He felt the Catholic faith would struggle in England without a legate – 'like [a] ship without [a] captain' – and he asked for a replacement to be sent. He was eventually replaced in June by William Peto, a former intimate of his and an aged and devout Observant Franciscan who had previously been a confessor to Katharine of Aragon. Peto was made a cardinal and legate to England, despite being very unhappy at his appointment. [28]

At the end of May 1557, Pole's main ally in Rome (and the Cardinal Protector of England), Giovanni Morone, was arrested for heresy along with the rest of Pole's previous allies and friends: all had been associated with the *Beneficio di Cristo*. In the eyes of Paul IV, Pole ran an 'apostate house ... Pole is the master and Morone ... the disciple.'[29] A list of eighteen charges had been drawn up against Pole, all based on his having been 'an aider and abettor of heresy and heretics'.[30] He now had to rely on his own emissaries and the English ambassador to put his case, but that was assuming that Paul IV would listen: one emissary had to wait almost two weeks before being granted an audience with the Pope. The emissary was to tell the Pope that Pole was ready to leave for Rome, and indeed to go to prison, but wished to justify himself.[31] Pole did so in an *Apologia* in which he wrote that he believed that no Pope had ever treated a cardinal so badly and that disaster (schism) would befall England if he left. He felt he was judged without the opportunity to defend himself. It was a very emotional plea for understanding and for a belief in his innocence. He was, however, still a believer in canon law and wanted the new legate, with letters of accreditation, admitted to the country. Sadly, it seems that Paul IV never read it.[32]

The Burning of Protestant Heretics

If the situation which Pole encountered regarding the clergy and the physical buildings of the Church was dire, could the same be said of the English? Were the English totally converted to Protestantism? It should be noted that Mary became queen because she was a Tudor and not because she was a Catholic. Yet much of the population accepted papal obedience and set about attending mass and restoring their churches to the best of their ability, although, as will be seen, by 1557 much still needed to be done.[33] Evidence from contemporary records shows a local enthusiasm for the return of Catholicism, 'an enthusiasm which produced large sums of money raised at great speed, to devote to popular ecclesiastical projects and civic festivities of the great feasts of the Church, curtailed under Edward'.[34] It seems reasonable to assume that Mary came to the throne with 'not only ... a deep well of sympathy for her own position but affection for the old ways and a large measure of revulsion against the sheer destructiveness of Protestant change'.[35]

However, all was not sweetness and light: there were large pockets of hard-headed Protestants, mostly from the artisan class, in London and the south-east and in Norfolk. Mary was terrified of them: before Pole's return she told Henry Penning, a Pole familiar, that she wanted Pole to come to England because 'she so feared these heretics, as they are desperate people'.[36] It fell to Pole and the queen to persuade them to adopt the old faith once more. Protestants must have heaved a collective sigh of relief when Mary announced at the beginning of her reign that although she very much wanted and would be glad if all her subjects embraced the Catholic faith, she 'did not intend to compel any of her said subjects until such time as further order by common assent may occur'.[37]

This (parliamentary) assent eventually arrived. The number of people burnt alive varies from historian to historian, but the most common figure given is 283. Others died in prison awaiting investigation and their fate.[38] It is impossible to look at these numbers from our twenty-first century perspective and not shudder. It was indeed a large number and involved some horrifying cases: the burning of a pregnant woman who gave birth in the flames, only to have the baby thrown back into the pyre; the burning of a blind woman whose twin brother shouted all the time she was roasting so that she would know that she was not alone; and the case of Thomas Benbridge, who recanted while in the fire and whose legs had been sorely burnt. He was taken out of the fire due to his recantation but later burnt again on the order of the Privy Council. The list goes on. It was 'the most intense religious persecution of its kind anywhere in sixteenth century Europe'.[39]

It was decreed in canon law within the Catholic Church that heretics should be burnt alive, and Pole was, when it suited him, a stickler for canon law. However, the aim was not to burn as many people as possible but to bring them back, repentant, into the arms of the Catholic Church: 'Those who show signs of recognising and repenting of their error ... should not face the punishment decreed by canon law.'[40] Pole was thus still trying to follow his previously expressed ideals of reconciliation, but with a caveat: those who could not, or would not, be reconciled were to be burnt. Indeed, the whole procedure was aimed at this: as Ridley notes, anyone denounced as a heretic was arrested and taken to the local bishop's court, where he was tried by an expert in canon law.

He was encouraged (at times very vehemently) to recant; if he refused he was told that he would be burnt and handed over to the secular arm (sheriff, justices of the peace and their officers) who then carried out the sentence on a specified date.[41]

The burnings started in February 1555, yet Mary had acceded to the throne more than a year earlier. Why the delay? Edward VI had repealed the heresy laws of his father and earlier monarchs and they had to be revived by Parliament, but the members of Parliament were precisely those who had benefitted from the distribution of lands after the dissolution of the monasteries and who would not pass a bill allowing heretics to be burnt until a compromise had been reached, as indeed it was, on the fate of their lands. Mary may also have wished to abdicate some of the responsibility for the burnings: the return to papal supremacy meant that heretics would be burnt under the authority of the Pope and 'for the heresy of denying papal supremacy as well as the doctrine of the real presence' of Christ in the Eucharist.[42] As the Pope's representative, this of course meant that Pole would be seen to be responsible, and indeed he was. In the 'Directions of Queen Mary to her Council, touching the reformation of the Church', Mary insisted that 'no moves against heresy were to be undertaken without the direct advice of the Cardinal'. Heretics were to be punished (ironically, in our eyes) without 'much cruelty' so that people would know that the proceedings were just. She also specified that a preacher should be at each burning, as should a member of the Privy Council if it was taking place in London.[43] The heresy laws were finally revived by Parliament in late 1554. The burnings could begin.

With the exception of the burnings, Cardinal Pole was never, in the opinion of any commentator whether contemporary or later, a hard or cruel man, but he was a man of the Church and the law in this case had to be followed. In September 1555 he wrote a letter to his bishops, emphasising the need for compassionate treatment of heretics and that attempts must be made to educate the ignorant. However, having finally become Archbishop of Canterbury on 22 March 1556, he 'instigated a systematic legatine visitation of all the dioceses in April 1556. Simultaneously, he established a heresy commission for his own diocese and … it was clear that the detection of heresy was to be a major consideration in all the visitations.'[44] He very much wanted to save souls, but if souls would not be saved then he was quite happy to burn bodies to match the fate which awaited their souls.[45]

Pole was not without mercy: he released twenty-two heretics who had been made to walk from Colchester to London in ropes in September 1556 and told Edmund Bonner (*c.* 1500–69), the Bishop of London, to treat heretics more leniently (he had a nasty tendency to shut them in his coal house while they awaited interrogation, and worse).[46] Yet in the same year, in a seemingly pointless and cruel gesture that was described by Foxe as Pole's 'harmless rage', he ordered the exhumation of the wife of Peter Martyr Vermigli in Oxford and had her buried in a dung heap and in 1557 he visited Cambridge and had the bodies of the Protestants Martin Bucer and Paul Fagius exhumed, tried and burnt.[47] But this was in fact an attempt to purify buildings of Protestant contamination.

One of the charges raised by the Inquisition against Pole was that he was indeed too merciful to heretics and favoured them. One of his *famiglia*, Antonio Giberti, who was in Rome, said that he had told those who criticised him for this that 'as many times as they proceed against him here, I have replied that they ought to consider what he is doing in England and how he is persecuting heretics if they wish to judge whether he is a heretic or not'.[48] In Kent, burnings had tailed off by the spring of 1556 but revived once Pole became archbishop: once again, the aim was reconciliation but the end punishment for the obstinate was always the same.[49] Pole even became focused and personally involved, possibly as a result of the charges in Rome. In the diocese of Canterbury his suffragans had previously acted as heresy-hunters, but in March 1558 he established an anti-heresy commission packed with his ardent supporters: five heretics, the last to be burnt in Mary's reign, were burnt there.[50]

Did Pole regard heretics as 'errant children … [who needed] to be disciplined but the hope was that they would see the error of their ways'?[51] Or did he see them as 'the declared enemies of Christ, servants of Satan who, once all attempts to reconcile them had proved futile, must be prevented from corrupting others: they must pay the penalty with their lives'?[52] Perhaps the answer is both: his mild nature pushed him towards a paternal concern for heretics and a need to help them recant, but the very nature of his position meant that he had to support the Church's view that an unrepentant heretic should be roasted alive. Indeed, Foxe noted how Dr Robert Farrar, the previous Bishop of St David's, was asked six times by the then bishop if he would recant and he refused. He appealed to Pole, but to no avail, and was duly burnt.[53]

As he wrote to Paul IV in his *Apologia*, 'God saved me to save others from heresy and cut off those who will not desist.'[54] In a sermon delivered to Londoners in 1557 after there had been expressions of sympathy at one burning, Pole made it clear that those who burned were not brave or martyrs, but manifested 'devilish pertinacity'.[55] The role of Mary in the burnings should not be understated: her instructions to the bishops on the burnings were echoed by Pole in his memorandum to the same and Mary herself personally intervened in certain cases; moreover, many of the supporters who had brought her to power were at the forefront of the movement. As Edwards notes, 'as for Mary herself, it seems impossible to deny her crucial responsibility for what happened' in her realm.[56] Yet, as Smith notes, 'Reginald Pole, despite having been a key figure in the *spiritualis*' attempts to secure religious reconciliation during his exile, orchestrated and directed the Marian programme of persecutions'.[57] He had set out his intentions in the second decree of his synod:

> We damn and altogether reject every heresy ... We prohibit and forbid any opinion which is at variance or does not agree with the same [Catholic] faith ... We damn and anathematise all Heretics of whatsoever description or kind, who believe, hold and teach otherwise than the same Church of Rome believes, holds and teaches.[58]

There can be little doubt that he was, and indeed had to be, responsible for what happened – and almost certainly Mary took her lead from him and from the Spanish theologians who had arrived at court – but at times he did do his best to mitigate things where possible.[59] This explains the almost positive review which the martyrologist John Foxe gave of Pole when compared to his opinions of Bonner or Gardiner (he called the former a 'Catholic hyena').[60] At the later trial of Carranza by the Inquisition in Spain, the Spaniard is said to have been unhappy with Pole's soft approach to the punishment of heretics.[61] Yet this was a second-hand opinion and one expressed to defend Carranza and to save him from the Inquisition. Often cited is the belief of the Spanish ambassador, the Count of Feria, that Pole was 'lukewarm' and 'moderate' and in the same month a 'dead man', and this comment has coloured perceptions of Pole to the present day, but it was made at a time when Pole was already ill and had refused the Jesuits entry into England against Feria's wishes. Indeed, Pole's personality in face-to-face dealings (he was better at expressing himself on paper or in small groups) was rarely forceful.[62]

Schenk accuses him of not stopping the burnings.[63] But how could he? The fate of unrepentant heretics was set in canon law and Pole generally set great store by obedience. As far back as 1539 he wrote to Contarini of the then Pope, Paul III, that '*omnia vincet mea erga illum obedientia*' (my obedience to him will conquer all), and his sense of duty was still as strong in 1555: he told Morone that he had always obeyed immediately whatever God ordered. He 'usually fairly quickly bowed to pressure and relied on simple obedience'.[64]

Were the burnings a success? Did they weaken support for Catholicism or even increase it?[65] Was the restoration of Catholicism now well embedded in the English Church, both physically and spiritually? These are difficult questions to answer. The documents detailing the visitations of the Archdeacon of Canterbury, Nicholas Harpsfield, to the diocese in 1557 paint a sorry picture of pitiful ruin: some churches are recorded as 'in great decay'; few have the necessary accoutrements for the altar, even lacking a cross (and in some cases parts of the altar are still on the public highway); windows have been smashed and not repaired; parishioners are not always on their best behaviour during the service; some churches are lacking a priest and parishioners have to travel to another church – the list goes on.[66] Yet some monasteries had been restored. The Observant Franciscans returned to Greenwich, Westminster Abbey was restored as a Benedictine monastery, a Franciscan friary was re-established in Southampton and four other Dominican houses had sprung to life again with the help of Carranza, leading Velasco Berenguer to conclude that 'there had been good progress in the restoration of English monasticism'.[67]

Was England spiritually Catholic? It seems very likely that this was the case. Certainly, some evangelicals escaped abroad and the more pragmatic may have recanted (if denounced) and adopted the Catholic faith while crossing their fingers behind their backs. Others were happy to return to the old ways and the old faith. In the summer of 1558 Pole wrote to Carranza that 'the campaign to restore Catholicism in England had turned the corner, and that religion in the country was at last "beginning to recover in its purest form"'.[68] Was he correct? Duffy, the expert on this period, believes that if Archbishop Pole had been alive when Elizabeth came to the throne 'he would indeed have presented his Protestant cousin with a formidable obstacle to any reversal of the Catholic restoration. It was the wholly unexpected double demise of cardinal as well as queen, not any gradual loss of direction or waning of determination, that halted the Marian project and the Marian burnings, in their tracks.'[69]

Pole's words to Parliament that 'I am come not to destroy, but to build; to reconcile, not to condemn' were thus both true and false: he had done his utmost to rebuild the Catholic Church in England and had reconciled it with Rome, but he had condemned and destroyed many lives in doing so.

10

REGINALD POLE AND THOMAS CRANMER: POLES APART?

One of those lives destroyed during Pole's time as papal legate and advisor to Queen Mary was that of Thomas Cranmer. It might seem that Thomas Cranmer and Reginald Pole had nothing in common other than both being priests who became Archbishop of Canterbury. But was that the case? An examination of their lives and relations both with each other and with others will reveal recurring themes, personal characteristics and decisions taken which suggest the truth is nuanced.

As far as we are aware, the two never met. This was partly a result of Pole's exile abroad for many years and then, after his return to England in 1554, Pole's refusal to meet with Cranmer. Their origins could not have been more different. Pole, born a noble and a relative of the king, had a sense of self-worth and, perhaps, entitlement, which the lower-born Cranmer could not emulate and indeed perhaps envied. Thomas was born on 2 July 1489, the son of a squire. He was thus a gentleman and not a noble. He went to Cambridge and was the holder of a fellowship at Jesus College, whereas Pole went to Oxford.[1] And here one of the main differences between them emerges: Cranmer, at this point not in holy orders, was interested in the opposite sex. At the age of twenty-five he married a woman who has come to be known in time as 'Black Joan of the Dolphin Inn'.[2] His marriage meant that he had to give up his fellowship, so he must indeed have been in love. Little is known of her: there has been speculation that she was a barmaid, but Foxe (Cranmer's great apologist) says that she was a gentleman's daughter and related to the wife of the owner of the Dolphin Inn. Joan died in childbirth, and thus, like Pole, Cranmer came to know great grief in his life. He was readmitted to his fellowship and seemingly at this point took solace in the Bible, taking holy orders within three years of her death. He gained his degree of Doctor of Divinity in 1526 and then pursued what has been described as an 'undistinguished' career at Cambridge. Pole was a far more brilliant scholar and was known as such throughout Europe.

The person who was to play such an important role in both their lives was, of course, Henry VIII. While Reginald was known to Henry as the son of Margaret Pole, the Countess of Salisbury whom Henry initially so esteemed, and benefitted from his position as the 'king's cousin', Cranmer had no such patronal or blood ties. He first came decisively to Henry's notice at a critical point: the Blackfriars trial to annul his marriage to Katharine of Aragon had ended with the matter having been referred back to Rome, with inevitable delays and no certain outcome in Henry's favour. At a dinner in 1529 at Waltham Holy Cross with Stephen Gardiner and Edward Foxe, both of whom had been closely involved in the marriage debacle, he advocated that the theologians of the European universities should be consulted (once again) on the validity of the king's marriage.[3] They reported this back to the king, and within a few months Cranmer had become intimate with the Boleyn family and was living in the palace of Thomas Boleyn where he was put to work providing arguments for the annulment of the royal marriage. His suggestion of consulting the universities was in turn to affect Reginald, who had applied to the king to study in Paris and was there by October of that year. Pole was soon asked by Henry to canvass the Paris theologians for their views on the marriage, a task which he fulfilled successfully but which, as we have seen, he did not necessarily enjoy.

Rome was, inevitably, to play a role in both men's lives and choices. Neither was favourably impressed by their trips to the holy city. In 1525 Pole had been in Rome 'three or four days, and seen the abomination of the cardinals, bishops, and other their officers, with the detestable vices of that city, he could in no wise tarry there any longer'.[4] Once resident at Rome and the curia, it is hardly surprising that he was a member of the council called by Paul III to reform the clergy; Pole's stance on the morals of the clergy was to remain, throughout his life, one of strict propriety. Cranmer had accompanied Thomas Boleyn to the Emperor at Bologna and then went on to Rome in 1530. Probably at Henry's request, the Pope appointed him the Grand Penitentiary for England (i.e. responsible for the granting and writing of dispensations in Rome for English interests).[5] It is difficult to dismiss the idea that what he saw contributed to his later view of the Pope as the 'Antichrist' and MacCulloch believes that 'having seen the Holy Father in Rome, Cranmer next made his first contacts with the evangelical reformers of Continental Europe'.[6]

The divorce was to run through the whole of their relationship, right until the bitter end. After Paris, Pole was moved to make his beliefs felt and wrote a letter (referred to in those days as a 'book') on the divorce. It is now lost and only known to us through Cranmer's comments on it in a letter to Thomas Boleyn. Reginald had by now come to believe that the divorce was anything but a good idea and made out 'a very strong case against the divorce on grounds of political expediency'.[7] We have no record of Pole's view of Cranmer at this point, but Cranmer admired Pole and wrote that he 'showed such wit and eloquence that he was worthy to be a member of the Privy Council, and he feared that if this document were read by the common people, it would be impossible to persuade them that Pole was wrong'.[8]

By January 1532 Cranmer was one of Henry's chaplains and had been appointed resident ambassador to Charles V. His encounter with Lutheranism in Nuremburg was to prove pivotal in his religious outlook. He certainly did not lack courage in his personal affairs: in the same year he married Margarete, the niece of the wife of the reformer Andrea Osiander (1498–1552). This marriage of a priest was illegal both in England and at the court of Charles V. It must have come as a great shock to him to learn in November of the same year that he had been appointed Archbishop of Canterbury. It was a clear sign of royal favour; there were far more able candidates, such as Gardiner. Cranmer eventually returned to England and was consecrated, with papal approval, on 30 March 1533. What happened at this ceremony was to prove a bone of contention for Pole and fellow Catholics later in life. He swore an oath to the papacy, but prior to this had uttered a protestation in front of lawyers that:

... his oath would not override the law of God and his loyalty to the king, or act to the hindrance of 'reformation of the Christian religion, the government of the English Church, or the prerogative of the Crown or the well-being of the same commonwealth … [he would] reform matters whatsoever they seem to me to be for the reform of the English Church'.

He duly read this out after swearing loyalty to the Pope and promising, among other things, to persecute heretics and rebels against the Pope.[9]

As MacCulloch notes, this was morally dubious: he had 'formally benefitted from papal bulls while equally formally rejecting their authority'.[10] Why had he done this? He seems to have had an absolute faith in royal absolutism: the vacuum previously occupied by the Antichrist Pope was now occupied by Henry VIII. Ironically, this exchange of authoritarian figures is what happened to Pole, but in reverse. Until he became interested in religion, Henry had been his much-idolised superior. Once he discovered God – and also realised that Henry had feet of clay, as demonstrated by his wish for a divorce – Pole turned to the papacy and the Pope and his obedience to him was almost as total as Cranmer's was to Henry.

This had huge implications for each of them. For Cranmer, even before the Act of Supremacy of 1534, it meant that he obeyed Henry's wishes in all things, even those which may have seemed questionable. He pronounced the marriage of Katharine of Aragon and Henry invalid.[11] Further requests to Cranmer regarding Henry's marital matters were all granted; furthermore he accepted religious changes which he almost certainly did not agree with – for example, the Six Articles – and acquiesced in the downfall of two people of whom he had been genuinely fond, even knowing that it would result in their deaths.

Yet, like Pole, he did not lack courage. Pole was sufficiently brave to strike out at and lambast Henry in *De Unitate*, but from abroad and at a safe distance. Cranmer was so brave as to express his sympathy for Anne Boleyn and Thomas Cromwell in letters to the king when they were each imprisoned in the Tower. Henry did not like contradiction, but Cranmer wrote of Anne, 'I never had better opinion in woman than I had in her; which makes me to think that she should not be culpable.' Yet, for Cranmer, Henry was infallible and 'I think your Highness would not have gone so far, except she had surely been culpable'. He was able to salve his conscience after speaking to Cromwell to agree that he was 'exceeding sorry that such faults can be proved by the Queen, as I heard of their relation'.[12] This was also reflected in his letter to Henry after the arrest of Thomas Cromwell in 1540:

> He that was such a servant, in my judgement, in wisdom, diligence, faithfulness, and experience, as no prince in this realm ever had … I loved him as my friend … but I chiefly loved him for the love which I thought I saw him bear ever towards your Grace, singularly above all other. But now, if he be a traitor, I am sorry that I ever loved him or trusted him, and I am very glad that his treason is discovered in time…[13]

Cranmer believed that the king 'was Christ's vice-gerent and vicar on earth, subject only to the judgement of God and therefore above all earthly restraint'.[14] On the other hand, Pole's view of Henry, and indeed of any monarch, was that 'in spiritual matters, kings were subordinate to priests: only the Pope was Christ's vicar on earth'.[15] And while some of Henry's orders and decisions may have caused Cranmer secret angst, he always gave the king what he wanted. After Henry's death in 1547 it must have been a source of great delight that the young boy who came to the throne as Edward VI was one who shared his reforming inclinations.

At the coronation of Edward, Cranmer declared him to be the new Josiah and as such he 'must see God truly worshipped, destroy idolatry, the Pope's tyranny and remove images'.[16] Under the guidance of Somerset and then Warwick (later Northumberland), Edward was able to assuage Cranmer's hatred of the traditional aids to worship: processions were banned; Candlemas candles, Ash Wednesday ashes and palms for Palm Sunday were to disappear. In short, the theatrical attributes of religion were abolished.[17] A new English Bible was planned; priests were to be allowed to marry; both kinds of communion (bread and wine) were allowed for the laity, but altars were removed.[18] There was organised and approved iconoclasm, as churches were vandalised and images destroyed. Mass was to be said in English and the Book of Common Prayer was introduced. What Cranmer sowed as Archbishop of Canterbury, his successor Reginald would reap and be forced to try to rectify. The disparities between their religious outlooks are glaring – there was no common ground here.

In London and the south-east, where reform ideas had taken root, these innovations were welcomed, but not everybody was accepting of the new changes: there were many who were conservative in religious outlook and went along with the changes for a quiet life. Equally, some rebelled. In the Prayer Book Rebellion of 1549 one of the rebels' demands was that Cardinal Pole should be recalled and be part of the government (with possibly the idea of him becoming the new Archbishop of Canterbury). Cranmer for once revealed his opinion of Pole: he thought him 'unworthy to live, for he had incited the Emperor and the French king to invade the realm'.[19] It is interesting that his dislike of Pole was not on religious grounds (as Pole's dislike of Cranmer was later shown to be), but on political grounds.

Pole is best known for his quarrel with Henry and for the burnings of Protestants under Mary I. Yet little mention is ever made of Cranmer and the burnings under Edward VI of Joan Boucher and George van Parris as Anabaptists. Of course, two is a much smaller number than the over two hundred and eighty unfortunates burnt by Mary and Pole, but Edwards points out that Cranmer had been planning a long list of heresies, including clerical celibacy, transubstantiation and others, only to have the canons rejected by the Lords. Heretics could also be denounced without any evidence having to be provided. They were then to be turned over to the secular arm for punishment. 'It is not clear whether or not this punishment might include burning, but the resemblances between what Cranmer was planning and what Mary [and Pole] did are strong and add their own twist to what the "bloody" Queen presided over subsequently.'[20] There were further similarities with Pole: Cranmer too was keen on trying to convert heretics and to be merciful when possible. Yet Foxe believed that Cranmer had bullied Edward VI into signing the death warrant for Joan.[21] Death was a last resort for both Pole and Cranmer, but neither hesitated to apply it if needed.

Cranmer made the most of Edward's evangelical sympathies to rewrite the country's religion. This, and his innate belief in the wisdom of the king, meant that he became involved in the unhappy matter of Edward's 'Devise' and the declaration of Lady Jane Grey as queen. Edward had deliberately excluded Mary from the succession as he believed that 'it would be all over for the religion whose fair foundation we have laid' and because Mary (and Elizabeth) were bastards.[22] He thus set out to make Lady Jane Grey queen. She was his Protestant cousin and the granddaughter of Mary Tudor, the sister of Henry VIII who had married Charles Brandon. She was married to Guildford Dudley, the son of Northumberland, and was thus Northumberland's daughter-in-law. With such a queen, the reins of power would reside in the latter's hands. More than a hundred prominent figures, including the council and judges, signed the letters patent – amid, it must be said, the provision of substantial grants of land and money. There was a separate document which bound them 'to uphold the new succession unto death'. Cranmer asserted himself and refused to sign, claiming that it would mean perjuring his oath made when Henry's will was drawn up.[23] That will had specified that if Henry or Edward should die without issue then the crown would belong to Mary and to her children and that it would be treason to go against the will. Cranmer asked to speak to Edward alone, a request which was refused, and after speaking to the king in the presence of other councillors, ever obedient, he eventually signed. He was thus guilty of treason and compounded his offence in the eyes of Mary by sending men to support Northumberland against her.

The reign of Lady Jane Grey lasted just nine days. Mary acceded to the throne by popular consent and, probably much to his surprise, Cranmer was not immediately arrested. Undoubtedly Mary would have acted against him at some point, but he hastened his own arrest by writing against the mass. On 14 September he appeared before the Star Chamber and was then sent to the Tower, accused of treason. Unsurprisingly, at his trial he pleaded not guilty because he was simply obeying the king's orders, but he then changed his plea. Found guilty, an act of attainder was passed on him in December and at that point he wrote to the queen. He abased himself in the letter as 'unworthy either to write or speak to your Highness' and but wrote 'with most penitent and sorrowful heart, to ask mercy and pardon for my heinous folly and offence in consenting and following the testament and last will of our late Sovereign Lord King Edward VI, your grace's brother'. It must have had some impact as on 17 December he, Lady Jane Grey and the Dudleys were allowed respite from their enclosed prisons and to walk in the Tower gardens.[24] Still Mary did not act against him, even after the suppression of the Wyatt Rebellion which saw the execution of Lady Jane Grey. She wanted him to be tried for heresy.

Cranmer, Hugh Latimer (*c.* 1485–1555) and Nicholas Ridley (*c.* 1500–55), with whom he had later been imprisoned, were then sent to Oxford. There, a Disputation was held and all three were condemned as heretics, but Mary was waiting for the return to papal supremacy which would allow her to burn all three of them, especially Cranmer. Reginald finally arrived in England in late 1554 and the mechanics for the heresy trial could begin to click into place. Rome issued a mandate for the trial on 19 June 1555 and it was received by Cranmer on 7 September, with his trial opening on 12 September. It examined everything: his oath which he had perjured; his marriage; his beliefs in the Eucharist. Once again, he manifested his disdain and contempt for anything representing papal authority while showing obedience to Mary as queen. He declared that 'he would never accept Roman jurisdiction within the realm'.[25] He was found guilty and was ordered to appear in Rome within eighty days. This was simply never going to happen, and he was returned to prison, but his life was saved for the next eighty days. Once again he wrote to the queen, protesting at being tried by an authority outside the country which he did not recognise:

… by authority coming from any person out of this realm, where the king and queen, as though they were subjects within their own realm, shall complain, and require justice at a stranger's hands against their own subject, being already condemned to death by their own laws.[26]

Like Pole, he never strayed from his beliefs, in this case that royal supremacy was all. He stuck to his oath to Henry VIII that he would 'never consent that the Bishop of Rome should have or exercise any authority or jurisdiction in this realm of England'.[27] The letter continues in the same vein, and at length (like Pole, Cranmer could be very prolix when the mood took him), and then developed his thoughts on the Eucharist, but to no avail. He had asked for an interview with Reginald, but Pole refused to see him and Pole's reply to Cranmer's letter to Mary of 25 October, which concentrated on the Eucharist, was long and at times meandering.[28] A second letter from Cranmer, requesting permission to go to Rome to plead his case, fell on deaf ears. Pole wrote again on 6 November, and it was not a comforting letter. Described by Mayer as 'vicious', it is more to the point in its accusations than Pole's first reply. It tackles his perjury at his consecration and his views on royal supremacy and the Eucharist.[29] It begins, 'May God give you repentance, as I pray daily myself, especially for [the] obstinate who need grace most' and ends, 'Any further reasoning [is] pointless, but I shall not cease to pray for you. May His Son forgive you.' Pole strongly believed that 'you fell through deliberate malice'.[30]

Ridley and Latimer were tried shortly after Cranmer and were burnt on 16 October: Cranmer was made to watch from the roof of his prison. In his first letter to Mary, Cranmer had left the door to a change of opinion slightly open:

And if it can be shown to me, that the Pope's authority is not prejudicial to the things before mentioned, or that my doctrine in the sacrament is erroneous, which I think cannot be shown, then I was never, nor will be, so perverse to stand wilfully in my own opinion, but I shall with all humility submit myself unto the Pope, not only to kiss his feet, but another part also.[31]

This had led to an influx of learned theologians who attempted to make first Cranmer, Latimer and Ridley recant, and then just Cranmer. Ridley's long and agonising death in the flames had affected Cranmer, who was seen to despair at the sight of such torment. Having initially refused to give any ground to the Spanish theologian Pedro de Soto, a period of emotional blackmail from his Catholic servant and discussions with theologians sent by Pole saw Cranmer weakening. Recantations, some genuine and some perhaps not, then followed, probably hastened by the arrival of the writ for his burning.[32] By this point he was attending mass and was granted a postponement of his execution. He 'had every reason for expecting last minute clemency; he was, after all, now fully repentant of his heresy ... and once more in perfect communion with the Church'. And he should have been granted mercy – canon law spared the lives of repentant heretics – but it was not to be.[33]

On 18 March a final and full recantation was signed. The date for his burning had arrived and on 21 March, in the church of St Mary's at Oxford, a sermon was read which explained why he had to burn: his involvement in the divorce, his heresy and because his death, with those of Ridley and Latimer, was revenge for the death of John Fisher.[34] Cranmer in turn was due to speak and publicly repent of his sins but instead he found courage at the last minute – if he was to be burnt then he would be burnt as a Protestant. He denied his recantations, which he had written because he feared burning, called the Pope the

Antichrist and was then hurried to the pyre. In the flames he made good his declaration in the church that 'forasmuch as my hand offended, writing contrary to my heart, my hand shall first be punished there-for' and put it into the flames.[35]

What was Pole's involvement in this? He certainly despised Cranmer and regarded him as a heretic with erroneous beliefs, as can be seen by his letters to him. But, as one who adhered to the law, why did he not intervene to save him? Ironically, like Cranmer himself, in this case he put obedience to his sovereign above that to the Pope and his laws. He 'allowed the necessities of power politics to prevail over his more humanitarian instincts'.[36] Mary had been quite relentless in her pursuit of the man who had engineered her mother's divorce and the declaration of her own illegitimacy. He could easily have been executed for treason, but she had preferred to burn him as a heretic. As he was *legatus natus* as Archbishop of Canterbury, she duly waited for papal condemnation before any sentence was put into effect.[37] She followed the rules on this, but not on saving him when he had recanted. The English ambassador in Venice reported that Mary had said that 'his iniquity and obstinacy was so great against God ... that ... clemency and mercy could have no place with him'.[38] She was almost certainly confirmed in her opinion that he deserved to burn by a sermon given by Carranza in which he said that burning him would be the only proper punishment.[39]

The death by burning of the person who symbolised all that had gone wrong in England since the mid-1530s was both more painful for Cranmer and an excellent example to set before all Protestants. (The fact that he recanted his recantations at the last moment was kept quiet for as long as possible and his previous six recantations were published immediately.) The Venetian ambassador, Giovanni Michieli, wrote:

> On Saturday last, the 21, Cranmer, late Archbishop of
> Canterbury was burned, having fully verified the opinion of him
> by the Queen, that he had feigned recantation thinking to save
> his life, and not that he had received any good inspiration, so
> she considered him unworthy of pardon.[40]

There is an irony in this: Foxe, based on first-hand evidence
and confirmed by a public letter written by Protestant exiles,
records that during the period when Mary refused to take
the Oath of Succession and acknowledge royal supremacy,
Henry would have sent her to the Tower if not for Cranmer's
intervention.[41] His tendency towards mercy was certainly
stronger than the queen's.

The papal condemnation, deprivation and excommunication
of Cranmer which took place in Rome in December 1555
meant that Mary needed a new Archbishop of Canterbury.
She had chosen Pole as the successor to Cranmer shortly after
she acceded to the throne, but Pole had refused to countenance
this until relations between Rome and England had been
restored. He was very keen on the residency of bishops, as
he wrote to his friend Morone in March 1555, and would
only accept it on that condition. He would do what the Pope
wanted but 'I would consider it a great liberty to remain
without such responsibilities, that I dislike so much, if not for
simple obedience'.[42] He had to obey: and Pole was declared to
be the new archbishop in consistory, and promoted to cardinal
priest, with Paul IV allegedly much praising his 'prudence,
goodness, learning and religion', and the paperwork arrived
in England in January 1556.[43] He was ordained bishop one
day after the death of Cranmer in the presence of the queen
and on 25 March he received the pallium (the symbol of his
office as 'metropolitan archbishop') in St Mary's Arches, one

of Canterbury's parishes in London (the queen had refused to let him go to Canterbury).[44] He was requested by the congregation to preach on that occasion and he set out his vision:

> Peace be unto you: peace to you men and women, peace to you old and young, and to every description of person here present be there peace ... God's peace, in which consists all the happiness that man can desire or imagine ... and this is the peace which not only gives quiet to man on earth, but, moreover, ineffable joy to the angels in heaven.

He had come to offer 'this peace ... [which] on the part of God, must be received by those who wish for its enjoyment, with great humility'.[45]

Like Cranmer, his reign as archbishop was cut short by his (far less painful) death. After his consecration Pole tried to rid Canterbury of traces of Cranmer: there was a general visitation and a 'diocesan special heresy commission was established'.[46] Although Pole was involved in sending a far larger number to the flames, his and Cranmer's reputations have both been darkened by the burnings. Both men were guided by the principle of obedience: both tried, when possible, to be merciful. Pole had freed spies sent by Henry VIII when he was in exile when a harsh punishment awaited them, and Cranmer, despite Cromwell calling for sterner punishment, forgave a priest who called him an ignorant ostler.[47] Both also tried to give heretics a chance to redeem themselves and, as Mayer notes, in this Pole's 'attitude was identical to Cranmer's'.[48] At Canterbury those who had accepted Cranmer's teachings were, where possible, to be re-educated rather than punished.[49]

They had in common their relationship with Henry VIII, but it was very different with each man. Henry loved the obedient Cranmer. Cromwell remarked, 'You were born in a happy hour I suppose … for, do or say what you will, the King will always well take it at your hand.'[50] There was no blood tie between Henry and Cranmer, just a relationship of patron and client or of king and subject. It was when Pole subverted his relationship of patron and client and told Henry that he was wrong and sinful that Pole fell out of favour with his prince. Pole had been part of the king's orbit because of his birth and his aptitude for learning, while Cranmer had been 'propelled into high office by the accidents of politics'.[51] Who emerged the victor, if there is any such thing? Posterity adapts its viewpoint depending on whether the commentator is Protestant or Catholic, but both men held unparalleled influence over the religious affairs of England. Pole is now almost forgotten by the general public, while most people have an awareness of Thomas Cranmer, his famous right hand and the Book of Common Prayer. Their lives ended in different ways – one in agony in the flames and one through sickness – and their different resting places reflect their differences: Pole is buried in Canterbury Cathedral, ironically the main church of the Archbishop of the Church of England, and Cranmer's ashes were left where he was burnt in Oxford. Yet despite their differences and their contrasting fates, they were not too dissimilar after all.

11

PHILIP I OF ENGLAND AND CARDINAL POLE: ANOTHER KING AND ANOTHER CONFLICT?

Few Tudor enthusiasts have much knowledge of our first, and only, Spanish monarch: Philip I of England and II of Spain. The aim of this chapter is to shed some light on this enigmatic figure and his role as husband, king and co-ruler of England and above all on his relationship with Reginald Pole. Was the conflicted relationship that Pole had with Henry VIII to be repeated with Philip? Was the Pope always to win Pole's loyalty in any battle over his allegiance? How much did Pole owe Philip for his return to England and the reconciliation of England with Rome? And finally did Philip, and the Spanish theologians whom Philip brought to England in his entourage, influence the burnings?

Philip was born on 21 May 1527 to the Emperor Charles V and Isabella of Portugal. Like Pole, and indeed typically of his princely status, his father had little hand in his upbringing due to his heavy workload and extensive travels. This was left to his mother, who, sadly, died in 1539 and Philip's upbringing was then entrusted to councillors, albeit with clear instructions from Charles. Philip gradually became an experienced ruler, trained in the administration of his territories and, perhaps unlike Mary, a natural ruler too.

He was married first to Maria Manuela of Portugal, a marriage which ended with her death in 1545, shortly after she had given Philip a son, Carlos (d. 1568). Plans were afoot for Philip to marry again and arrangements were well under way to marry (another) Maria of Portugal when Edward VI of England died and Mary Tudor came to the throne. Charles V was delighted and although too old and ill to marry Mary himself (they had, of course, been engaged when Mary was but a child), he was very keen that she should marry his son, Philip. It is fairly obvious that no father would want his son to marry a much older woman (and close relative too, but that mattered little in that era) unless it would bring great benefits to himself and his son, and this was very much the case for the proposed marriage of Philip and Mary.

Charles wanted Philip to marry Mary because the marriage would mean uniting 'the government of England with that of the Low Countries [part of his empire] and bringing them both into an alliance with his enemy, France. This would give him ports and bases in England that would help defend his possessions in the Netherlands.'[1] Such a marriage would consolidate Habsburg predominance in the north of Europe.[2] Philip's reply to the suggestion that he should be the one to marry Mary was both dutiful and unenthusiastic, almost attempting to shirk his duty. He wrote to his father that he was glad of her succession to the throne, not least because it would help Charles in his never-ending battles with France for the domination of Europe, but he was less cheery on the prospective match:

> If she should decide on marriage with your Highness and should find you so inclined, that would be most appropriate, but in case your Majesty decides on me, and if you wish to arrange things for me, your Highness knows that, since I am such an obedient son, I have no will but yours, even more so in a matter of such obvious import and moment.[3]

This obedience to his father was like that of Pole to his father figure, the Pope. Clearly, this was never to be a love match on Philip's side, but it was a more successful marriage than many earlier commentators have believed: as we will see, a mutual affection developed. But what would Mary gain from such a marriage? As Geoffrey Parker notes, Mary would have a husband who could command in wartime and carry out other manly duties.[4] She would also have help, from a devout Catholic, in restoring England to Rome. Furthermore, marrying Philip meant that England was now actively involved in territories in a way that would have been unthinkable with any marriage to an English noble, to Reginald Pole or to another European prince. It strengthened the 'cultural and commercial ties with their neighbours from across the Channel [...] and, if children were born of the marriage, they would be poised to inherit England, Ireland, and the Low Countries (and if Philip's son, the Infante Carlos, died, the whole Spanish inheritance, too)'.[5] It made England a European country, and potentially a very powerful one, instead of being an outsider in the wings of the stage occupied by Charles V and Henri II of France.

The Marriage Treaty and the Power Assigned to Philip

The marriage treaty was drawn up by Charles with little or no involvement on Philip's part, and it must have come as a surprise when he read its terms. One part of the treaty regarded the succession and much of the rest was designed to allay anti-Spanish sentiment in the government and in the country. Philip's role was clearly to be an inferior one to that of the queen, despite his title of king. Among the many restrictions laid down was the fact that no Spaniards were to hold offices in England or be part of the Privy Council. No treasure or jewels – nor indeed Mary or their children – were to leave the country, and no English assets were to be given to anyone outside the kingdom. He was to have no control of forts or castles. Particularly relevant, given later developments, was the clause which forbade England joining the Emperor's war against France.[6] Mary made her own initial position clear to Charles V: she would love and obey Philip, but 'if he wished to encroach in the government of the country, she would not be able to permit it'.[7] Parker believes that Philip was aware of the contents of the treaty and this is reflected in a notarial act he had drawn up in January 1554, even before the treaty was signed, in which he said he would 'approve, authorize and swear to the said articles so that his marriage to the most serene queen of England may take place, but this does not bind or oblige him and his possessions, or his heirs and successors, to execute or approve any of them'.[8]

This was heady stuff and it did not augur well. Ironically, it recalls Cranmer's opting out of the oaths to the papacy sworn when he became Archbishop of Canterbury, yet it was also unnecessary: the situation changed rapidly after the marriage took place. However, Philip's lack of enthusiasm for the contract was reflected in the extraordinarily long time it took him to reach England (partly because he was waiting for a papal dispensation to marry Mary, partly because, as ever, he had very little money to fund the venture and partly because it was, we can assume, not an attractive prospect), and in his lack of direct communication with Mary until he was prompted by his father. In March 1554 a proxy marriage took place but Philip only left Spain for England in July of that year, arriving seven days later.[9] The happy couple were married in a rain-soaked Winchester on 25 July and in approval of the wedding Charles appointed Philip as King of Naples. He was at least a king to her queen.

The treaty had been passed in Parliament in spring 1554, having been made public three months previously. It was clear from it that Mary was to be queen regnant and the Act for the Queen's Regal Power was passed, confirming that regal power was Mary's 'as fully and absolutely as ever it was in any of her most noble progenitors kings of this realm'.[10] Something – perhaps Philip's affability (he tried very hard to make himself amenable to the English, including wearing English dress at the wedding feast and for the entry into London), perhaps imagined love on Mary's part or perhaps the realisation by queen and council that the treaty was unworkable – prompted Mary and the Privy Council to soften the blows. Before the wedding Mary had stipulated that Philip was to be kept informed and 'to be obeyed and to receive good advice'.[11] Yet only two days after the wedding Philip's participation in government was noticeably widened. All matters of state dealt with by the council were to be reported in Latin or Spanish (Philip had little or no English), both Mary and Philip were to jointly sign 'all matters of Estate' and a royal governmental stamp would be made featuring both their names.[12] In other words, Philip's role in government was to be an active one, so much so that in September of that year he felt able to write, 'I have begun to deal with the business of this kingdom and a good start has been made.'[13] Alexander Sansom believes that theirs was in fact a 'co-monarchy'.[14]

Philip, Pole and the Reconciliation of England to Rome

The start of the relationship between Reginald and Philip did not bode well. Both the Pope and Charles V believed that Reginald was against the marriage. Encouraged by the Pope to be more positive in his outlook, Pole wrote to Cardinal Morone to say that he had never written to Mary about marrying as she had never requested his opinion, and he thought that she should have stayed single. Yet Pole was a pragmatist and once the marriage was inevitable he regarded it as 'the greatest arm for establishing matters of religion', believing that no one would work harder than Philip.[15] He was aware of how powerful an ally Philip could be and wrote to him on 21 June 1554 congratulating him on the forthcoming marriage and hoping that Philip would help both in uniting England to the Roman Church and establishing peace.[16]

Philip responded warmly; writing in the September after the wedding, he told Pole that his good wishes were welcome and that he would act as quickly as possible for the rest.[17] It is unlikely that Pole had received this letter when he wrote in strong terms to Philip:

But you, Catholic prince, to whom divine providence and benignity has bestowed that other high title of Defender of the Faith which further elevates and adorns the kings of England through Peter's apostolic authority, consider within yourself, how does it serve your piety that all ambassadors sent to you from all princes have had open access to you and have been able to congratulate you on the obtention of such title, yet Peter's successor, who sent to you … his own legate to this and to bring forth the peace and grace of Him who excels over all kings, shall not be admitted?[18]

It is interesting that Pole felt sufficiently confident to write in this way, perhaps protected in his mind by the power of the papacy, and it is clear that this was going to be a relationship between equals, not one of king and subject. Perhaps even more interesting is the fact that Pole clearly saw Philip, and not Mary, as the person to be contacted for help. Pole had also contacted Carranza and other Spanish theologians for their help and this, as Velasco Berenguer notes, 'placed Philip and his Spaniards at the centre of the efforts to re-Catholicise England'.[19]

The main difficulty for Pole's return to England as legate for the reconciliation with Rome was the thorny problem of the Church property which had been distributed after the dissolution of the monasteries. Philip played with a strong hand: he told Pole that he could not enter England with the current authority granted to the cardinal by the Pope as it left too much to Pole's discretion. He had already understood Pole's character all too well: in Pole's eyes the property had to be returned to the Church. Instead, Philip approached Rome for more satisfactory powers to be granted to the cardinal and also sent Simon Renard to reason with Pole. It worked. As Loades notes, 'by the end of October [1554] Renard had succeeded in convincing Pole that the restoration of England to the Church and even Mary's survival as queen, depended upon the willingness of the legate to surrender his discretion entirely to the king'.[20] Haste was of the essence as Parliament was due to meet on 12 November and Philip took the initiative, certain of papal approval (which duly came as Julius pre-dated a bull to 1 August giving free title to those holding Church lands). As Mary later wrote to her father-in-law, the reconciliation with Rome, including the resolution of the problem of Church property, was 'largely ... to the wise guidance of my said Lord'.[21]

Pole could now return to England, and duly did so in some pomp and with the attainder against him repealed. When he arrived by river in London he was greeted by Gardiner and many others and on entering the palace of Whitehall was 'welcomed with great affection by His Majesty the king'.[22] They then went together to see the queen, who was waiting in the next room. The meetings between Pole and Philip then gathered pace: on 27 November Philip went to see Pole at Lambeth Palace and 'it was believed that he purposely visited Pole himself, rather than wait for the cardinal to visit him, to emphasise the respect that ought to be paid to the legate as a representative of the papacy'.[23] The following day Pole 'privately' visited the king to talk about his legation, but before he reached Philip the king did him the enormous favour of coming out to greet him with, in his hands, the important brief from the Pope regarding Church property.[24] This was a sign of intimacy, and another meeting took place on 29 November. The following day, the feast of St Andrew's, England finally returned to the Catholic fold.

The Search for Peace and Problems with Rome
Although Philip remained in England until the summer of 1555, relations between Pole and the king are not so easy to trace during this time. Undoubtedly Reginald was at court and enjoyed great favour from the king and queen, employing his powers as legate to call a synod and to take steps to revive the

English Church. But he was also legate for peace in Europe, and this was a role he took seriously throughout the reign of Philip and Mary. England was initially neutral and there was a clause in the marriage contract which strictly enjoined that the marriage could not lead to England's intervention in the Habsburg–French war.[25] In other words, England was not to be subsumed into Habsburg disputes. With a view to this, and with the continuing wars between Charles V and Henri II throughout the European peninsula, both France and Rome at the start of Mary's reign regarded her 'whether acting in tandem with Reginald Pole or not – as a potential mediator between Charles V and Henri II'.[26] Pole, inherently peace-loving by nature, was determined to pursue this line. He would be impartial in his search for peace, and above all wanted to serve the 'common good'.[27] His was the main impetus behind the Conference of Marck in May 1555 and, despite ill health, he was there himself as a mediator between France and the Habsburgs. He presided over the talks between six delegates from each side. Perhaps surprisingly, Philip himself was also in favour of peace at that time.[28]

Pole wanted a peace which would protect the unity of Christendom and said as much in his 1554 work *Discorso di Pace*. Christians needed to be united to face the threat of the Turks, and this was one part of his legation.[29] However, for a variety of reasons English attempts at neutrality at the conference failed and the country, and Pole and its delegates, were viewed as being pro-Habsburg, a contention which it was ultimately difficult to refute, despite Pole's call for independent arbitrators to be summoned to resolves the disputes. Pole was politically naïve in his dealings at the conference and indeed not sufficiently astute to realise that the mounting tensions and the election of the virulently anti-Spanish Gianpietro Carafa as Pope Paul IV in May of that year meant that France had a strong new ally.[30] The talks ended in failure and England was no longer seen as neutral; indeed both sides 'denounced the English mediators for incompetence and partiality and the diplomatic venture which had been intended to restore English prestige to the high days of 1518 resulted only in ignominy and helplessness'.[31] 'Helplessness' would not help either Pole or England against a hostile Pope.

The election of Paul IV followed on from the sudden death of Marcellus II, who was Pope for only twenty-two days. Pole could, of course, have attended the conclaves for both, but he refused, feeling that his duty called him to remain in England. Mary was keen for him to offer himself as a candidate following the death of Marcellus, commending his 'sincerity of life' to others, but it was too late: Carafa had already been elected.[32] (Although Pole, not present in Rome, missed being elected by only two votes.) Of some note is the fact that Philip did not support his candidacy: did he consider him too essential to England to lose him to Rome, or was he already having doubts about Reginald's character? Loades believes that 'neither Philip nor Charles was wholeheartedly in favour of the Englishman, distrusting both his sympathies and his judgement'.[33]

The Select Council of Philip I and His Correspondence with Pole

It is difficult to agree totally with Loades' assertion as cited above, certainly at this point in their relationship: Philip placed great trust in Pole when he left England, literally entrusting him with the queen and the country. In late August 1555 the 'Select Council' was founded in anticipation of Philip's departure. Based on a similar council in Spain, it is now believed to have been an effective governmental organ designed to ensure Philip's participation in, and awareness of, government.[34] It was formed of eight members of the Privy Council who were to have 'the special care of all matters of state, [as well as] of financial and other grave matters of the kingdoms'. Perhaps most importantly, it was to be headed by Cardinal Pole 'when he wishes to do so and conveniently can'.[35] Philip particularly wanted to know about 'all the business and proposals to be considered by the domestic parliament in writing before its meeting'.[36] His was a keen interest in English affairs. The council set to work and sent him memoranda in Latin on which he noted his opinions and instructions. These then became letters and there was regular correspondence. Government affairs will also, of course, have been discussed in his (mostly lost) correspondence with his wife, Mary, and he intervened directly on several occasions, including the nomination to the post of Chancellor and the refurbishment and re-organisation of the English fleet.[37]

Reginald also corresponded with him directly and the tones of these letters are at times intimate and certainly not submissive: he wrote to Philip as an equal, secure in his closeness to Mary and in his position as cardinal and later as archbishop. The first letter of 2 September 1555 notes that 'the first duty you assigned me was to console [the] queen during your absence' and he reports how she liked his letters and was kept very busy with government business.[38] In another letter of 16 September, he describes how sad Mary was without her husband and hopes for his quick return and on 8 October how she was working too hard.[39] Contradicting those who see it as an unhappy marriage, Pole notes in late October that 'I learn you welcome my news of the queen. I take that as [an] order to write more, which [I] do gladly ... She [is] very happy about your concern for her health, which makes her know she is loved.'[40]

Pole has been described as 'Mary's mainstay' during Philip's absence in the Netherlands. He was at court a lot and the Venetian ambassador Michieli wrote how 'nothing was done without his advice'.[41] He was, as he wrote to Cardinal Morone in September 1556, heavily involved in both secular and ecclesiastical affairs.[42] The Venetian ambassador praised him the next year for ending the factional politics of Mary's councillors and offered that 'one could say that really the king and prince was he'.[43] King and prince in the eyes of some he may have been, but there was soon to be a call on his loyalties to both the king and to the Pope.

Paul IV and Philip I: The Two Father Figures in Pole's Life

The election of Paul IV as Pope did not bode well either for Pole (whom Carafa had long viewed as a heretic, notwithstanding attempts by an earlier Pope to mend the breach between the two when they were cardinals) or for Philip. Paul, as a proud Neapolitan, hated the Spanish. The Venetian ambassador reported that he called them 'heretics, schismatics and accursed of God, seed of Jews and *Marranos*, scum of the earth; deploring Italy's misfortune that it was forced to serve people so vile and despicable'.[44] He wanted them out of Italy and above all out of Naples, and did little to work with Philip, instead trying to provoke him. Philip was to find that it was very difficult to live up to his early letter to Paul in which he had written that he hoped 'your Holiness will know that the Holy See has never had a more obedient son than I, nor one more desirous to preserve and increase her authority'.[45]

The first obstacle to good relations between the papacy and the king of Spain and England was the Pope's nomination of Bernardino Scotti (*c.* 1493–1568) to the archbishopric of Trani in the diocese of Naples. He was neither a native and nor was he likely to be resident in the see, as Charles V had stipulated that any holder must be and as Philip was determined should be the case.[46] Pole urged him to accept the nomination and Philip initially refused: although always happy to do what the Pope wanted, he could not 'contravene Charles V's promise, confirmed by himself to nominate only [a] native'. There were two huge egos involved in this struggle – those of Philip and Paul IV – and the prickly (and longstanding) topic of Church authority in the distribution of benefices. The signs of a struggle for Pole were emerging: as he told Cardinal Carafa in October 1555, with Philip 'I pressed as hard as I could'.[47] Throughout this period and in the coming months Pole repeatedly asked Philip himself and, via Philip, his father to make peace with France, and wanted him to be 'the king of peace'; he himself 'never cease[s] to pray to God to illumine all hearts for peace'.[48] As the situation regarding territory deteriorated between Philip and the Pope and war began to seem likely, Pole's sense of urgency increased. He wrote that war with the Pope would not be a good thing and that there was no cause to fight; he would, however, do all that he could with the Pope.[49] In late summer 1556 Philip ordered troops to be moved on to papal territory: Rome was isolated, without being attacked, and battles occurred in nearby towns.[50] The situation continued into the new year and Paul called on his ally, France. Henri II broke the 1556 truce he had negotiated with Philip, sending troops to threaten the Flemish border and also into Naples, hoping to receive it in exchange. Philip asked the Privy Council for England's support but they stuck to the marriage treaty, saying that this was just a continuation of existing hostilities and not a new war.[51]

That situation would change with the Stafford rebellion of late April 1557. Supplied with ships and men by France, Thomas Stafford took Scarborough Castle with the aim of eventually overthrowing Philip and Mary. War was proclaimed in England on 1 June 1557. This placed both Reginald, a cardinal, and Mary, a pious and loyal Catholic, in huge difficulties. Even before the outbreak of war Mary had been 'very displeased to be caught in the middle' and Pole was waiting, in vain, for instructions from the Pope on how to comport himself.[52] Paul, as can be imagined, was less than pleased with both. He was forced to surrender in early September 1557. The Pope's 'ignominious surrender delivered control of all of Italy to Spain'.[53] The war with France continued. In November 1557 Pole heard from Cardinal Morone that the Pope was happy to

… see your proper attitude for cardinal and Christian and your plan to approach Philip, either by letter or in person. But [he] does not see how any Christian can stay in contact with [the] worst example in Christendom and wants you to return to Rome to assist him, avoid communicating with enemy of the Church, and be where your status says you should be.[54]

Pole was to choose: England, Mary and Philip; or the Church. In Rome he was viewed with suspicion as an agent of the king and queen. Worse was to follow: Pole wrote to Paul saying that he had written to Philip asking for peace but to no avail, and in December he was told that the Pope suspected Philip of wanting to overthrow the papacy. He threatened to excommunicate the Spanish king.[55] Certainly, if Philip had been in England then Mary could well have prevented the escalation of matters. When Philip returned in 1557 Pole did his best to avoid split loyalties by leaving London for Canterbury and then, his powers as legate having been revoked by Paul in that March, he visited Philip as a private individual.[56] He was walking a tightrope and could not pacify the figures stood at each end. Rome's silence was ominous. He continued to work for peace, badgering Philip again in letters, yet emphasising repeatedly his obedience to Paul in letters to Rome: he told Cardinal Carafa in December 1557 that he was still waiting to hear from the Pope 'and more than ready to obey'.[57] Obedience was always important to Pole and the choice was taken out of his hands: Mary refused to send him back to Rome and to accept any new legate. Pole was tied to England.

Philip and the Burnings

Philip's attitude to Protestants and the burning of these heretics is a series of contradictions. He frequented Protestants, and did so quite happily: as Geoffrey Parker notes, between 1550 and 1551 he 'ate and drank, danced and jousted, hunted and talked with Lutherans, and his surviving letters to Lutheran rulers from this period exude warmth'.[58] Indeed, Sansom regards Mary as 'the more intransigent, principled and less pragmatic of the two monarchs'.[59] Philip had spent time in the Netherlands where 'he became familiar with an environment where the existence of heresy was accepted as almost natural'.[60] This was in part a result of his father's necessary, if unwelcome, accommodations with the Lutherans of 1548 and later, and was certainly not to be the case in England.

As we know, the burnings began in February 1555 and some foreign onlookers were horrified: 'I do not think it well that Your Majesty should allow further executions to take place,'

Renard wrote to Philip.[61] But Philip had no power to intervene in the legal process and possibly for this reason his confessor, Alfonso de Castro, then preached a sermon to the court speaking out strongly against the burnings and urging that the Protestants should be converted. Was this Philip trying to save face? The sermon was surprising as de Castro was a known hater of heretics: he had published *Adversus omnes haereses* (*Against All Heretics*) (Paris, 1534) and *De iusta haereticorum punitione* (*On the Just Punishment of Heretics*) (Salamanca, 1547). *Adversus* was republished in 1556 and dedicated to Philip and *De iusta* was reprinted in 1556 with a dedication to Charles V.[62] As Kelsey notes, initially Philip was aiming for moderation.[63] Yet there was not total agreement among Philip's Spanish clergy and advisors. Pedro de Soto was very hostile to Protestants (and was briefly summoned to England by Pole). Bartolomé Carranza, who was to prove of special help to Pole in the Synod, was an active supporter of the burnings. He is believed to have advised Philip to 'attend first to God's affairs through the punishment of heretics' and he was very close to Mary.[64] Sansom views him as 'intimately involved in pushing forward the persecuting agenda, alongside Pole and Mary herself'.[65]

Where did Philip stand in this? Absence was no excuse for his non-intervention and all the above indicates that he approved of the burnings. He certainly knew of them as he was kept informed by the Select Council. He seems to have been a keen proponent of burnings as the last resort, although his influence is hard to trace, but he certainly did nothing to stop them or to moderate the stance of Mary and Pole. Indeed, some years later he boasted that 'many heretics had been burned and many others converted' during his reign in England.[66]

Conclusion

Pole's relationship with Mary was 'the relationship of a private and intimate counsellor. The queen depended on him heavily and trusted him entirely.'[67] As we will see, his relationship with Vittoria Colonna followed these same lines. Mary and Reginald were, as a previous chapter showed, the main forces behind the burnings. But if Mary counted on Pole, what was Philip's opinion of the cardinal? Here, the waters are more muddied. I think he was always a cardinal to Philip, and was thus essential to Philip in his attempts to reconcile England with Rome, and it is at this point that their relationship seems to have been at its warmest. Difficulties arose when it came to the question of war. Pole proved inept at the Marck peace conference, and although he tried to argue for peace with Philip and at best remained neutral in the king's conflict with the Pope, he was clearly not on Philip's side. On the surface there was respect and accord – for no other reason would Philip have appointed him as head of the Select Council – but it seems that this attitude may have faltered with time and Philip was suspicious of his overarching obedience to the papal see.

Pole wanted to return to Rome when summoned by the Pope, despite almost certainly knowing that the outcome of his return to Rome was likely to be arrest by the Inquisition. He had stayed in England because Mary refused to let him receive the papal summons. Loades describes Reginald's adherence to the Pope and the authority of the Church (however badly the Pope treated him) as 'the only sure and immovable foundation for true belief and the Christian life'.[68] Philip had also not supported his candidacy for the papacy. Was he suspicious of his orthodoxy? Did he believe that Pole was too essential in England to lose? We will never know.

What is clear is that Pole did his best in a difficult situation. And he clearly felt that he could count on Philip to do the right thing after his death: on 23 September 1558, when he was already very ill and recognised that this illness might kill him, he accepted Philip's kind offer of help and recommended to him 'those few of my *famiglia* that I brought with me from Italy and whom I have never myself been able recompense as I would very much have liked. They have served me with great loyalty and love', and he asked him to help them as much as he was able.[69]

This patronage was the only favour Pole asked of Philip. With the death of Mary, Philip's authority in England ended, but he could, of course, have offered places and pensions in his other courts. Sadly, there is little evidence that he did so.

12

CARDINAL POLE AND THE WOMEN IN HIS LIFE

It is very easy to see Reginald Pole as a two-dimensional figure: a cardinal who was loyal to the Catholic Church and the papacy while standing up to Henry VIII and his religious reforms who then proceeded to burn Protestants under Mary Tudor. He was more than that, and if we look at his relations with the women in his life, we get a far more rounded picture of Reginald. The women were few in number: Pole was no Casanova cardinal. He is not associated with any Renaissance courtesans, nor are there any reliable reports that he had love affairs or fathered any illegitimate children. Beccadelli records a rumour that he had 'a natural daughter, whom he had secreted in a convent in Rome'. But she was 'an unhappy orphan, the daughter of an English lady deceased, whom the cardinal had taken under his protection to save her from being abandoned', and he left sufficient funds to provide a dowry for her. This was 'one of his silent acts of beneficence, which he performed without sounding his own praises'.[1] Indeed, Pole was a deeply spiritual man who, as we have seen, came to spirituality a little late in life. This allowed no room for romantic dalliance and instead his relations with women can be divided into two clear types: the female members of his family, not just his mother but his sister and his nieces, and also those who shared his religious interests and beliefs.

Ursula Pole, Baroness Stafford (d. 1570)

The birthdate of Ursula Pole, Reginald's sister, is unknown but the event which led her to figure in the documents of the day and in Tudor history books was her marriage on 16 February 1519 to Henry Stafford (1501–63), the heir of Edward Stafford, Duke of Buckingham. Stafford was an exceptional catch for the Pole family, and, as Adam Pennington notes, like many daughters of the nobility, Ursula 'married up'.[2] The future must have seemed very bright to Ursula: she, like Henry and Arthur Pole, accompanied the king to the Field of the Cloth of Gold, and lived in splendour, but things changed for the worse with the downfall of the Duke of Buckingham in 1521. She and Stafford were almost penniless. Margaret Pole took one of their daughters into her household and although Henry VIII returned some of the late duke's lands, it was not enough as the income from the lands was limited, especially with such a growing family.[3] In 1537 her husband wrote to Cromwell begging for help and threatening to leave the country because they were so poor.[4] Ursula and Henry had seven children in the first ten years of their marriage and a further seven arrived over the coming years.[5] At one point they were reduced to living in an abbey for four years.

Ursula's husband converted to Protestantism (though he switched back later in life when it was required and became quite conservative in his beliefs). He was politically astute enough to conform to Henry's wishes and neither he nor his wife were implicated in the Exeter Conspiracy. Ursula seemingly had stronger Catholic beliefs: she was very intimate with Elizabeth Howard, her sister-in-law and the wife of the ultra-Catholic Duke of Norfolk, who left 'sister Stafford' a bequest in her will of jewellery and apparel.[6] There is a portrait in the Courtauld Gallery, dated 1536 but with no details of the sitter, which is traditionally identified as Ursula Pole: if it is indeed her, the portrait confirms her religious beliefs and her status as a Plantagenet as she holds a white rose and a ciborium. The dating is also intriguing: 1536 was the year of the Pilgrimage of Grace and the arrival of Pole's *De Unitate*: the hypothesis that it is Ursula – which is unlikely to be confirmed as we have no other surviving portrait of her – would make this very much a statement piece on the part of the Pole family.

The Staffords lived a quiet life in Stafford during the rest of Henry's reign, with Henry Stafford acting as justice of the peace. He prospered under Edward VI, becoming Baron Stafford and publishing a translation of Edward Foxe's justification of the royal supremacy (this would have been anathema to Reginald, but Stafford had a large family to feed). After helping to raise men to secure the throne for Mary Tudor in 1553, he was suitably rewarded for his father's loyalty and that of his wife's family to her mother, Katharine of Aragon. As he wrote to Mary, the Poles 'chose death rather than consent to your disinheritance in your tender years' and he seemingly benefitted from Reginald's role as Archbishop of Canterbury: many of his father's lands were returned to him and he enjoyed a position at court as chamberlain of the Exchequer.[7] They had returned to splendour again.

Although Reginald did not have a very high opinion of Ursula's husband, relations between Ursula and Reginald seem to have been warm, although one wonders how he felt when

Fig. 2. Cardinal Reginald Pole. (Classic Image/Alamy Stock Photo)

Fig. 3. Margaret Pole. (Chronicle/Alamy Stock Photo)

Fig. 4. Henry VIII. (Walker Art Library/Alamy Stock Photo)

Fig. 5. Mary Tudor. (Lebrecht Music & Arts/Alamy Stock Photo)

Fig. 6. Thomas Cranmer. (The Print Collector/Alamy Stock Photo)

Above left: Fig. 7. Santi Nereo ed Achilleo, Rome. (Author's photograph)

Above right: Fig. 8. Santi Vito e Modesto, Rome. (Author's photograph)

Right: Fig. 9. Santa Maria in Cosmedin, Rome. (Adobe Stock/ Valery Rokhin)

Fig. 10. Pope Paul IV. (Penta Springs Limited/Alamy Stock Photo)

Fig. 11. Vittoria Colonna. (Archivio GBB/Alamy Stock Photo)

Fig. 12. Bagnoregio, Italy. (photo courtesy of Claudio Grande, unsplash.com)

Fig. 13. The English Hospice in Rome (now known as the Venerable English College). (Author's photoraph)

Above: Fig. 14. Print by Philips Galle, after Frans Floris, *Tabula Cebetis Cartae Vitae* (1561). (© British Museum, London)

Below left: Fig. 15. Cardinal Pole's chapel 'Domine quo vadis' on the Via Appia. (Author's photograph)

Below right: Fig. 16. Lambert Lombard, *Christ on the Cross*. (Kupferstichkabinett, Berlin) © bpk / Kupferstichkabinett, SMB/Jörg P. Anders.

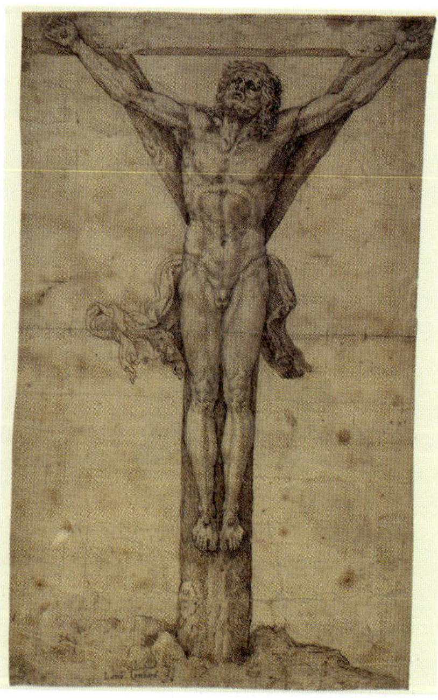

Fig. 17. Michelangelo Buonarotti, *Crucifixion.* (© British Museum, London)

Fig. 18. Michelangelo Buonarotti, *Ragusa Pietà* (*c.* 1545). (Private collection)

Fig. 19. Sebastiano del Piombo, *Portrait of Cardinal Pole*, held in the Hermitage Museum in St Petersburg. (Photography © The State Hermitage Museum/photo by Vladimir Terebenin)

Fig. 20. The tomb of Cardinal Pole in Canterbury Cathedral. (Author's photograph)

her son (and his nephew) Thomas Stafford was executed in 1557 for his conspiracy to overthrow Mary I. Unfortunately, there is no surviving correspondence between the two, but it is clear from other sources that he was fond of her and grateful for her relations with their niece Catherine Hastings *née* Pole. Ursula was, as befitted her actual status, very much an aunt.

Catherine Pole, Countess of Huntingdon (1508–76)

Catherine was the eldest daughter of Henry Pole, Lord Montagu, and his wife, Jane Neville. She was, as Routledge notes, a direct descendant of Richard, Duke of York (the father of king Edward IV) and thus a prime catch.[8] An illustrious marriage was in store for her and indeed, in 1532, she married Francis, Lord Hastings (1513/14–60), son of the Earl of Huntingdon and Anne Stafford, who was the daughter of the late Duke of Buckingham. The Poles thus consolidated their relations to the Stafford family and the marriage would 'further help to consolidate the Pole family's influence in the south'.[9] Catherine at the time was Montagu's co-heir, and, as this was before the disgrace of the Poles, must thus have seemed an attractive prospect to the Hastings family. Another of Montagu's daughters, Winifred, then married Hastings' younger brother, Thomas.

Hastings' father, George, 1st Earl of Huntingdon, despite attempts to implicate him, survived unscathed from the storm of the Exeter Conspiracy and continued to flourish as a royal intimate. Leaving aside the potential benefits of the marriage to the Poles, the family seems to have been genuinely fond of Hastings: in 1534 when Montagu heard that he was seriously ill he rode straight to him, an act repeated by Margaret Pole in 1536.[10] He was also popular at court: he became a Knight of the Bath in 1533 and 'participated at both the baptism of Prince Edward and the funeral of Jane Seymour'.[11] In 1539 Hastings was part of the reception party for Anne of Cleves. His eldest son, Henry, was educated with Prince Edward, and he himself was prominent in the political events of Edward's reign, favouring and in turn being favoured by the Earl of Warwick and becoming a member of the Privy Council. His son Henry married Katherine Dudley, youngest daughter of Warwick, who was now Duke of Northumberland.[12] Hastings' support for Lady Jane Grey should have meant disgrace when Mary Tudor ascended the throne, and he and his son were briefly imprisoned in the Tower but both were then pardoned.[13] He proved his loyalty to the throne by moving against the Wyatt rebellion. Claire Cross correctly describes him as 'a *politique* driven forward by his desire for family aggrandisement, a realist who … knew how to bend with the times'.[14]

If Mary's accession had initially seemed to threaten Francis Hastings, it was a boon for his wife, precisely because she was the granddaughter of Margaret Pole. Catherine and Winifred Hastings were restored in 1554 'to the blood and estates of Henry Pole, Lord Montague'.[15] These estates were extensive, including lands in Hampshire, Wiltshire, Devon and Somerset. Her husband continued to flourish under Mary (and the presence in England of Cardinal Pole can surely have done his prospects no harm) and Catherine was a favoured attendant of the queen.[16] He was clearly a personable man (indeed, he continued to thrive under Elizabeth I) and it was seemingly at happy marriage.

Catherine wrote two (lost) letters to her uncle Reginald before his arrival in England, and his reply of 21 June 1554 survives:

I read with no small joy to see my hope confirmed that I ever had of your marriage that it should be comfortable unto you and to all your friends, and also of your own person to see how God has worked to make you a good wife and a good mother withall, bringing well up your children that God has given you to his honour, having that comfort of my good lord your husband that you can desire...[17]

These were the first letters that he had received from his family in many years, and he was moved:

I could not read your whole letter, though it was not long, at once, for the sorrowful remembrance it brought me of the loss of those which I left in good state at my departing, to whom you were most dearest.

It is signed, 'By your loving uncle R. Pole, cardinal legate.'[18] Although Reginald was not yet in England, it is clear that in some way he was home: he had his family back.

By July 1555 Catherine and her husband were sending Pole gifts of red deer pasties and he, in addition to wishing them the protection that he sincerely hoped God would grant them in their various illnesses, was also encouraging their son Henry to translate into English a work on nobility (a concept never far from Pole's mind, as we have seen).[19] He was looking forward to receiving her at Richmond and he was, as ever, 'your loving uncle'. By 25 November of that year he had heard from Ursula that she was with Catherine while her husband was away to give her comfort (and Catherine went to stay with Ursula the following year), and he had finally seen their sons Edward and Walter, to his delight. At her husband's request he had become Walter's godfather and he recommended that the boy stay with Catherine for a while, seemingly advising against sending him to another noble household as was the custom with sons. He thought both boys would be 'servants of God'.[20]

The affectionate relationship between uncle and niece continues: in December she had sent him, among other things, napkins. He is clearly enamoured 'of my little Walter', as he writes in a letter of 2 January 1556.[21] Reginald had, in effect, become a father figure in both his eyes and in those of the Hastings family: in a letter likely dated to 20 January 1557 he worries about the marriage of her daughter and whether she is too young. Of some interest is his comment that he had in the 1530s attempted to defer her own marriage because of her youth.[22] Having lacked a family for so many years, he is extremely solicitous of Catherine's health and is sorry in May 1557 that it is no better. He worries about her idea of taking the baths at Buxton as 'although they do good to some, the complexions are not all alike', again entrusting her and her family to God's protection, 'specially my son Wa[l]ter'.[23] His feelings for Walter had almost certainly been increased by knowing him better: Walter seems to have been a part of his household, albeit for a short period: in July 1556 Catherine had written to thank Reginald for helping 'our little Walter' and hopes he will continue to benefit from 'your grace's good education'.[24] Reginald seemingly had some influence on Walter: Cross believes that in the reign of Elizabeth I Walter was 'almost certainly a crypto-Catholic'.[25]

The picture of Reginald that these letters paint is very different from the man we have come to know: God and religion are mentioned, as befits a man of the Church, but more than that they show 'the tenderness and simple piety of the great cardinal's private life'.[26]

Margaret Pole, the Cardinal's Mother

It is perhaps easy for modern readers to see Margaret Pole as simply an unfortunate old woman who suffered a horrible death at the hands of an inexperienced executioner on 27 May

1541. With the exception of the late introduction by Cromwell of an embroidered tunic, supposedly symbolising the marriage of Reginald to Mary, Margaret was indeed never implicated in the Exeter Conspiracy and was unjustly put to death because she was a Pole and the mother of Reginald. Tragic as this is – as Sharon Bennett Connolly notes, she surely had the right to spend her contented later years surrounded by a brood of grandchildren – she was much more than that and a swift analysis of her life, and indeed of her actions, helps shed light on her character and on her relations with Reginald.[27]

Margaret could not help but be conscious of her ancestry and her status: she was the daughter of the Duke of Clarence and the niece of Edward IV. She spent her early years at court, married a man who was half-cousin to Henry VII, became lifelong friends with Katharine of Aragon and was governess to her daughter Mary. Her restoration to her brother's lands as Countess of Salisbury in 1512 meant that she was one of the wealthiest and most influential nobles in the kingdom. Her life was, however, illustrative of the vicissitudes of fortune: born into wealth, she then found herself the impoverished daughter of an attainted traitor before being welcomed back to court under Henry VII and Elizabeth of York, married to a steady man who was elevated to prominence while Prince Arthur was alive and then, like Katharine of Aragon, she fell into penury after her husband's death. Her fortunes revived when Henry VIII ascended the throne and married Katharine and she became Countess of Salisbury.

She was, as imperial ambassador Chapuys noted, 'a very honourable and virtuous lady', devoted to the Princess Mary, but also very status-conscious, pious, litigious and at times quite ruthless.[28] These all affected her relationship with Reginald. Margaret was very devout: at Clavering, one of her properties, she regarded the erection of a new tabernacle as of greater importance than more urgent repairs.[29] It is generally believed that it was poverty that made her dedicate Reginald to the Church, and he was to throw this action back at her later in life. In his letter of 15 July 1536 he wrote:

> ... from my childish years ... you had given me utterly unto god ... in me you had so given all right utterly from you ... and possession utterly of me that you never took any care to provide for my living, nor otherwise, as you did for others, but committed me all to god to whom you had given me...[30]

Reading this, it is hard not to believe that in some way he blames his mother for his future actions and feels she has no right to criticise him for sending *De Unitate*. If she had not given him to the Church would a quieter, less eventful future have awaited Reginald and, given the consequences of his actions, the Pole family?

Margaret recognised the debt that she owed the king – in the document of her restoration of 1512 she acknowledged that she was the king's 'poor kinswoman and [had] no living but by help of your highness'.[31] Yet, like Reginald, her gratitude for the king's patronage and kindness was not infinite. She challenged the king in a long legal dispute over lands which she claimed as her own as part of her restoration. This seemingly started around 1517 and was still ongoing in 1531. Why did she not bow to the inevitable and give up the lands? As Pierce notes, 'anything other than sycophantic gratitude and utter submission to Henry's will would always provide fertile ground in which to sow the seeds of the king's suspicions ... Margaret had continued to underestimate the king.'[32]

She certainly did not improve the king's perception of her when she refused to surrender Mary's jewels to him until receiving his orders in writing, and it is little wonder that Henry told Chapuys in February 1535 that 'the countess was a fool, of no experience'.[33] This sense of self-righteousness and of putting one's own conscience before what was advisable was inherited by Reginald: *De Unitate* reeks of Reginald's conviction that his was the only correct point of view. Seemingly unaware of her own folly, she was more than aware of the 'folly' of Reginald's actions in sending his book to Henry and the danger in which this placed them all. Prompted by Lord Montagu, she said that she 'took her son for a traitor and for no son, and that she would never take him otherwise'. Almost certainly the letter would have been seen by the council, but it surely is a more strongly worded letter than most historians believe:

> And now to see you in his grace's high indignation ... I am not able to bear it. Trust me, Reginald, there went ... the death of your father or any children ... Wherefore, upon my blessing I charge you to call your spirits ... and take another way [or] you will be the confusion of your mother. You write of a promise made of you to God ... that was to serve God and your prince whom if you do not serve with all your will, with all your power I know you cannot please God, and your bounden duty is so to do above all other. ... I shall deeply pray to God to give you grace and to make you his servant or else to take you to himself.[34]

In other words, she wishes for him to repent or die. Stern stuff, and from a woman of strong character. There is no reason to doubt the sincerity of her words. But how did this affect Reginald? Hugh Holland, a servant of Geoffrey Pole, Reginald's younger brother, met with Reginald in Flanders in around 1537. Reginald sent messages to his family, including one to his mother which showed his love for her but also his own ruthlessness: Holland was to remind Margaret that 'she and I looking upon a wall together read this, *Spes mea in deo est* [my hope is in the Lord] and desire her blessing for me. I trust she will be glad of mine also.' Yet Reginald was also convinced that his way was the only way: he added that if she was 'of the opinion that other be there, mother as she is mine, I would tread upon her with my feet'.[35] Mother and son were similar in their determination to have their own way. Indeed, on the death of her son Arthur Pole, Margaret and Lord Montagu had kept his death secret for a month and when they revealed it to his widow, Jane, they forced her to take a vow of chastity so that she could never remarry and thus they could protect the Pole inheritance. She was only able to renounce the vow and remarry after Montagu's death and Margaret's imprisonment.[36] Reginald was clearly cut of a similar cloth.

Yet he felt her death deeply, as Mayer correctly notes. An incident which his biographer, Lodovico Beccadelli, notes is telling. Until her death he had

> ... believed that the lord God has given me the grace to be the son of one of the best and most honoured ladies of England and I have gloried in that ... But he has wished to honour me more and increase my obligation, for he has also made me the son of a martyr, whom that king, because she was constant in the Catholic faith, has had publicly decapitated, even though she was more than seventy years old [*sic*] and his aunt. Thus he has rewarded the efforts which she took for a long time in raising his daughter. God be praised and thanked.[37]

Reginald then retired to pray and came out, composed, after an hour. As we shall see, the role of mother that another woman, shortly to be examined, assumed in his life indicates that there was a vacuum that an hour's prayer simply could not fill. As Reginald wrote to Granvelle, the Emperor's councillor, on 11 April 1539, Henry had killed his brother who was 'the person I loved most in the world, except my mother'.[38] We can only imagine how he suffered at the news of her execution, and a botched execution at that. She may have been 'condemned to eternal life', but was this sufficient consolation?[39] Her loss still smarted eleven years later: he wrote to Mary I in early December 1553 of 'such monstrous injuries as he did, especially in killing my mother'.[40] It would surely have been of some comfort to him that she was beatified under Pope Leo XIII in 1886 for having died 'for the truth of the orthodox faith'.[41]

Vittoria Colonna (1490–1547)

The relationship between Pole and Colonna was a complex one, and not easy to decipher given the fragmentary nature of the surviving evidence. It is too easy to view it in anachronistic terms, and we do need to remember the depth of religious and spiritual feeling in both Pole and Vittoria and in many others of that period.

There is no doubt that Vittoria Colonna was an extraordinary woman. Born into the nobility and with a high-profile marriage to Francesco Ferrante d'Avalos, Marchese of Pescara, she started writing poems (initially to her late husband) following his death in 1525. Very few women were poets, and none had ever had a book of poems published before the printing of her *Rime* in 1538.[42] She was very pious from an early age – even wanting to become a nun in 1525 – and favoured charismatic preachers such as Bernardino Ochino. She was relatively intimate with

Paul III, who consulted her on some matters.[43] Colonna also came to know the unorthodox Renée d'Anjou (and possibly the works of Calvin) when she stayed at Ferrara.

The friendship with Pole was 'undoubtedly a friendship based on the spiritual guidance and good Christian advice which the Cardinal provided to the tormented and disorientated soul of the Marchioness of Pescara in her incessant search for piety, and that she reciprocated … with an admiration that bordered on adoration, and a maternal affection'.[44] They almost certainly met after his first failed legation when he was a curia cardinal and based in Rome. He saved her both spiritually and physically: in the late 1520s Paolo Giovio had commented on how she chastised her flesh through fasting, flagellation and constant prayers, and Pietro Carnesecchi later confirmed to the Inquisition that Pole saved her from 'a state of skin and bones'.[45] At some point, probably 1540, she wrote a poem to Pole about his mother, comforting him in his grief for her imprisonment. In it she already refers to herself as his 'second mother':

> My son and master, if your first and true
> mother abides in prison, yet still her wisdom
> is not stolen from her nor her noble spirit defeated
> nor the many virtues from her unconquered companions.
> To me, who seem to move about unburdened and free
> and keep my heart confined and buried in a small plot
> I pray you turn your eyes from time to time
> so that your second mother does not perish.[46]

She later offered herself to Pole as his new mother after the brutal death of Margaret Pole.[47] Reginald happily accepted, and this was so well known that he was even indirectly referred to as 'your son' by Pietro Bembo.[48] She joined him, and the other *spirituali*, at Viterbo, staying in a local convent from 1541 to 1544, and met with him occasionally but was at times discouraged from doing so by others of the circle. It is important to remember, however, just how negligible the role of women had previously been in religious life outside of the convent and in discussions at this time, and there may well have been some hostility towards this 'interloper'. Vittoria Colonna and Giulia Gonzaga were, with others, trailblazers who took an 'active part in the project of religious reform'.[49]

Colonna loved Pole because 'you help me to know myself, to humble myself and make myself nothing, and live entirely in Him who is all consolation', and she can sense 'the smell of Christ which you bear' – and not because she 'had fallen deeply in love' as some now believe.[50] She 'came to find Jesus Christ in the personality of Pole, to the point of divinizing him',[51] a situation which seemingly made Pole uncomfortable. When accused by Pole's familiars of being too fond of him and wanting to spend too much time with him (one can just imagine their dismissive attitude towards this pesky woman), Colonna wrote to Priuli that Pole himself sees nothing wrong with this and that she believes that her relationship with Pole is 'so perfect, my affection so right, due and holy, so helpful to my soul and so dear and right in God's eyes'.[52] Cardinal Morone, in his trial by the Inquisition, said that although they spent time alone, it was to talk of 'godly matters, because both of them took more pleasure in that subject than in any other'.[53] Other letters to him are full of devout religious sentiment.

He was for her 'a true and sincere servant of God'.[54] Although she reproached him for his short replies to her many letters, Pole recognised that he owed her more time and attention when he was reprimanded for being remiss in this by his servant, George Lily.[55] She may well have missed him and wanted his company, but this was because 'you continually helped me (more than I could ever believe) to know myself, to humble myself, to reduce myself to nothing and live only in He who is our every good, consolation, joy and happiness'. She was far from 'erotically' drawn to Pole, as recently argued. She had never 'seen anything in his Lordship but Christ'.[56] He was her spiritual master, and this was very much in line with Valdés' belief that through such contact with a master and through examining one's soul a person 'could slowly approach an ever greater purity and proximity to Christ'.[57] Such was her trust in him (and indeed in Cardinals Morone and Sadoleto) that she appointed them as executors to her will and left 9,000 *scudi* in her will in trust to Pole to be used for charitable works. Her family was unhappy with this, and Pole later returned the sum for the dowry of her nephew's daughter.

As Brundin notes, it is clear that Vittoria needed the cardinal far more than he needed her. His feelings towards her are not as clear-cut as we might like, but he treats her as a follower and disciple and nothing more. In a letter of October 1546 he acknowledges in fact that in the face of her 'more than maternal love', 'neither in deeds nor words have I reciprocated even the smallest part of so much love, but have rather done the opposite'.[58] But this surely, in the eyes of Pole, is the correct, and only possible, response of a spiritual master to a disciple, believing that 'the divine will shall amply reward you'.[59]

Giulia Gonzaga, Countess of Fondi (1513–66)

Born into a minor branch of the Gonzaga family, Giulia was famous in her lifetime (and indeed since) as a great beauty and a woman of great piety. She was married at thirteen to Vespasiano Colonna and widowed less than two years later.[60]

From late 1535 she spent the rest of her life in Naples residing in a convent, and it was there that she again met, and became a disciple of, Juan de Valdés, who was to prove the link between Giulia and the *spirituali* at Viterbo under the aegis of Reginald Pole. In the same year she met Pietro Carnesecchi, who was to prove another link to Pole and the *spirituali*.

Valdés had visited Giulia at Fondi, her late husband's fiefdom, and wrote to her cousin Cardinal Ercole Gonzaga of her 'divine conversation and kindness'.[61] He had probably been asked by Cardinal Ercole, to whose household in Rome he had belonged, to help Giulia in a legal dispute with her stepdaughter. Valdés was a charismatic layman with strong Lutheran leanings, supporting especially the idea of *sola fide* (justification by faith alone as the way to redemption).[62] Their relationship soon became one of spiritual master and follower, especially after she had heard Bernardino Ochino preach his Lenten sermons in Naples in 1536.[63] She became part of the group surrounding Valdés, which included Marc'antonio Flaminio (another later link to the Viterbo *spirituali*), and in turn introduced Pietro Carnesecchi to the group.

So inspired was Valdés by his conversations with Giulia that he wrote the *Alfabeto Cristiano* (*Christian Alphabet*). This focussed on the inner being and the figure of Christ and his role as saviour, casting aside all the practices traditionally considered essential to Roman Catholicism: the sinner 'confesses directly to God, not to a confessor'.[64] The Naples Valdesian group concentrated on spreading his works, to the extent that Giulia had the *Alphabet* published in Venice, albeit attributed to an anonymous author.[65]

At his death in 1541 Valdés left Giulia all his manuscripts. She was already in contact with the group in Viterbo via her friendship with Flaminio and Carnesecchi. In early

1542 Flaminio sent some of Valdés' religious writings to Viterbo via Apollonio Merenda, Pole's chaplain, and a member of Valdés' group.[66] Carnesecchi was by now very close to Giulia and in 1546 visited her in Naples before joining Pole at Bagnoregio. Flaminio's correspondence with Giulia is unfortunately lost, but Carnesecchi and she were regular correspondents. Colonna also wrote to Giulia: on 8 December 1541 she recalls their meeting in years past in Fondi and thanks her for sending the 'so many and such good things to the Cardinal and to those other gentlemen ... which he received with immense pleasure, seeing such affection and charity in them'. Pole, she writes, is 'extremely busy'.[67] Vittoria then thanks her for sending Valdés' commentary on St Paul to the group.[68] Giulia's relationship with Flaminio was clearly a close one and one of shared religious sympathies: he referred to her as a 'most honourable patron' to whom he was a 'most dedicated servant'. The *Meditations* which he wrote were 'an exposition of the *sola fide* doctrine written in the spirit of Valdés'.[69]

Giulia apparently then sent Valdés' writings to Flaminio to have them printed in Italian.[70] There can be little doubt that it was the legacy of Valdés which bound Giulia and Flaminio together and almost certainly his relationship with Valdés which further made him of interest to Pole: Cardinal Morone, when interrogated by the Inquisition in 1557, claimed that 'many people believed that he kept him [Flaminio] with him because he was a pupil of Valdés and of Bernardino da Siena [Ochino]'. If Pole is to be believed, this was also to save Flaminio from the error of his ways, and indeed it should not be forgotten that Flaminio died a good Catholic.[71] At Viterbo Flaminio had Valdés' *Commento sopra li Psalmi* and his *Considerationi*, which he had translated into Italian for Giulia.[72]

Once in England, Pole did not forget her: Carnesecchi wrote in a letter to Giulia of 1 March 1555 that he had news of England from Bartolomeo Spadafora that 'of Cardinal Pole and Priuli he does not write anything except that they are well, and regarding the first, [...] he most cordially expressed his desire to know about you, which desire I satisfied amply in my [letter to him]'.[73] Giulia, like Colonna, clearly saw him as a spiritual master as she did Valdés: as Russell notes, she, with others faithful to Pole, tried 'with a fierce desire' to have Pole's works published in the 1560s, both 'for the glory of God and also for the glory of Pole'.[74]

So what do we learn about Pole from his relationships with the women in his life? He was a man who was attached to his family, one who welcomed renewed relations with them and who was happy to act as a father figure to its younger members. His love for and interest in Walter, his great-nephew, is touching and presents an unexpected side to his character. He was a man who preferred a few close personal relationships, who had a small and loyal circle of people surrounding him, and he was happy to add his relatives to this group. He had a close, albeit conflicted, relationship with his mother, and sought and found a second mother in Vittoria Colonna. Yet in his role as a cardinal, as in so much of his life, he obeyed the rules and felt relatively uncomfortable with the apostolic devotion that she showered up on him. It is easy to believe that he felt more comfortable in his relationship with Giulia Gonzaga, which was conducted, as far as we know, at a distance. It was a more equal relationship: they shared religious literature and indeed followers, and above all they shared religious beliefs. As is the case with all of us, Pole was not as two-dimensional as he seems at first glance: he was not just a man of the Church but also a man of feeling.

13

CARDINAL POLE AS GOVERNOR AND PATRON OF TOWN AND HOUSEHOLD

The Governorship of Bagnoregio

It was a rather offended Reginald Pole who wrote to his friend Cardinal Morone, a man who 'know[s] me inside out', on 28 May 1554 to refute all accusations of taking 'every opportunity to withdraw from the things of the world to return to my private life [studies]'.[1] Pole was amazed that Morone could possibly think this, not least because Reginald held that 'we, following His [God's]will should not avoid the opportunities that he sends us'. He fears that people believe 'I have always been keen to withdraw to my studies, never taking part in action nor showing any desire for those positions which mean dealing with affairs, leading them to believe that either I am very cowardly, or that I place my private studies above any form of action'.[2]

The irony is, of course, that this was written when he was waiting in the Low Countries for permission to go to England to, indeed, involve himself in action. He was, as he said, 'always willing to serve those who were in a position to command and who know how to and want to command well [and he will always be willing to serve] the honour of God and … [for] the good of others'.[3] Even more ironic is the fact that he had to fend off these accusations after serving the Pope as perpetual governor of Bagnoregio (fig. 12), a small town in the papal states.

It was a paid post, but the salary of 75 *scudi* per annum was surprisingly negligible and as Edwards notes he 'probably lost on the transaction'.[4] The reason for this is unclear: other governors had received more. Did the Pope think Pole would devote little time and attention to Bagnoregio and thus renumerated him accordingly? If this was the case, then he was to be surprised. Reginald was appointed in January 1547, and it was not a position he could refuse. Indeed, he approached it with alacrity. There had been cardinal governors of Bagnoregio since 1496, but Pole was to prove remarkably different from the majority of previous governors, many of whom had viewed the post as a recognition of favours given to the Pope of the time and rarely, if ever, visited, ensuring that a lieutenant did all the donkey work of ruling the township instead.[5] As we shall see, Pole visited regularly and was happy to immerse himself in the town's business and problems.

He had visited the town on two previous occasions that we know of: he had accompanied the Pope on a papal visit in September 1540 and in a letter from the summer of 1541 he writes that he had recently seen Vittoria Colonna at Bagnoregio and thanked the then governor of the town, Cardinal Antonio Pucci (r. 1531–44), for the care and hospitality shown to Colonna.[6] On these, and future visits, Reginald would stay in the convent of Sant'Agostino. On 3 February 1547 Pole's auditor, monsignor Girolamo Pecorino, took possession of Bagnoregio in his absence, by which time Pole had appointed Gabriele Bianchello to act as his lieutenant when he was not present in the town.[7] Pecorino read aloud a letter to the assembled councils and the community which, in essence, set the tone for Pole's governorship: they were to 'let him [Reginald] know in full all that you know to be necessary, as we will not fail to quickly provide all that is needed for the common benefit of this town and in particular of all of you'.[8]

He requested that two orators be sent to him to advise him of the community's needs. Of most interest to the populace was the question of the borders with Bolsena, a neighbouring town. Pole was quick off the mark and the affair had been sorted by 13 March 1547.[9] In April of that year the town was getting ready for his arrival. He did not come alone: Marc'antonio Flaminio and Pietro Carnesecchi also accompanied him, and thus, as at Viterbo, spiritual discussions were clearly still on the agenda. He was still there at the end of May when he met with members of his household and other witnesses to amend the bequest to him of 9,000 *scudi* which had proved so contentious in Vittoria Colonna's will. He stated that he would willingly direct the money away from charitable works (as per Vittoria's bequest) and give it for the dowry of Ascanio Colonna's daughter. As Targoff notes, 'the pressure Ascanio and his allies must have put on him was no doubt immense' and we can only think that Pole must have found it a bitter pill to swallow; his only consolation was that he was able to stipulate that if no children were forthcoming from her marriage then the money was to be returned to him and used for charitable causes in Rome.[10]

Yet personal matters were not foremost in Pole's dealings with Bagnoregio: he had to deal with requests to reduce the tax payable on horses, clarify a boundary dispute with Viterbo and protest at the sequestration of cattle by the *Viterbesi*.[11] These must have seemed small fry to a man of so lofty a mind as Pole, yet he dealt with them efficiently and quickly. He visited Bagnoregio again, possibly in November 1547, when he had withdrawn from Rome due to ill health, and definitely in December. The town, presumably delighted with their attentive governor, sent him a Christmas gift of forty pairs of capons, a roe deer and three hares.[12]

The year 1548 saw him active on the Pope's behalf in Rome, returning to Bagnoregio in the autumn. He had appointed a new lieutenant (and two more in the coming year) and sent someone to learn about and to deal with the trials for some crimes committed in the town. In 1549 he was there once again in early summer and his intervention was sought on the price of weapons.[13] Later that year he was in Rome for the conclave following the death of Paul III, returning to the town by June 1550 and remaining there until the end of September.[14] Again, he intervened in the daily life of the town: he had to sort out the quarrels between some citizens.[15] He was then summoned by the Pope to return to Rome to discuss with Cardinals Morone and Cervini some of the reform ideas which had not been discussed at Trent.[16]

It is in November of that year that we find his largest contribution to the well-being of Bagnoregio and its populace. On 28 November he ordered the general council to set up a wool industry (*valcheria*) so that the many young and unemployed men who loitered and lazed around the town's gates would have an occupation to keep them busy.[17] It was a labour-intensive operation and perfect for keeping idle hands busy. Money was raised to start the building of the machinery and work began in December 1550. Those working at the *valcheria* were in theory to be paid between 25 to 30 *scudi* per annum (at least a third of the salary Pole received for being governor!).[18]

The project went so well that the enterprise needed to be expanded, and on 1 August 1551 the general council applied to Pole (who had been in Bagnoregio the previous month) for a loan of 100 *scudi*. The cardinal, keen that the unemployed should find work because doing nothing was the 'the cause and origin of many evils', duly lent the money, with the understanding that it was to be reimbursed within seventeen months.[19] So successful was the industry that it required further expansion and in September 1552 the council requested another loan of 100 *scudi*. Pole, who was resident in Bagnoregio at the time, once again agreed, this time without stipulating a date for the reimbursement of the money. All this was for nought: a violent storm in January 1554 meant that the river flooded and the machinery and thus the industry were destroyed. As Cipriani notes, Pole was not there later in the year to offer his moral support for a rebuilding of the site and in 1555 the council decided to build a windmill for processing grain instead.[20] There is no evidence that Pole, never a wealthy cardinal, ever received repayment of his loans.

He was able to help the general council in April 1552 with advice regarding the expense of a loan to be made on papal orders to the *Camera Apostolica* for the war against the Turks and was present in Bagnoregio in September.[21] But the following year saw the accession of Mary I to the English throne and Pole sent Vincenzo Parpaglia, whom we shall discuss shortly, who then wrote to the councils to say that Reginald would soon be leaving for England. Concerned, the town sent an ambassador to Parpaglia to see if a successor would be nominated.[22] Pole clearly thought that Cardinal Alvise Corner (1517–84) would be a suitable replacement as he wrote to him in late August asking him to keep an eye on Bagnoregio, but by late September it was Cardinal Alessandro Campeggi (1504–54), as deputy governor, who approved a loan for the council.[23] Campeggi was a stopgap and in October 1553 Pole was finally able to inform the council that Cardinal Corner would indeed act for him while he was in England.[24]

Yet although absent, he had not forgotten the town: in March 1557 he sent a gift of 100 ducats, specifying that the money was to be used to repair the town's walls.[25] On hearing of the death of Pope Marcellus II, the town decided to hold processions and prayers asking for the election of Pole as Pope. They were clearly attached to the cardinal, but that boat had sailed and Carafa, Pole's enemy, was elected pontiff.

In short, Pole was a conscientious and attentive governor and, as Mayer notes, 'enjoyed the place'.[26] The only other cardinal governor of this period who exceeded him in generosity (if not in visits) was Cardinal Domenico Grimani (r. 1513–23), who rebuilt the *palazzo comunale*. As he wrote to Cardinal Morone in 1554, Pole was always ready to undertake 'the smallest action that I could take for the benefit of the humblest person in the world'.[27]

Cardinal Pole as Governor of His Household

Detailing Pole's household is not an easy task, and little work has been done on it. However, it is worth pursuing because it throws up some interesting themes: the loyalty that those who benefitted from his patronage, small as it was, felt that they owed, or did not owe, to Pole; how an impecunious cardinal such as Pole could reward his entourage and how this entourage was influenced by his disgrace in the reign of Henry VIII and indeed by the pull of the king's patronage.

Were friendship and previous Polean patronage more important than to be in Henry's good graces?

As a prince of the Church, a cardinal was supposed to embody magnificence and largesse, extending the latter to the servants and friends who surrounded him. Writing in *De Cardinalatu* (*On the Cardinalate*) in 1510, Paolo Cortese prescribed 'sixty upper servants and eighty lower servants'.[28] In the census of late 1526 the average size of a cardinal's *famiglia* was 134 members. A *famiglia* of fewer than 100 members was to be considered small and was not that common. As Mary Hollingsworth rightly notes, 'the size of one's household ... was the indicator of rank, and for the most prosaic of reasons – a large household was very expensive to maintain. In addition to salaries, there was food and accommodation.'[29]

We have no surviving household accounts for Pole and his *famiglia* in Rome and given that, until late in life, he was an impoverished cardinal, it is difficult to imagine him maintaining a large household. He was poor as much of his own volition as anything else: he once refused a benefice because he could not be resident in it and in 1539 complained to Contarini that he was 'without provision and without money', to which would be added hunger.[30] But as Beccadelli notes, 'he had a pleasure in seeing his table genteelly covered, but always managed with such economy, as to measure his expenses by his income, which, till within the last year[s], had always been very inconsiderable'.[31] Yet there is no doubt that, whether large or small, he perforce did have a household and some insight can be given into some of its members and their roles and indeed their rewards. As Thomas Mayer notes, 'Pole by most definitions of a Renaissance patron was a failure'.[32] He should have been able to offer protection to his servants or intervention in disputes, but there are only three examples of this and none was brilliantly successful. Nor was he particularly adept at recommending his servants to other, hopefully better-off, masters. He also had little to offer in more 'tangible rewards' because of his poverty, and even in England he was not particularly wealthy. There was a one-off incident at Trent, clearly worthy of recall in Beccadelli's eyes:

> Four thousand ducats of his Granada pension were brought to him there which from some accident or other had been in arrear to him; but having supported himself for so long without feeling the want of it, and kept clear of all debts by his usual good management, he very liberally divided the whole sum among his domestics and dependants in proportion to their stations, without regarding that he was but a poor cardinal himself.[33]

Mayer believes that he only paid two pensions, and this at a time when such things were a typical currency of patronage.[34] So what did he have to offer? First, travel and new experiences: as legate he covered huge distances and his servants, despite the inconveniences of Renaissance travel, were able to visit new countries; second, proximity to one of, if not the, greatest seats of power in the period: the papacy; and third, he could offer himself: a charismatic, upright, sober figure who radiated simple faith and spiritual hope in his role as leader of the *spirituali* and the renewal of the Church. To be in Pole's orbit reflected well on those who served him and nurtured and reflected their own spiritual beliefs. They were, as Mayer says, 'true believers' in Pole.[35]

Any cardinal's household was divided along the same lines as the Pope's and that of any secular lord, namely into upper and lower offices. Within the household the *familiares continui commensales* (literally, the continuous members of his family) had their own status, were generally resident in the cardinal's palace or rooms in the Vatican and held the more important positions in the household.[36]

Vincenzo Parpaglia, the Long-standing and Well-travelled Servant

The *maestro di casa*, or major-domo, was the most important person in a cardinal's *famiglia*. He selected and supervised some of the lower-rank servants and had a judicial role within the household.[37] In 1560, after Pole's death, a Vincenzo Parpaglia was described as having held this role, probably after the death of another right-hand man, Bartolomeo Stella, in 1554. Parpaglia was certainly suited to be Pole's *maestro di casa*: he had held just such a role running the household of Pole's friend Cardinal Contarini at the colloquy of Regensburg in 1541.[38] Yet he was much more than that: he at times represented Pole or the Pope himself. In 1543 Francesco Priscianese described the *maestro di casa* as needing to be 'a very excellent and wise person, practical and discreet', and Parpaglia seems to have embodied these qualities.[39]

We first learn of him in 1539, when, in his role as an auditor/referendary (i.e. an advisor), he accompanied Pole on his travels as legate. He was clearly trusted by Pole, who also appointed him as vice-legate of Viterbo and the Patrimony of St Peter, and he stood in for Pole at Bagnoregio on the odd occasion.[40] At some point he took holy orders and became the Abbot of San Saluto. He was to cover many miles in Pole's service: in March 1539 he was sent from Spain to France to give Francis I a letter from Pole. Returning from France, he reported directly to the Pope at Frascati in April of the same year. Apparently, he travelled from Carpentras to Frascati in only eight days. Both he and his horses must have been exhausted. Such was his understanding and so high was the esteem in which he was held that he had that rarest of things: an immediate and long audience with the Pope.[41]

He was not just a servant of Pole, but also an intimate and one who shared Pole's interests: in a letter Pole wrote to Contarini from Carpentras in July 1539, he says that Priuli and Parpaglia send greetings and tells how they were staying with the Franciscans and 'all study philosophy and history' and indeed were still doing so in a letter of the following month.[42] The mammoth journey from Carpentras to Frascati was to be anything but Parpaglia's last: in August 1539 he was sent by Pole from Carpentras to the Pope to plead for leave for an exhausted Pole to stay in France.[43] He eventually moved from Viterbo to Trent to be by Pole's side and in the 1540s went to Bologna, Rome and Trent, and when Pole was at Maguzzano in 1553 he was often on relay between the cardinal and the Pope.[44] In August 1553 such was his intimacy with both Pole and the Pope that the latter wished to see him every day.[45] Parpaglia was clearly a man of upright character: Pole himself wrote in 1539 that he was 'a person of good intellect and experienced in these courts' and in 1553 Cardinal del Monte wrote to Pole that Julius III was happy to send Parpaglia to the French court because he was sure that 'for his great prudence and God's inspiration he cannot err'.[46]

Parpaglia's travels did not end when he arrived in England. He was once again Pole's trusted messenger on diplomatic missions. When moves were afoot for a peace conference in 1555, it was once again Parpaglia who was sent, this time to the Emperor; in June he was sent to Ardres, and in December he was sent to Philip II in Brussels before going on to France.[47] In May 1556 he was en route to Italy and returned via France. Parpaglia was, by Pole's own admission, 'our familiar and *continuus commensalis*' and Pole had 'long experience of Parpaglia, and I trust him'.[48] So why, then, did Parpaglia leave Pole at some point in 1556? Was he unrewarded by Pole? Yet the pension paid to him and his nephews when they left Pole's service was one of just two pensions that Pole ever provided. Parpaglia was not to benefit from any relatively conspicuous rewards, and nor did his other servants, but this was due to circumstance rather than to stinginess on Pole's part. Was there a waning in Pole's charisma and Parpaglia's faith in him as a 'sincere instrument' who was keen to reform the Church?[49] Had the incessant to-ing and fro-ing proved too much? Had he seen that there was little future for him with Pole, against whom Paul IV was irrevocably pitched? Or did he simply want a quieter life in Rome? Certainly, after Pole's death Parpaglia flourished: Pius IV appointed him as papal nuncio to England in May 1560 – a mission doomed to failure given Elizabeth I's hostility towards Catholicism – before he was recalled in the September of that year. What happened to him after that is unknown.

George Lily (aft. 1495–1559), a Loyal Servant

The son of the first headmaster of St Paul's School, Lily was an educated man who had studied at Magdalen College, Oxford and went on to study at Padua. He probably entered Pole's service in 1529.[50] He was also a man of sincere religious feelings – as Pole was to prove to be – and at one stage was considering joining the strict order of the Theatines. He was thus well-suited to become Reginald's 'domestic chaplain'. Interested in history, and indeed in geography, he contributed an essay attached to Paolo Giovio's *Descriptio Britanniae* (1548) and produced the first map of the British Isles to be printed. Pole's involvement in both these projects in unclear, although there is some suspicion that Lily edited the

Descriptio in which a very saintly and indeed 'fully fleshed out' description of Pole and his motives in his legations appears.[51]

Lily also acted as Pole's secretary, moving with him to Rome and, unlike some, did not leave him in his exile. He is one of the few servants for whom we have records confirming the rewards Pole gave him for his loyal service. These rewards were dependent on Pole's own financial circumstances, and it is no coincidence that in 1529, when Pole was still in the good graces of Henry VIII, he was able to give Lily a prebend in Wimborne Minster. Such was Lily's loyalty to Pole that in England he was outlawed for treason.[52] Once in exile, Pole's resources in England dried up and he was reliant on the scant help he could give his servants in Rome itself. When Reginald was appointed *de facto* head of the English Hospice in Rome when it came under papal, rather than royal, control (fig. 13) in 1538, Lily was given accommodation, food and a small stipend through the hospice before moving with Pole to Viterbo. At various points over the following years, he acted for Pole as warden of the hospice.[53] A man of some sensitivity, he was not blind to his master's faults and upbraided Pole for his treatment of Vittoria Colonna.[54]

He joined Pole in Brussels in 1554 and followed him to England, where finances improved for both Pole and Lily. He acted as proctor for various clergy in their appeals to Pole and was appointed to the vacant position of subdeacon in Santa Maria in Cosmedin, Pole's titular church in Rome, in February 1556 and in the same year was given a prebend in St Paul's Cathedral. Mayer describes him as having an 'important role in Pole's administration' and a further reward for this was his appointment to the vacant first prebend in Canterbury Cathedral in early 1558. A good churchman, he took up residence in Canterbury and soon wrote to Alvise Priuli that he missed Pole's household. He was to die in Canterbury on 14 July 1559.[55] Lily is the perfect example of what to Pole must have seemed an ideal servant: loyal, religious and with few expectations of reward.

The same cannot be said of another Englishman who, albeit briefly, formed part of Pole's entourage.

Richard Morison, Friend of Pole Turned Government Propagandist

Morison encapsulates all the dilemmas of sixteenth-century patronage: to whom do you owe your loyalty? Probably born in Yorkshire to a family that was not wealthy, he depended on others for his future and his earnings. He entered Wolsey's Cardinal College at Oxford in about 1526 and was at some point granted a lifetime pension by Wolsey.[56] At some point he transferred to Cambridge and when there his evangelical leanings, which were later to come to the fore, were perhaps initiated by meeting Cranmer. In 1532, like so many Englishmen, he set out for Padua, stopping first at Paris where he met Pole and Thomas Starkey and then on to Italy and the university in Padua where he studied law and Greek (perhaps teaching George Lily the latter) among other subjects. He was a 'scholar-companion' to Thomas Winter, Wolsey's illegitimate son.[57] It was in Padua and Venice that Morison became close to Pole and other English students. He was poor precisely because his patron, Winter, was poor and had to borrow money from others including Starkey. As Sowerby notes:

At one point Morison was so poor that he could not even afford to clothe himself, joking to Starkey that he must be Michael Throckmorton's [a friend and servant of Pole] servant as he was dressed in his livery.[58]

He seems to have left Winter around 1534 when Winter left Italy.[59] In the summer of 1535 Morison moved to Venice and lived in Pole's household in a house which Pole shared with Edmund Harvel, a man who was acting as *de facto* English ambassador, and Pole supported him financially, although this financial support probably ended when Pole left Venice. Yet he was still regarded as one of Pole's household: George Lily described him as 'one of our flock'. He had been so poor that he had had to resort to pawning his books: Pole helped him recover one of them.[60] Morison made repeated pleas to Thomas Cromwell for patronage and a place in his household, all against the background of providing Cromwell with news from Italy: his pleas were heard and in May 1536 he left Italy for success in England. The events of the following months – the arrival of *De Unitate*, Pole's refusal to moderate his stance towards Henry, and ultimately his acceptance of the cardinalate – meant that Pole and Morison were to be on a collision course. As Sowerby notes, Morison believed that 'it was the scholar's duty to put his education to the service of his country. Intellectual ability and "virtuous qualities" were gifts from God; anyone who possessed them should not "take the fruits and profits" thereof "to his own use".'[61]

This was precisely why Henry had paid for Reginald's expensive education and why he was so angry and exasperated by his ingratitude. Yet Morison's bile was not immediately spilled at Pole's expense, as it would be during the next two years. He was asked to write a precis for Henry of *De Unitate* and 'considerably toned down the extent of Pole's challenge to Henry VIII'.[62] Some affection and concern for Pole's well-being clearly remained, but that was soon to change. Morison was now a royal servant and, not to put too fine a point on it, Cromwell's lapdog. Yet his denouncements of Pole are so vitriolic that it is difficult to believe that he did not believe what he wrote. As he wrote to Pole in an undated letter – and this must have pricked Pole's conscience because of the similarity of his erstwhile position with Morison's current one – 'No one was ever more obliged to his prince than I. The king thought his aid to you and your family should have produced better results.'[63] If Pole would moderate his stance, Morison would help him (and here we have a reversal of the patronal situation as the servant is now in a position to benefit the master): he would act as his best friend to reconcile Henry and the deviant Pole. Reginald, who was hesitating about how to proceed at this point in the summer of 1536, had written in a (lost) letter to Morison such that the latter concluded 'you write in your letters that you are at my command'. Strange times.

Morison was not alone in being disappointed in Pole: Thomas Starkey, who had benefitted from knowing Pole and was the one who had encouraged him to set on paper his thoughts on the divorce and the primacy, wrote to Cromwell on various occasions, declaring on 24 July 1536 with reference to Reginald that 'no man is more disappointed than I – not his own mother, who now repents having brought him to light, nor yet his most dear brother, who, by his act, is deprived of a great comfort of his life'.[64] There were also others who had previously been close to Pole, and benefitted from his early hospitality and patronage, who later denied Pole and his views: for example, Cuthbert Tunstall in his sermon preached before the king on 31 March 1539 roundly condemned Pole and the Pope and the threat of invasion of the country.[65]

Morison's attacks on Pole were printed by the royal printer and the first was above all for distribution abroad. *An Invective against the Great and Detestable Vice, Treason* was published in 1539 in no fewer than three editions. It was English royal propaganda and dealt with the Exeter Conspiracy. Its aim was to calm foreign concern about Henry's actions and the executions of the plotters. It was a well-informed work, based closely on the trial records and 'accused the conspirators in some of the same terms and with the same evidence that was actually used to condemn them in court'.[66] Reginald was described as 'the very pole [pool, reflecting the contemporary pronunciation of Reginald's surname] from whence is poured all this poison'; he was an 'arch traitor', an 'English Judas, hated by God'. His attempts to encourage the invasion of his country and the ingratitude shown by himself, his family and the Courtenays were underlined.[67] Morison was seemingly unaware of the irony that their betrayal of the king's kindnesses mirrored his own betrayal of Pole's. Did this book have any effect? It is known that the warmth of Emperor Charles V towards Pole apparently cooled as a consequence of this portrayal.[68]

Pole himself was extremely hurt. As Edwards notes, Reginald said he had 'never expected to be so hurt by one who owed him so much. In Italy, Morison had been his *germanus frater* [we would say true, or blood, brother] but he was now turning violently against him'.[69] What we have is only a draft reply, and we don't know if it was sent, but it was vehement in its denial of Morison's accusations and in turn accused Morison of changing his tune to further his own career. Ever one to make the best of a bad situation, and indeed to use adversity to show himself as a martyr, Pole said he was glad of the suffering that Morison had brought upon him. In another draft of the same period, he tells Morison that he had exaggerated any danger from Courtenay and the accusations against Montagu, Pole's brother, were not proved.[70]

Yet Morison did not stop there: in the same year, again in the face of threats from abroad, he wrote the *Exhortation to Stir All English Men to the Defence of Their Country* and again this went through three editions. It lambasted Pole for the league with the Pope and their plans for England. He was 'vilified … as England's archenemy … was referred to as "Reynard" (the fox) with all the implications of sleight and deceit that entailed. In both works, Morison played on the pronunciation of Pole's name, using watery imagery when referring to him. Pole's influence was thus portrayed as fluid, insidious, dangerous and flowing from Rome.'[71] He even called for violence against Pole (as if the various assassination attempts were not enough): 'Shall we … not make this traitorous Cardinal's bloody hat, cover a bloody pate?'[72] Morison was adamant that those who had been his friends in the past 'wish for no traitor's death so much as they do for yours'. 'He is much more thy friend, that wished you dead than alive.'[73]

But Morison's actions contradicted his own view of friendship: he wrote to Cromwell that 'friendship should be like a marriage, for better or for worse, for richer for poor, til death depart'.[74] Yet not only had he turned against Pole in the most violent terms in print, he also benefitted from Pole's disgrace, taking over Pole's prebend of Yatminster Secunda in 1537. Morison's ambition and desire for money and position saw him acquire many offices and become a member of the Privy Chamber and later an ambassador.[75] What price friendship and loyalty? The pull of loyalty to the king and his country (although it has to be said that Pole had acted out of his concern for the welfare of both king and country, albeit in a way that Morison was convinced was wrong) was infinitely more potent than any friendship or debt that he ever felt to Reginald Pole.

It is clear that Pole was indeed a willing, effective and fair governor of Bagnoregio. To apply these adjectives to the ruling and running of his household is more complex: he was hindered by a lack of money and could offer little in terms of material rewards, yet the loyalty that Parpaglia and Lily showed him (and there are other examples of long-standing, poorly rewarded servants who remained loyal to Pole) shows that they considered him to be the master they wanted. Morison was ambitious and motivated by money and power: for him, Pole's personality and spiritual qualities were not enough. The lure of the power and patronage which Henry could offer won him over. Yet he was the cuckoo in the nest: proof that Pole was indeed a good governor of his household, even if his patronage lay outside the traditional framework of Renaissance patronage. His staff were loyal and served him because they wanted to serve him: there were certainly more affluent cardinals in Renaissance Rome. So, yes, he was indeed a fair and effective governor of his men.

14

CARDINAL POLE'S ARTISTIC PATRONAGE

Renaissance cardinals were nearly always patrons of the arts: they used the arts to show how rich and magnificent they were as 'princes of the Church'. Their palaces were decorated with panel paintings, frescoes and tapestries; they commissioned portraits of themselves, friends and family to hang on their walls and expressed their religious beliefs through paintings and sculptures both in their homes and in their cardinalitial churches. Cardinal Pole's art patronage has rarely featured in discussions of the patronage of cardinals and has passed almost unnoticed in the studies of his life, with authors believing it was almost non-existent or of little value. It has recently been described as 'fairly modest'; yet it casts a valuable light on Pole's lifestyle, his role as a cardinal and patron and also on his religious beliefs.[1]

Lambert Lombard (1505/6–56)

The first example that we know of Pole's patronage of an artist came two years after he was elevated to the cardinalate. They had been tempestuous years and Pole was living in fear of his life because of the assassination attempts on the orders of Henry VIII. His first mission as a papal legate – ostensibly to garner peace, investigate the spread of heresy and announce a general council, but in reality to (belatedly) take advantage of the uprising in northern England known as the Pilgrimage of Grace – proved frustrating and he took shelter in neutral Liège with the Cardinal-Prince Érard de la Marck from the end of May to late August 1537. He was not warmly welcomed, but the stay proved fruitful for both sides.[2]

Lambert Lombard had been long established as de la Marck's court painter, and, with a view to educating Lombard in classical and Italian art, de la Marck asked Pole to allow Lombard to accompany him to Rome; once there, the artist could buy antique and contemporary works of art for his palace.[3] Pole, an impecunious cardinal, could hardly refuse: de la Marck had been a more than generous (if mostly absent) host, and, to boot, he, rather than Pole, would pay Lombard a pension while in Rome. They left on 22 August and arrived in Rome on 18 October. Travelling via land and sea also gave Lombard the opportunity of visiting other artistic centres, such as Verona and Ravenna. The painter was, in fact, working for two people in de la Marck and Pole, and if the financial benefits accrued from his Liégeois patron, still Pole was a man of 'importance in political, church and humanist circles and was thus a prestigious patron'.[4] In fact doors were opened for Lombard and he saw churches, palaces and collections and met artists of the calibre of the sculptor and painter Baccio Bandinelli (*c.* 1493–1560) and the artist Francesco Salviati (1510–63), both Mannerists and an influence on Lombard's later style.[5] He thus had free bed and board, a prestigious patron and access to circles he could never have imagined frequenting – yet Pole also stood to gain. He could, of course, commission works of art from Lombard.

There is only one documented work by Lombard for Pole and that is a *grisaille* (grey and white painting) of the *Tabula Cebetis* (*Tablet of Cebes*). It is mentioned by Dominic Lampson, Lombard's biographer and also secretary to Cardinal Pole during his archbishopric of Canterbury (1554–58). He writes how Alvise Priuli, Pole's close friend and right-hand man throughout much of his life, told him how he and Bartolomeo Stella, Pole's major-domo and a member of the *spirituali* at Viterbo, 'had never seen a better painting from a man born outside Italy than that which Lombard had completed in Rome, based upon the dialogue of the Theban philosopher Cebes ... at the behest of Reginald Pole'.[6] Although lost, we have some idea of its appearance from a later print by Philips Galle after a design by Frans Floris, Lombard's pupil, which was published in 1561 with a commentary by Lampson (fig. 14).[7] Lampson's commentary is important because it tells us what the painting was meant to represent: it shows a walled garden representing human life and the moral choices we make on our way to salvation, that is to say it was a guide for the Christian soul. The whole concept was clearly of interest to Pole with his inclination towards justification by faith alone, and indeed in 1538 a new Greek edition of the *Tablet of Cebes*, dedicated to Cardinal Pole, was published in Venice.[8]

Of some interest is the temple in the print, which bears a resemblance to the oratory Pole erected on behalf of the English Hospice on the Via Appia, probably shortly after his appointment as its head. Its small size and intimacy reflect, as will be seen, Pole's taste for small works of art (fig. 15). The oratory is called *Domine quo vadis* and refers to an apocryphal episode when Peter, fleeing martyrdom in Rome, met Christ on this road and asked him where he was going.

Christ's reply that he was going to Rome to be crucified again led Peter himself to return to Rome to his own death.[9] Its size means that its purpose is unclear: it was almost certainly too small for mass to be heard inside it, but the two doors would have allowed worshippers to enter and pray (or venerate the remains of martyrs, perhaps). It is now bricked up and closed to the public but in 1900 still contained frescoes depicting some of the events of Peter's later life, including the meeting with Christ.[10] The date of execution and the artist are unknown, and so it is impossible to examine Pole's involvement in the frescoes.

Lombard's time with Pole was short lived: de la Marck died suddenly on 18 March 1538 and Lombard's pension died with him. With a wife in Liège, he inevitably returned home, probably in early to mid-1539. All the works that he had acquired to fill de la Marck's palace were sold in Rome at his heirs' instructions. Yet there is one drawing which survives from this period which was almost certainly completed by Lombard for Cardinal Pole: the drawing of *Christ on the Cross* (Kupferstichkabinett, Berlin) (fig. 16). It is a personal interpretation of a drawing by Michelangelo for Vittoria Colonna, now in the British Museum, and is generally dated to the late 1530s or early 1540s (fig. 17).[11] Both Vittoria Colonna and Michelangelo were members of the circle of *spirituali* who met in Viterbo under Pole's leadership in the early 1540s. Michelangelo produced three drawings for Colonna as gifts to mark their friendship and devotion to each other, and indeed produced other drawings for those for whom he also felt 'profound personal attachment … they were carried out for love rather than duty'.[12] They are presentation drawings, not preparatory sketches for a painting, are complete in themselves and were given as gifts, with nothing expected in return.[13]

Michelangelo's drawing in the British Museum is unique in the history of the depiction of the Crucifixion from the tenth century to the late 1530s: whereas Christ had previously been shown as dead and with closed eyes, here Christ is alive and his face is upturned, in communion with his Father.[14] As Chapman notes, the simplicity of the drawing is 'reminiscent of Catholic *spirituali* writers' and preachers' injunctions for the faithful to focus their devotions on the image of Christ's crucifixion'.[15] Condivi believed that Christ was asking God why he has abandoned him and was 'suffering in bitter torment'.[16] Indeed, such was the impact of the drawing that Colonna wrote to Michelangelo that she had 'seen the *Crucifixion*, which has crucified in my memory as no other picture that I have seen has done, nor can one see anything better done, more alive and a more finished image and I certainly could not explain how subtly and wonderfully it is done'.[17]

If Michelangelo's depiction of a Christ alive and suffering was unique, then Lambert Lombard's drawing echoed its originality. Was it based on an engraving of the Michelangelo drawing? Almost certainly not: the engraving by Giulio Bonasone (*c.* 1510–aft. 1576) after Michelangelo contains a landscape but, with the exception of that, is very close to the original drawing. Lombard's is a personal interpretation of Michelangelo's work – the cross is different, there are no *putti* and Christ's side has still not been pierced. It resembles in style the drawings he produced in Rome around 1538 and its depiction of a live and suffering Christ is 'so completely exceptional in the history of Netherlandish art' that it has been suggested that 'Lombard produced it in direct response to the concerns of his patron in Rome, the embattled English cardinal Reginald Pole'.[18] The Lombard drawing was not shared with his pupils and was almost certainly not brought back to Liège from Rome as the majority of his drawings were then found in his personal archive on his death. Its provenance until the nineteenth century is sadly unknown, but Wouk believes it is very much in the vein of 'the drawing as a gift', perhaps from one grateful client to his patron (Pole) who had afforded him the chance to see Italy and Rome.[19] It is, rarely for Lombard, signed with his signature and the word '*fecit*', meaning 'Lambert Lombard made this'. Did Lombard see that this drawing was a way to reflect Pole's Christocentric beliefs and spirituality, just as he had done in the *Tabula Cebetis*: that by gazing on Christ's sacrifice we achieve salvation and are dependent on it?

The giving of works of art with nothing expected in return does, of course, fall outside the normal patterns of Renaissance patronage and was to be continued within the circle of the *spirituali*. They 'tried to develop a very specific and well-defined visual culture, the keyword of which was closeness'.[20] Namely, that a close examination of, or meditation on, the works in question by the recipient would bring the onlooker closer to Christ. The fact that the *Tabula* was monochrome (Michelangelo's presentation drawings also used a limited colour range) meant that there was little or no distraction from the subject depicted. It is this type of art and patronage which, among other things, would closely link Reginald Pole, Vittoria Colonna and Michelangelo.

Michelangelo, Vittoria Colonna and a Painting for Reginald Pole

It was with Michelangelo that Vittoria Colonna had 'one of the most celebrated friendships of the Renaissance', exchanging sonnets, letters and also drawings.[21] They probably met after Michelangelo moved permanently to Rome in 1534. It is very clear that there were strong links between Michelangelo and the *spirituali*.[22] His assistant and biographer, Ascanio Condivi, described how the artist had 'gladly retained the friendship of those from whose enlightened and learned conversation he could benefit and in whom there shone some ray of excellence: such as the most reverend and distinguished Monsignor Polo for his rare virtue and singular goodness'.[23] Not only was Michelangelo friends with Pole, he corresponded with Bartolomeo Stella, Pole's major-domo and a founding member of the Oratory of Divine Love in Rome sometime around 1517, and was also friends with Pole's later biographer Beccadelli and with Cardinal Morone, for whom he executed a lost cartoon.[24]

Michelangelo is mentioned in letters by members of the Viterbo group: in one from Colonna to Carlo Gualteruzzi (1500–71), an intimate of Colonna and Pietro Bembo and an outlier of the *ecclesia Viterbiensis*, she writes of 'our excellent in everything Michelangelo' and in 1543 she wrote to Alvise Priuli that Michelangelo had arrived in Viterbo. Beccadelli himself wrote of 'our Michelangelo'.[25] He was, of course, not a theologian, despite his reform-leaning beliefs. He was there as an artist and one who, with his beliefs and the skill and poignancy of his art, could best express what they needed from art: something which helped a meditation on Christ's sacrifice.[26]

It has long been known that Cardinal Pole at some point in the 1540s owned a *Pietà* by Michelangelo. Based on the description of it as a drawing by Giorgio Vasari (the touchstone, for many, of Renaissance art), it has always been assumed that this was exactly that: a drawing, probably a variation of a *Pietà* for Colonna that is now in the Isabella Stewart Gardner Museum in Boston. There are now very good grounds for believing that it was, in fact, a painting. Pole had evidently taken (or been sent) a *Pietà*, presumably for his own meditation, to Trent where he was a legate to the council. There is a series of letters between Pietro Bertano, Bishop of Fano, and Cardinal Gonzaga, beginning on 12 May 1546 in which Gonzaga requests a 'Cristo' by Michelangelo. He is told by Bertano that Pole has one, in the form of a *Pietà*, but that the whole of Christ's body can be seen. He will happily give it to Gonzaga as he can easily obtain another via Vittoria Colonna.[27] The reply from Gonzaga to Bertano of 21 May 1546 clearly describes it as a '*quadro*' (painting), not a '*disegno*' (drawing) and it is mentioned as such again in a letter of 11 June 1546. It has only recently been highlighted that Vasari himself makes it clear at one point in his *Vite* that the term '*quadro*' refers to a painting or '*tavola*' (painted panel) and further confirmation can be found in the funeral oration given by Benedetto Varchi at Michelangelo's funeral in Florence on 14 July 1564 when he speaks of a 'most compassionate Deposition from the cross, which he [Michelangelo] gave to the most pious, indeed most holy, and no less learned than she was eloquent Donna Vittoria Colonna'.[28] So it was very much a painting and not a drawing – and, as Forcellino notes, Gonzaga was the son of Isabella d'Este (one of the great Renaissance patrons of artists) and certainly knew his paintings from his drawings.[29]

Where is this painting and how did Pole acquire it? There is every reason to believe that it was a gift from Vittoria Colonna and originally painted for her. She, in turn, then gave this object to Pole (either personally, or she dispatched it to him) to 'bolster Pole's spiritual strength in the difficult task ahead' (the discussion of justification by faith alone at the council).[30] One of her sonnets of these years 'refers to the shipment of a depiction of Christ to a personage who is not identified. However, the sonnet employs personal terminology similar to that which the poetess reserved for other correspondence and compositions intended for Reginald Pole.'[31] This is sonnet S1, 142 of the *Rime Spirituali*, which begins (my emphasis):

> Because your mind, girt and adorned well
> With the eternal light, preserves of God
> The likeness in that innermost abode
> Where never may unfaithful image dwell,
> Haply, since ardent longing doth impel,
> Which never knows fulfilment but increase,
> As is true lovers' wont, even this may please,
> *And prove in painted form acceptable,*
> *And thinking thus, my lord, your humble, new*
> *Mother and handmaid send the work to you*
> *A better master fashioned in your heart...*[32]

The fact that Colonna describes herself as the recipient's 'new mother' (*nuova madre*) means that in all likelihood (who else's 'new mother' was she?) the sonnet is addressed to Pole. Maria Forcellino believes – correctly, in my opinion – that the sonnet was composed by Colonna on the occasion of the shipment of Michelangelo's *Pietà* painting to Pole, then linked to the resulting discussion in the Gonzaga–Bertano papers.[33] It is thus clear that Colonna received a painting from Michelangelo and, given the Gonzaga letters explored above and the sonnet, sent Pole a painting that was certainly small, as it was portable, and had clearly been completed by 1546 or earlier (when her *Rime* were published), but most probably left Rome in the winter of 1545.[34]

It is Antonio Forcellino whom we have to thank for identifying this painting. By detailed archival work and that little bit of luck that so often comes with research, he has shown, by tracing the provenance of the painting and by technical and stylistic analysis, that it is a lost Michelangelo *Pietà* now in a private collection in America and generally known as the *Ragusa Pietà* (fig. 18).[35] As a result of in-depth restoration and examination, it is clear from the underdrawing that the painting is an original and not a copy.[36] So what do we learn from this? It is evident that Colonna, Pole and Gonzaga esteemed Michelangelo as the artist who could portray the simplicity and devotion to Christ and His sacrifice which they so treasured. He produced for them drawings and a painting which could be examined (at times with a mirror and a magnifying glass in the case of Vittoria Colonna) to deepen their own religious experiences and their 'intimacy of faith'.[37]

It has recently been suggested that the beliefs of Pole and the *spirituali* actively influenced much larger paintings: two of the frescoes by Michelangelo in the Cappella Paolina in the Vatican, *The Conversion of St Paul* and *The Crucifixion of St Peter* (both *c.* 1542–9).[38] Yet until concrete proof in the form of letters or a theological plan for the frescoes is forthcoming, we have to view the frescoes as, respectively, a depiction of an event described in the Bible (Acts 9) and an imagined depiction of a legend.

Yet Michelangelo was not the only artist who had links with the *spirituali*. Sebastiano Luciani, commonly known as Sebastiano del Piombo (1485–1547), came from Venice to Rome in 1511 in the train of the Sienese banker Agostino Chigi. He brought with him a Venetian understanding of colour and successfully combined it in his early years in Rome with the robustness of Michelangelo's drawings – which the latter cheerfully provided – and a later innovative technique for painting. The two became firm friends until 1536 when Sebastiano overstepped the mark by trying to teach Michelangelo, something which the elder master most definitely did not appreciate, and their friendship ended.[39]

Sebastiano was seen as a rival to Raphael (1483–1520) and became Rome's foremost painter after the latter's death. He was the darling of the rich and affluent members of the curia – including ambassadors and popes, namely Clement VII, with whom he fled into the Castel Sant'Angelo during the 1527 Sack of Rome, and Paul III – and of the city itself and, perhaps most importantly, was associated with many patrons with reformist inclinations. In 1516 he had painted the innovative (if incoherent) group portrait of *Cardinal Bendinello Sauli and Three Companions* (National Gallery of Art, Washington): Sauli and his family had many links to the early reform movement.[40] The frescoes of the Borgherini Chapel in San Pietro in Montorio followed a programme devised by another energetic reformer, Cardinal Bernardino López de Carvajal (1456–1523).[41] His most recent biographer believes that he is 'central in the artistic responses to the religious controversies of early Catholic reform' and it is thus no surprise that he is known to have been on the outer rings of the Viterbo circle.[42]

In the years after his arrival in Rome, Sebastiano had been active in Viterbo, painting his *Pietà* and *Flagellation of Christ* for Giovanni Botonti, a clerk in the *Camera Apostolica*, and cannot have been unaware of the reform ethos of Egidio da Viterbo (1469–1532) prevalent in that town. He was also intimate with Vittore Soranzo, a member of the *spirituali* circle and later a friend of Colonna, and is described by him as 'Sebastianello nostro Venetiano' (our little Sebastian the Venetian). The diminutive denotes a sense of affection, too.[43] Sebastiano also painted Pietro Carnesecchi, Vittoria Colonna (a much-damaged possible copy exists in Museu Nacional d'art de Catalunya, Barcelona) and Giulia Gonzaga (Museum, Wiesbaden) in the 1530s. His portrait of Gonzaga, if this is indeed the original, was commissioned by Cardinal Ippolito de' Medici (1511–35) in 1532 and from the life – Sebastiano went to Fondi to visit her in June of that year for this purpose – and there are various copies and versions, all arousing much speculation as to their authenticity.[44]

This, and perhaps the fact that Pole was still in touch with the Sauli family at various points in his life (even influencing the religious beliefs of Stefano Sauli), explains why Pole chose him to paint his portrait as a cardinal (Hermitage Museum, Leningrad) (fig. 19).[45] It has to be said that the authorship of the portrait has been debated at certain times, including recently, but there is also no doubt that the most important art historians of the past century and the Hermitage itself believe that the painting is by Sebastiano. The most recent attribution of the painting in 2018 to Piero Bonaccorsi (known as Perino del Vaga) (1501–47) is far from convincing: from a purely aesthetic viewpoint it seems in fact too good to be by Perino. It has a subtlety and emotion lacking in his extant works and the connections between Pole and Perino suggested by Agosti and Balzarotti are tenuous at best. Until further evidence emerges to the contrary, it seems reasonable to accept it is by del Piombo: the quality of the depiction of the hands alone are, in my opinion, enough to ascribe the painting to him.[46] There is no record of the commission, and the datings vary, but it was painted (obviously) after Pole became cardinal in 1536 and thus either in the late 1530s or early 1540s, but a dating to 1543 or earlier is more likely, given that the positioning of the hands echoes those in *Paul III* by Titian (Naples, Museo di Capodimonte). Whether the portrait of Pole (a papal favourite) influenced the depiction of Pope Paul III or vice versa is open to debate, but the Hermitage portrait lies firmly within the tradition of cardinal and papal portraits.[47]

Why did Pole, a man who shunned ostentation and who had little wealth, require a portrait of himself? If we accept the earlier dating, it may have been to celebrate his elevation to the cardinalate, as was the case for some other cardinals, for example Sebastiano's *Portrait of Cardinal Rodolfo Pio da Carpi* (Kunsthistorisches Museum, Vienna) who was elevated in the same consistory as Pole, or because 'portraits of Pole were in demand in the 1540s' as his fame as a saintly cardinal and opponent of Henry VIII spread. Colonna had promised to get a portrait of Pole for Cardinal Madruzzo and had herself 'expressed the wish to have always with her portraits of Contarini and Pole'.[48] Michael Hirst convincingly dates the portrait to the 1540s on stylistic grounds and this dating may well explain what Burckhardt called 'the rendering of a controlled but profound grief', perhaps after the execution of his mother.[49] Of some interest is the fact that Sebastiano was still following the ideas of the *spirituali* at the end of his life. His will of 1547 ordered that his body 'should be taken to burial without priests, friars and ceremonies and there should be no payment for candles. All the money which would have been spent on that was to be given to poor people for the love of God.'[50]

Pole returned to England as papal legate in 1554 and died there in 1558, leaving four short years in which much needed doing to reform the English Church. Time was too short for his artistic tastes to influence or bring into being an 'English renaissance'. Indeed, was he even interested in doing so? Little is known of his artistic patronage in England other than some miniatures, for the most part commissioned by his *famiglia*, which show once again his and their taste for a personal, simple art.[51] The reconciliation of England with the Church of Rome and the reform of the English Church were more important.

15

THE DEATH OF CARDINAL POLE, HIS LEGACY AND HIS REPUTATION

By November 1558 Cardinal Pole had been ill for several months, seemingly from the 'double quartan fever', although now generally believed to be from the influenza epidemic which had swept the country. Already by 23 September 1558 he had written to Philip I that he was aware that he was mortally ill.[1] Pole's illness progressed, and he was unable to shake off the paroxysms which accompanied the fever. At the same time Mary fell ill from the same epidemic. Their Catholic legacy hung in the balance: if either one had survived we might now be living in a Catholic country, but fate intervened.

On 17 November, Mary died at seven in the morning and Cardinal Pole died later that day 'with that piety that you would expect'.[2] Both he and Mary, although in separate palaces, had confessed regularly and heard mass with great piety during their illness and each had received extreme unction two days previously.[3] It had been decided that Pole should not learn of Mary's death in order not to distress him, but a servant let it slip and Pole, in tears, remarked that 'in all his life he had received no greater pleasure or consolation than to think of ... how God's providence... had shown a great conformity in both the queen's life and his own and how for her and for himself their lives had been difficult because of the same cause [Henry's divorce] and then it had pleased God that she should come to the throne'.

They were, he said, united 'not only by their blood but by the great conformity of their souls'.[4] He died quietly and following his death (mistaken) rumours of his wealth caused the officials of the new queen to rush to draw up inventories of his goods. They were to be disappointed: the inventories are a turgid list of beddings, clothes and hangings. After a period of mourning the cardinal was then transported to Canterbury where, as he requested in his will, he was buried in the corona of St Thomas Becket in a simple chest tomb with a now lost monument painted on the wall by one of his *familia*, Dominic Lampson, on 15 December 1558 (fig. 20).[5]

Alvise Priuli, 'my intimate friend and familiar of twenty-five years, of great piety in God and singular faith and love towards me', wrote to inform others of his death and told Queen Elizabeth that if she had known Pole's 'great sincerity and his other rare qualities' better and for longer he was sure that she would have esteemed him as much as her late sister had done. Pole, he was sure, would pray for her in the other life that God would give her 'a tranquil, happy and long reign in God's service'.[6]

This was to prove to be mostly the case, but not to the advantage of the Catholic cause. As Duffy notes, by midsummer 1559, 'the Acts of Supremacy and Uniformity were back in place, and Pole's most important reforms had been undone by legislation returning First Fruits and Tenths to the crown, and brazenly allowing Elizabeth to asset-strip any diocese during Episcopal visitations'.[7] Yet his upper clergy were loyal both to Pole and to the Catholic Church: both houses of convocation affirmed their belief in papal supremacy and the Catholic mass, and a large number of upper clergy and the heads of Oxford and Cambridge refused the Oath of Supremacy.[8] As already noted, only one of Pole's bishops agreed to serve the new queen.

In his lifetime those who had known Pole personally were fulsome in their praises: in 1535 Cardinal Contarini recommended Pole to Charles V as someone he knew intimately: 'I will speak only of his superior religion, for he thinks and takes care about nothing else but to act in some cause for the honour of God and the utility of Christianity.'[9] Charles himself, having met Reginald on many occasions, said, 'I know of no better priest in the whole of Christendom than the Cardinal of England.'[10] Pietro Bembo described him as 'possibly the most virtuous, learned and grave young man in the whole of Italy today'.[11] His probity was constantly emphasised by others: Sadoleto wrote to Giberti of Pole's 'exceptionally high standard of behaviour and excellent manner'.[12] Sir Edward Hastings, who was sent to escort Pole back to England in 1554, described him as 'a man full of God, full of all godliness and virtue, ready to humble himself to all fashions that may do good'.[13] Cardinal Ercole Gonzaga described him as 'a saint, with excellent judgement when it came to things of this world, of vast learning'.[14]

He is even one of the few cardinals to have escaped the caustic tongue of Pasquino (or that of the poets who appended the poems to the statue). To say that nearly all *pasquinate* are close to the bone is putting it mildly (today, the libel trials would be endless), but Reginald even merited a laudatory poem. In a series in which Pasquino writes the epitaphs of the cardinals, Pole's reads:

> Here lies the Cardinal of England
> Learned, decent, Catholic and divine
> And who loved him was I, Pasquino
> A thing unheard of and never seen before on earth.[15]

Indeed, his learning and piety were always noted at the time, as was his shyness (or what Longolio called his taciturnity): Seripando described him at the Council of Trent as a man '*cui nihil erat proprium, quam tacere*' (to whom nothing was proper but to be silent), and although his shyness lessened with age, he was always more at ease with people he knew well.[16]

Pole was always immensely kind and loyal to both his servants and friends: he defended More and Fisher valiantly in *De Unitate* and defended Flaminio when alive and after his death. As Fenlon notes, 'loyalty, in the end, was his most signal virtue'.[17] He tried to avoid confrontation and conflict, for example leaving England rather than openly express his views on Henry's divorce and leaving Rome rather than criticise Contarini's thesis on justification. Indeed, Pole wrote of himself:

> ... by my natural accord, I tend to avoid all strife and contention. My custom of acting in this way extends from my boyhood to the present ... To such an extent have I avoided arguments with others that I do not think there is a word that causes greater distress to my soul than the word contention itself.[18]

It was only when religion and the Church were at stake that he was willing to stand up and be counted: his address to the

Council of Trent was trenchant in its criticism of the clergy's woeful behaviour. He was likewise confrontational and, to put it mildly, outspoken, in his denouncement of Henry's divorce and the separation from Rome. Yet his sense of obedience meant that he only wrote *De Unitate* because he was ordered to do so (and the consequences be hanged). He also obeyed the Pope: he did not openly contradict the Church's view on justification once it was decreed. His only disloyalty and disobedience was his decision to put his country before the edicts of Paul IV and to continue as legate despite being recalled. Most notably, he obeyed the law when it came to dealing with heretics.

Doubts about Pole's religious beliefs continued to swirl around him in his lifetime. William Thomas, the tutor of Edward VI, wrote in 1547 that he 'secretly professes to be a Protestant and openly maintains the papacy'.[19] Carafa's attack on his 'heretical' views in the conclave of 1549 led to a *pasquinata* in which he is described as 'l'Inglese/Ch'e' Lutherano palese' (the English [cardinal]/ who is openly Lutheran') and exiled Protestants during Mary's reign regarded him as a Nicodemist, or a closet Protestant.[20] He was persecuted by Paul IV for being, in his eyes, a heretic, and Pietro Carnesecchi in 1567 at his own heresy trial said that Pole died 'in the opinion of Rome a Lutheran, and in Germany a papist' (and this despite his burning of 283 Protestant heretics!), yet even under torture Carnesecchi maintained to the last that Pole was 'completely faithful to the teaching of the Church'.[21] Under Paul III he was, as Cranmer wrote to Henry VIII in 1535, 'made much of, and much set by, and received of the Pope himself very gladly': it was the vitriol of Paul IV which darkened his name.[22] Yet he died a Catholic death and very much in the arms of mother Church, much to the consternation of Giulia Gonzaga and Pietro Carnesecchi who 'both disapproved of the Cardinal's declaration immediately before his death of his obedience and loyalty to the Catholic Church'.[23]

In England the die was cast when he sent *De Unitate* to Henry and he was slandered by Henrician propagandists such as Richard Morison, not just for his ingratitude to Henry but also for his encouraging Charles V to invade. Morison had benefitted from Pole's patronage when in Padua but, like Pole himself, turned against his erstwhile patron when the claims of his new patron, the king, proved stronger. Relations between England and Pole remained frosty during the reign of Edward VI, when he was viewed as an unnatural Englishman who had chosen Rome over his own country. He was welcomed by cheering crowds when he eventually returned to his homeland and Parks references a number of pamphlets praising Pole. Giovanni Michieli, the Venetian ambassador to England during this period, wrote a final report in 1557 in which Pole is described as one who does not 'deceive the promise of integrity and sincerity and great value' and that God had saved him from becoming Pope so that he could save England. He was of 'so great learning and so great goodness as to lead people to such new ways ... being completely unmoved ... by every sort of human prejudice and material interest'. He judged individuals by their worth and apparently refused to promote people on the basis of their rank or family.[24]

The hagiography of Pole began immediately after his death, first with his funeral oration and then with Beccadelli's biography. The oration was probably written by George Lily. It emphasised his lack of ambition, his dedication to his 'ecclesiastical studies', the idea that God saved him from becoming Pope so that Pole in turn could save England, his high probity and his household, which was 'implicitly likened to a monastery that turned away all "dissolute men"'. He was '*Sancte educatus, sanctus vixit, sanctissime mortuus est*' (educated to be a saint, lived like a saint and died in a most saintly fashion)'.[25]

Beccadelli in turn ended his life of Pole with the words, 'And I doubt not but whoever will examine the calamitous events of his story, the persecutions he suffered in his own person, and the share he bore in the misfortunes of his friends and family, will think him worthy to be enrolled among the order of martyrs.'[26]

Was he a martyr? In the eyes of many he was just that. His written works, though few, survived and perpetuated his fame among Catholics. *De Unitate* 'became a template for future generations of English Catholic martyrologists, propagandists and polemicists'.[27]

All this was damaged, if not destroyed, in the eyes of some by the Anglican Matthew Parker's *De Antiquitate Britannicae Ecclesiae*, published in 1572. As Edwards notes, Parker helped 'to provide the basis of a Protestant "Black Legend" that would be influential for centuries'.[28] Among many other things, he criticised Pole's disloyalty to a king who had been so generous to him and accused him of becoming Italian and the Pope's man instead of a Christian and of being a traitor; of fathering illegitimate children; of hoping to marry Mary; of being the butcher of the Anglican Church; and persecuting Cranmer so that he could become Archbishop of Canterbury.[29] Much of this could be refuted on a point-by-point basis, but mud still sticks. We can at least thank Parker for a description of Pole's physical appearance: no, not some monster, but of 'medium height, slim build with a red and white complexion, a broad face and cheerful eyes reflecting a calm temperament'.[30]

Often depending on their religious affiliation (or their view of Mary Tudor, as the burnings always figure large in portrayals of Pole), later authors have veered between the ecstatic and the damning. The two most recent biographies are those by Mayer and Edwards. The latter gives a reasoned and impartial account of Pole's life and is highly recommended for further reading. Mayer's biography is also vital reading, but it is a complex and intricate work which at times follows some of the author's own theses rather than the evidence. He believes that because Alvise Priuli was in all likelihood a homosexual, then so was Pole (or that he at least had homosexual inclinations).[31] There is simply no evidence to support this, despite his claim that it 'is not too much to say that he and Priuli were married'.[32] Theirs was what Beccadelli called it – a 'long friendship' – and, turning to Edwards once again, Pole 'was in many respects a reformer, with a personal life of austerity and purity ... [there is] no specific evidence that Pole went beyond warm friendships with other men, as was condoned, and even required, in the Church and society of his day'.[33] Homosexuality was made illegal in civil law in England in 1533 with the Buggery Act: surely if Henry VIII, who was so willing to slander Pole at every turn, had caught even a whiff of any homosexual inclinations or practice, he would have shouted it from the rooftops – but he didn't.

So, who was Reginald Pole? He was a man who was very conscious of his nobility of birth and profited from it in his youth and when abroad. When he returned home and addressed Parliament in 1554, his speech showed that 'Pole never forgot his royal status, and expected others to appreciate it'.[34] This royal kinship had led to his patronage by the king, who had, in turn, inverted everything Pole held dear: loyalty to the Church of Rome and zero tolerance for the opposing views of More and Fisher who had previously been the king's friends. Pole, faced with the impossibility of staying silent on these horrors – and, indeed, instructed to give his opinion by the Crown – sent Henry the lambasting *De Unitate*. His love for the Pope and the supremacy of the Roman Church, and indeed for his country, left him no choice, even though he knew that he was putting his family at risk, as so sadly proved to be the case. He was not a coward, as the sending of *De Unitate* shows, and he bravely faced the multitude of plots to assassinate him (and as we have seen, these were not 'comic opera plots') and continued with what passed for a normal life at that time.[35] He was a man of deep religious feeling, a feeling which was, in his earlier days, inclusive rather than confrontational, but when faced with the evidence of heresy he was not afraid to act as required by the law. He inspired devotion and loathing but was pious, and 'quintessentially, and in all things a man of prayer'.[36] A man who had much to contend with, and some of it his own doing, but who did his best.

NOTES

Abbreviations

AAV	Archivio Apostolico Vaticano
D.B.I.	*Dizionario Biografico degli Italiani* (online)
CRP	*The Correspondence of Reginald Pole (Vols 1–3)*
O.D.N.B.	*Oxford Dictionary of National Biography* (online)
TNA	The National Archives

1 The Pole Family and Early Family Fortunes

1. Edwards, J., *Archbishop Pole* (Abingdon 2021), p. 3.
2. Higginbotham, S., *Margaret Pole, The Countess in the Tower* (Stroud, 2016), p. 8, Edwards, *Archbishop*, p. 3.
3. For Simnel and other claimants to the throne of Henry VII, see Amin, N., *Henry VII and the Tudor Pretenders. Simnel, Warbeck and Warwick* (Stroud, 2020).
4. Cunningham, S., *Prince Arthur, The Tudor King Who Never Was* (Stroud, 2016), p. 80; Pierce, H., *Margaret Pole, Countess of Salisbury, 1473–1541, Loyalty, Lineage and Leadership* (Cardiff, 2003), p. 12.

5. Schenk, W., *Reginald Pole, Cardinal of England* (London, 1950), p. 1.

6. Pierce, *Margaret Pole*, pp. 13, 20; Cunningham, p. 80.

7. Cunningham, p. 109.

8. For the most recent discussion on the survival or death of the Princes in the tower, see Langley, P., *The Princes in the Tower, Solving History's Greatest Cold Case* (Cheltenham, 2023).

9. Roe, A., *Perkin, A Story of Deception* (London, 2004) for Warbeck; Higginbotham, pp. 19–20 and Amin, pp. 299–306.

10. Ellis, H. (ed.), *Hall's Chronicle* (London, 1809), p. 490.

11. Paul, J., *Catherine of Aragon and her Friends* (New York, 1966), p. 9.

12. Higginbotham, p. 26.

13. Starkey, D., *Henry, Virtuous Prince* (London, 2008), p. 308.

14. Pierce, *Margaret Pole*, pp. 31–2.

15. Ibid., p. 33; Pierce, H. 'Pole, Margaret, suo jure countess of Salisbury' in *O.D.N.B.*

16. Haile, M., *The Life of Reginald Pole* (second edition, London, 1911), p. 8; CRP 1, no. 331, p. 272; Pierce, *Margaret Pole*, p. 35; Starkey, *Henry*, p. 308.

17. Higginbotham, p. 39.

18. Pierce, 'Pole, Margaret'.

19. Pierce, *Margaret Pole*, p. 52.

20. Ibid., pp. 61, 81.

21. Ibid., p. 81; Harris, B. J., *Edward Stafford Third Duke of Buckingham 1478–1521* (Stanford, 1986), p. 55.

22. Porter, L., *Mary Tudor, The First Queen* (London, 2010), p. 6.

23. Harris, p. 43.

24. Beccadelli, L., *The Life of Cardinal Reginald Pole, written originally in Italian by Lodovico Beccatelli, Archbishop of Ragusa* (trans. & ed. B. Pye, London, 1766), pp. 8–9.

25. Guy, J., *The Children of Henry VIII* (Oxford, 2013), p. 23.

26. Loades, D., *Henry VIII* (Stroud, 2013), p. 119; Davies, C. S. L., 'Stafford, Edward, third duke of Buckingham' in *O.D.N.B.*

27. Guy, *The Children*, p. 29.

28. Harris, p. 61.

29. Ibid., p. 210.

30. Pierce, *Margaret Pole*, pp. 86, 89; Paul, p. 54.

31. CRP 1, no. 103, p. 102, note no. 78.

32. Ibid.; TNA, SP 1/139 fos 132r-v.

33. Edwards, *Archbishop*, p. 9.

34. Ibid., p. 10.

35. Ibid., p. 9.

36. Antony, C. M., *The Angelical Cardinal: Reginald Pole* (London, 1909), p. 6 and see also Gasquet, F., *Henry VIII and the English Monasteries* (2 vols, third edition, London, 1888) I, p. 22.

2 *The King's Cousin and the King's Scholar*

1. CRP 1, no. 5, p. 40.

2. Woolfson, J., *Padua and the Tudors, English students in Italy 1485–1603* (London 2020), pp. 4, 109; Parks, G. B., *The English Traveller to Italy* (2 vols, Rome, 1954), I, p. 475; Brigden, S., 'The Early Life of Reginald Pole' in *Reformation Cardinal. Reginald Pole in Sixteenth Century Italy and England* (ed. J. Willoughby, Oxford 2023) pp. 7–13, p. 8.

3. CRP 1, no. 5, p. 40.

4. Parks, p. 476; Gasquet, F. A., Cardinal, *Cardinal Pole and his early Friends* (London, 1927), p. 14.

5. Schenk, p. 218.

6. Sanuto, M., *I diarii di Marin Sanuto* (59 vols, Venice 1879–1903), vol. 30, col. 176.

7. Ibid., col. 298.

8. Parks, p. 488; Woolfson, *Padua*, p. 222.

9. Schenk, p. 219; Williamson, H. Ross, 'Cardinal Pole in Italy' in *History Today 20* (1970), pp. 20–27, p. 20.

10. Woolfson, J., 'John Claymond, Pliny the Elder and the Early History of Corpus Christi College, Oxford' in *English Historical Review Vol. 112* (1997), pp. 882–903, p. 895; Woolfson, *Padua*, 83.

11. Schenk, p. 6 and Woolfson, *Padua*, p. 77.

12. Murphy, J., 'Cardinal Reginald Pole: Questions of Self-Justification and of Faith' in *Royal Studies Journal Vol. 4* (2017) pp. 177–95, p. 183; CRP 1, no. 3, p. 39; ibid., no. 9, pp. 43–44.

13. Gwyn, P., *The King's Cardinal, The Rise and Fall of Thomas Wolsey* (London, 1990), p. 301; Mayer, T. F., 'Pole, Reginald (1500–1558)' in *O.D.N.B.* and see also Brigden, 'The Early Life', p. 11.

14. Beccadelli, p. 16; Woolfson, *Padua*, p. 286.

15. Ibid., 111; *The Genius of Venice, exhibition catalogue* (eds Martineau, J. & Hope, C., London, 1983), pp. 369–70.

16. Fowler, T., *The History of Corpus Christi College with its list of members* (Oxford, 1893), p. 58; Mayer, 'Pole, Reginald'.

17. Gee, J. A., *The Life and Works of Thomas Lupset with a critical text of the Original Treatises and the Letters* (London, 1928), p. 120; Mayer, T. F., 'Lupset, Thomas (c. 1495–1530) in. *O.D.N.B.*

18. Simar, Th., *Christophe de Longueil, humaniste (1488–1522)* (Paris, 1911), pp. 9, 37.

19. Ibid., p. 89, Hyde, H., *Cardinal Bendinello Sauli and Church Patronage in Sixteenth Century Italy* (Woodbridge, 2009), p. 56.

20. Ross Williamson, p. 21.

21. Simar, p. 92.

22. Woolfson, *Padua*, p. 111; Parks, G. B., 'Did Pole write the 'Vita Longolii'?' in *Renaissance Quarterly, Vol. 26* (1973) pp. 274–85.

23. Hyde, pp. 55–8. The unexplored ties between Pole and the Sauli family will be discussed in a future publication.

24. Wade, T., 'Reginald Pole and Humanism in Padua' in *Reformation Cardinal, Reginald Pole in Sixteenth Century Italy and England* (ed. J. Willoughby, Oxford 2023) pp. 15–25, p. 20.

25. CRP, 1, p. 58, note no. 93; see Woolfson, *Padua*, p. 110 for other scholars (of less importance to this narrative) who visited and stayed with Pole in Padua.

26. Mayer, T. F., 'Starkey, Thomas (*c.* 1498–1538), humanist and royal servant' in *O.D.N.B.*

27. Schenk, p. 16.

28. Hyde, pp. 55–56.

29. Haile, p. 31; Walsh, G. G., 'Cardinal Pole and the Problem of Christian Unity' in *The Catholic Historical Review Volume 15* (1930), p. 391.

30. Prosperi, A., *Tra Evangelismo e Controriforma. G.M. Giberti (1495–1543)* (Rome, 1969), p. 111.

31. Higginbotham, p. 65.

32. Schenk, p. 21.

3 The King's Great Matter: Reginald Pole and the Divorce

1. Guy, *The Children*, p. 10.

2. Murphy, B. A., *Bastard Prince, Henry VIII's lost son* (Stroud, 2001), p. 5.

3. Starkey, D., *The Reign of Henry VIII, Personalities and Politics* (second edition, London, 2002), p. 34.

4. Starkey, D., *Six Wives, The Queens of Henry VIII* (London, 2003), p. 123.

5. Whitelock, A., *Mary Tudor, England's First Queen* (London, 2010), p. 32.

6. Starkey, *Henry*, p. 7.

7. Williams, P., *Katherine of Aragon* (Stroud, 2013), p. 227.

8. Scarisbrick, J., *Henry VIII* (London, 1988), p. 152.

9. Guy, J., & Foxe, J., *Hunting the Falcon, Henry VIII, Anne Boleyn and the Marriage that shook Europe* (London, 2023), pp. 34, 416; Ives, E., *The Life and Death of Anne Boleyn* (first edition, Oxford, 2004), pp. 18.

10. Emmerson, O., & McCaffrey, K., *Becoming Anne, Connections, Culture, Court* (Norwich, 2022), p. 80.

11. Scarisbrick, *Henry VIII*, p. 149.

12. Whitelock, p. 40.

13. Loades, p. 192; Bernard, G. W., *Anne Boleyn, Fatal Attractions* (Yale and London, 2010), p. 25.

14. Rex, R., *Henry VIII* (Stroud, 2009), p. 46.

15. Scarisbrick, *Henry VIII*, p. 156.

16. Ibid., p. 203.

17. Ibid., p. 188.

18. Ibid. pp. 188–9.

19. Ibid., p. 227, citing the contemporary commentator, Edward Hall.

20. Ibid. p. 255.

21. Beccadelli, p. 20; Edwards, *Archbishop*, p. 17.

22. Higginbotham, p. 65; Edwards, *Archbishop*, p. 22.

23. Scarisbrick, *Henry VIII*, p. 23; Haile, p. 67; Edwards, *Archbishop*, p. 23.

24. Mayer, T. F., 'A Fate worse than Death, Reginald Pole and the Paris Theologians' in *English Historical Review Vol. 103* (1988), p. 883.

25. Edwards, *Archbishop*, p. 22 and ibid., p. 23 for the importance of the Paris theologians.

26. Gasquet, *Cardinal Pole*, p. 110.

27. Mayer, 'A Fate', p. 883.

28. Edwards, *Archbishop*, p. 29.

29. Ibid., p. 30; Scarisbrick, *Henry VIII*, p. 24, Mayer, 'A Fate', p. 884.

30. Mayer, 'A Fate', pp. 873 ff.

31. Paul, p. 134.

32. Fletcher, C., *The Divorce of Henry VIII, The Untold Story* (London, 2013), p. 146.

33. Scarisbrick, *Henry VIII*, p. 260.

34. Edwards, *Archbishop*, p. 41.

35. Wabuda, S., *Thomas Cranmer* (Oxford and New York, 2017), p. 49; CRP I, no. 60, pp. 69–70; Mayer, 'A Fate', p. 889.

36. CRP 1, no. 74, pp. 78–9; ibid., no. 97, pp. 97–8.

37. Mayer, 'A Fate', p. 890, note no. 2; CRP 1, no. 60, pp. 69–70.

38. Schenk, pp. 28–9.

39. Smith, F. E., *Transnational Catholicism in Tudor England. Mobility, Exile and Counter-Reformation, 1530–1580* (Oxford, 2022), p. 40.

40. Mayer, 'Pole, Reginald'; Haile, p. 89, Higginbotham, p. 70.

4 Fireworks from Rome: Cardinal Pole and the Events of 1532–37

1. Lipscomb, S., 1536, *The Year That Changed Henry VIII* (Oxford, 2009), p. 40.

2. Higginbotham, p. 71.

3. Scarisbrick, *Henry VIII*, p. 311.

4. Haile, p. 109; Higginbotham, p. 76.

5. Higginbotham, p. 76; Haile, p. 109.

6. Haile, p. 112; Paul, pp. 184–5.

7. Loades, p. 236.

8. Waduba, p. 89.

9. CRP 1, no. 64, pp. 71–2.

10. Scarisbrick, *Henry VIII*, p. 45; Vos, A., 'The 'Vita Longolii', Additional Considerations about Reginald Pole's Authorship' in *Renaissance Quarterly* Vol. 3 (1977), pp. 324–44, p. 332.

11. Barrington, R., 'Two Houses both alike in dignity: Reginald Pole and Edmund Harvell' in *The Historical Journal* Vol. 39 (1996), pp. 895–913, p. 900.

12. Ibid.

13. Dodds, M. H. & Dodds, R., *The Pilgrimage of Grace 1536–7 and the Exeter Conspiracy 1538* (2 vols, London, 1971), I, p. 21.

14. Scarisbrick, *Henry VIII*, p. 3.

15. CRP 1, no. 77, pp. 81–2; Scarisbrick, *Henry VIII*, pp. 65, 82.

16. Woolfson, *Padua*, pp. 94–7; Parks, pp. 484–5.

17. CRP 1, no. 74, pp. 78–9; ibid., no. 73, pp. 77–8.

18. Ibid., no. 76, pp. 79–81.

19. Lipscomb, p. 40

20. Marshall, P., *Heretics and Believers, A History of the English Reformation* (New Haven and London 2017), p. 224.

21. Woolfson, *Padua*, p. 222.

22. CRP 1, no.2, p. 39; Gasquet, *Cardinal Pole*, pp. 58–9.

23. Guy, J., *Thomas More, A very brief history* (London 2017), p. 70; Higginbotham, p. 85.

24. CRP 1, no. 82, p. 86; Ibid., no. 85, p. 88.

25. Marshall, p. 236.

26. Pole, R., *Pole's Defense of the Unity of the Church* (trans. and with introduction by Joseph G. Dwyer, Westminster, Maryland 1965), pp. 2, 297, 17.

27. Ibid., pp. 72, 38

28. Ibid. pp. 285, 262.

29. Ibid., pp. 185.

30. Ibid., p. 283.

31. Ibid., pp. 196, 237.

32. Ibid., p. 189

33. Edwards, *Archbishop*, p. 55.

34. CRP 1, no. 77, pp. 81–2.

35. Pole, *Pole's Defence*, pp. 336, 322.

36. Merriman, R. B., *Life and Letters of Thomas Cromwell* (2 vols, Oxford, 1902), I, p. 203.

37. Mayer, T. F., *Reginald Pole, Prince and Prophet* (Cambridge, 2000), p. 41; CRP 1, no.97, pp. 97–8.

38. Wabuda, p. 119.

39. CRP 1, no. 101, pp. 100–01.

40. Marshall, p. 236.

41. CRP 1, no.102, pp. 101–2.

42. Ibid., no. 106, pp. 103–4.

43. Ibid., no. 115, pp. 111–13.

44. LP 11, no. 451 and reproduced in Higginbotham, pp. 112–113.

45. CRP 1, no. 12, pp. 118–9.

46. See Dodds, I, passim; Loughlin, S., *Insurrection: Henry VIII, Thomas Cromwell and the Pilgrimage of Grace* (Stroud, 2016), passim.

47. AAV, Arch Concist. Acta Vice Canc. 5, fo. 45v; ibid. Acta Camerarii 3, fo. 125r.

48. Eubel, C., & Van Gulik, G. (eds), *Hierarchia catholica medii et recentioris aevi sive summorum Pontificum, SRE cardinalium, ecclesiarum antistitum series* (second edition, Munster 1913–2001, Volume III, p. 25.

49. Beccadelli, pp. 40–2.

50. CRP 1, no. 142, p. 127; ibid., no.144, pp. 128–30.

51. Marshall, p. 236.

52. Dodds, II, p. 338.

53. AAV, Arch Concist. Acta Vice Canc. 5, 48v; Dodds, II, p. 280; CRP 1, no. 153, p. 134; Loades, p. 282; Whitelock, p. 100.

54. Pastor, L. F., *The History of the Popes, From the Close of the Middle Ages* (ed. R. F. Kerr, Volumes XI-XIII, London, 1912–51), XII, p. 467.

55. Marshall, p. 254.

56. AAV, Arch. Concist. Acta Vice Canc. 5, fo. 68v, ibid. Acta Camerarii 3, fo. 140v.

57. Loades p. 283.

5 'Pity it is…'

1. *Original Letters, illustrative of English History; including numerous royal letters: from autographs in the British Museum and one or two other collections* (ed. H. Ellis, second series, volume II, London 1827), letter 218, p.88. The quote is from a letter written by Thomas Cromwell to Michael Throckmorton.

2. CRP 1, no. 155, pp. 136–141.

3. Pastor, XII, p. 467: '... desperatissimo et malcontento al possibile ... con simili altre parolaccie per le quali anchor si vede chiaramente l'animo di quell re'.

4. Brigden, S., 'Bryan, Sir Francis [called Vicar of Hell]' in *O.D.N.B*; Ogier, D. M., 'Mewtas [Mewtis], Sir Peter (d.1562) soldier & courtier', in *O.D.N.B.*

5. Edwards, *Archbishop*, p. 66.

6. Dodds, II, p. 282; Hutchinson, R., *Henry VIII, The Decline and Fall of a Tyrant* (London, 2019), p. 18.

7. Beccadelli, p. 49.

8. MacCulloch, D., *Thomas Cromwell* (London, 2019), p. 459.

9. Soberton, S. B., *The Forgotten Tudor Women: Gertrude Courtenay: Wife and Mother of the Last Plantagenets* (published by author, 2021), pp. 129–30.

10. Dodds, II, pp. 282–3; CRP 1, no. 178, pp. 158–9; ibid., no. 182, pp. 162–5, p. 165; ibid., no. 198, p. 175.

11. CRP 1, no. 181, pp. 161–2. p. 161; MacCulloch, *Thomas Cromwell*, p. 436.

12. Mayer, 'Pole, Reginald' in *O.D.N.B.*; Beccadelli, p. 52; CRP 1, no. 193, p. 171.

13. Scarisbrick, *Henry VIII*, p. 361.

14. Edwards, *Archbishop*, p. 57.

15. *Chronicle of King Henry VIII, of England: Being a Contemporary Record of Some of the Principal Events of the Reigns of Henry VIII, and Edward VI* (trans. & ed. M. A. S. Hume, London, 1889), p. 132; Brigden, S., *Thomas Wyatt*, The Heart's Forest (London, 2012), p. 405.

16. Soberton, *The Forgotten Tudor Women*, p. 140.

17. Higginbotham, pp. 162–3, 81.

18. Soberton, *The Forgotten Tudor Women*, p. 54.

19. Pierce, *Margaret Pole*, pp. 161–2.

20. Borman, T., *Henry VIII and the men who made him* (London, 2019), p. 325.

21. Dodds, II, p. 310; Higginbotham, p. 119.

22. Dodds, II, p. 310.

23. MacCulloch, *Thomas Cromwell*, p. 478; Scarisbrick, *Henry VIII*, p. 361.

24. Dodds, II, 326; *Chronicle of King Henry VIII*, p.133.

25. *Correspondance Politique de MM. de Castillon et de Marillac Ambassadeurs de France en Angleterre (1537–1542)* (ed. J. Kaulek Paris, 1885), p. 176.

26. Pierce, *Margaret Pole*, pp. 142–3; see also Smith, F. E., 'From Royal Servant to Arch Traitor, Pole, Henry VIII and *De Unitate*' in *Reformation Cardinal, Reginald Pole in Sixteenth-Century Italy and England* (ed. J. Willoughby, Oxford, 2023), p. 38.

27. Smith, *Transnational Catholicism*, p. 144.

28. Dodds, II, p. 311.

29. Borman, pp. 322–3.

30. Pierce, *Margaret Pole*, p. 170.

31. *Correspondance Politique*, p. 87.

32. Pierce, *Margaret Pole*, p. 170.

33. *Original Letters*, II letter 131, pp. 114–5.

34. Pierce, *Margaret Pole*, p. 173.

35. Soberton, *The Forgotten Tudor Women*, p. 161.

36. CRP 1, no. 290, pp. 243–4.

37. *Correspondance Politique*, p. 309.

38. Ibid., p. 309.

39. Ibid., p. 317; Pierce, *Margaret Pole*, pp. 176–7.

40. *Correspondance Politique*, pp. 318, 315, 321.

41. Pierce, *Margaret Pole*, p. 142 and CRP 1, no. 241, pp. 206–7 in which a similar sentiment is expressed to Charles V.

42. Scarisbrick, *Henry VIII*, p. 362.

43. CRP 1, no. 242, p. 207; Edwards, *Archbishop*, 81; Brigden, *Thomas Wyatt*, pp. 429–35; Beccadelli, pp. 55–9.

44. CRP 1, no. 294, p. 246.

45. Haile, p. 270; Beccadelli, p. 59.

6 Danger for Pole from within the Church

1. Fenlon, D., *Heresy and Obedience in Tridentine Italy, Cardinal Pole and the Counter Reformation* (Cambridge, 1972), p. 36.

2. Overell, M. A., 'An English Friendship and Italian Reform, Richard Morison and Michael Throckmorton, 1532–1538' in *The Journal of Ecclesiastical History Vol. 57* (2006, pp. 478–493), p. 488.

3. CRP 1, no. 64, pp. 71–2; Ross Williamson, p. 23.

4. Olin, J. C., *Catholic Reform from Cardinal Ximenes to the Council of Trent 1495–1563* (New York, 1990), pp. ix, x.

5. Olin, *Catholic Reform*, p. 13.

6. Olin, J. C., *The Catholic Reformation, Savonarola to Ignatius Loyola* (New York, 1992), p. 183; Haile, p.185; Beccadelli, p. 37.

7. Smith, 'From Royal Servant', p. 33.

8. CRP 1, no. 179, pp. 159–60; Mayer, 'Pole, Reginald' in *O.D.N.B.*

9. Ryrie, A., *The English Reformation, A very brief history* (London, 2020), p. 7.

10. Edwards, *Archbishop*, pp. 96–7.

11. Overell, 'An English Friendship', p. 488.

12. Fenlon, *Heresy and Obedience*, p. 43.

13. Overell, M. A., 'Pole and the Spirituali' in *Reformation Cardinal, Reginald Pole in Sixteenth Century Italy and England* (ed. J. Willoughby, Oxford 2023), pp. 41–55, p. 43; CRP 1, no. 332, pp. 263–5; ibid., no. 328, pp. 268–71, Edwards, *Archbishop*, p. 100.

14. See Fenlon, *Heresy and Obedience*, p. 72 for the list of members of the group, which included for a short period the Jesuit Bobadilla and also Murphy, 'Cardinal Reginald Pole'. p. 186.

15. Schenk, p. 108.

16. McNair, P., *Peter Martyr in Italy, An Anatomy of Apostasy* (Oxford, 1967), p. 285.

17. Maddison, C., *Marcantonio Flaminio, Poet, Humanist, and Reformer* (London, 1965), p. 147, note no. 65; Smith, *Transnational Catholicism*, p. 80.

18. Overell, 'Pole and the Spirituali', p. 45.

19. CRP 1, no. 341, p. 278.

20. Vowles, S., 'Vittoria Colonna' in *Michelangelo. The last decades* (eds Vowles, S. & Lewis, G., London 2024), pp. 77–110, p.86.

21. Fenlon, *Heresy and Obedience*, p. 72, note no. 8.

22. Pastor, Vol. XI, p. 497.

23. Fenlon, *Heresy and Obedience*, p. 52.

24. Olin, *Catholic Reform*, p. 15.

25. Edwards, *Archbishop*, p. 101.

26. Fenlon, *Heresy and Obedience*, p. 74.

27. Ibid.

28. Murphy, p. 187.

29. Beccadelli, p. 62.

30. Targoff, R., *Renaissance Woman, The Life of Vittoria Colonna* (New York, 2018), p. 236.

31. Overell, 'Pole and the Spirituali', p. 53.

32. Pole, R., *Causes of Christian Disunion, Cardinal Pole's Legatine Address at the opening of the Council of Trent, 7 January 1546* (ed. & trans., V. McNabb O.P., London, 1935), p. 5; Pole, R., *De Concilio liber Reginaldis Poli cardinalis* (Rome, 1562), fo. 57 v.

33. Pole, *Causes*, pp. 7, 8, 9, 14.

34. Fenlon, *Heresy and Obedience*, p. 133.

35. Smith, *Transnational Catholicism*, p. 87.

36. Woolfson, *Padua*, p. 102; CRP 2, no. 159, p. 142; ibid., no. 216, pp. 186–7; CRP 2, no. 520, p. 12; CRP 3, no. 1185, p. 87.

37. Beccadelli, p. 63. Fenlon, *Heresy and Obedience*, p. 153 believes that he had a breakdown and was suffering from a psychosomatic illness, yet Massarelli said Pole had been ill for forty days.

38. CRP 1, no. 501, p. 363; Mayer, *Prince and Prophet*, p. 156; Fenlon, *Heresy and Obedience*, p. 189.

39. Mayer, *Prince and Prophet*, p. 161.

40. Ibid, p. 163.

41. Fenlon, *Heresy and Obedience*, p. 200.

42. Fenlon, D., 'Pietro Carnesecchi and Cardinal Pole: New Perspectives' in *Journal of Ecclesiastical History Volume 56*, no. 3 (July, 2005) pp. 529–533, p. 529.

43. CRP 1, no. 473, pp. 350–1.

44. Edwards, *Archbishop*, p. 159. Merenda was released by the Inquisition in 1553, deprived of his benefices and thus disgraced: Russell, C., *Giulia Gonzaga and the religious controversies of sixteenth century Italy* (Turnhout 2006), p. 116.

45. Hughes, P., *Rome and Counter Reformation in England* (Birmingham, 1941), p. 43.

46. Mayer, T. F., 'The War of the Two Saints, The Conclave of Julius III and Cardinal Pole' in *Cardinal Pole in European Context* (ed. T. F. Mayer, Aldershot, 2000) IV, p. 4, citing the viewpoint of Cardinal Gonzaga.

47. Murphy, p. 188.

48. Mayer, 'The War of the Two Saints', p. 9; Ross Williamson, p. 26; Pastor, XIII, p. 14.

49. Pastor, XIII, p. 15.

50. Hughes, p. 45.

51. *Pasquinate del Cinque e Seicento* (ed. V. Marucci, Rome 1988), p. 191. My translation of '... non ti vergogni, .../d'aver l'Inglese cosi male trattato/Il poverio uccellava al papato/E tu, in presenza d'ogni cardinal/ Per eretico marcio imperial/Con mille prove l'hai canonizzato.'

52. Mayer, 'The War of the Two Saints', p. 9; Fenlon, *Heresy and Obedience*, p. 229.

53. Ryrie, p. 10.

54. CRP 2, no. 572, p. 77; Flaminio, M., *Lettere* 2 vols (ed. A. Pastore, Rome, 1978) I, p. 190.

55. Smith, *Transnational Catholicism*, p. 149.

56. Beccadelli, p. 70.

57. Fenlon, *Heresy and Obedience*, p. 233.

58. Smith, *Transnational Catholicism*, p. 91.

7 Danger from Henry VIII and England Waxes and Wanes

1. Ryrie, p. 9.

2. Hutchinson, *Henry VIII*, p. 18.

3. CRP 1, no.173, pp. 152–4; ibid., no. 181, p. 161; ibid., no. 198, p. 175.

4. Ross Williamson, p. 25.

5. CRP 1, no. 182, pp. 163–5.

6. Pastor, XII, p. 468; Ross Williamson, p. 25.

7. Hutchinson, *Henry VIII*, p. 147.

8. CRP 1, no. 250, pp. 216–7; ibid., no. 290, pp. 242–4, Haile, p. 270.

9. CRP 1 no. 374, p. 294; ibid. no. 375, pp. 294–5; ibid. no. 378, p. 295.

10. Parks, G. B., 'The Parma Letters and the Dangers to Cardinal Pole' in *The Catholic Historical Review Vol. 46* (1960), pp. 299–317, pp. 304–5.

11. Ibid., p. 305 and CRP I, no. 439, p. 333: 'che esso, per la cui causa io son perseguitato, e molto magiore, et più potente di colui, che mi perseguita'. My translation.

12. CRP 1, no. 428, pp. 326–9, p. 328.

13. Scarisbrick, J., 'The plot to depose Henry VIII' in *Catholic Herald, December 20 2018*, online. I have based my account of this episode on Scarisbrick. There is a fuller, and at times conflicting, account in Brigden, *Thomas Wyatt*, pp. 512–4.

14. Ibid.

15. Ibid.

16. CRP 1, no. 306, pp. 252–3.

17. Hutchinson, *Henry VIII*, pp. 70–1; CRP, 1, no. 334, pp. 274–5.

18. Harrison, E., 'Henry the Eighth's Gangster: the affair of Ludovico da l'Armi' in *Journal of Modern History Vol. 15* (1943), pp. 265–274; Hutchinson, *Henry VIII*, pp. 154–9, 304–5, 332–3.

19. Hutchinson, *Henry VIII*, p. 155.

20. Harrison, p. 265.

21. Hutchinson, *Henry VIII* p. 156; Harrison, p. 267.

22. Harrison, p. 268.

23. Ibid., pp. 270–1.

24. Ibid., p. 266.

25. CRP 1, no. 428, p. 326.

26. Ibid., no. 421, p. 324 and no. 424, p. 325; Schenk, p. 112.

27. CRP 1, no. 423, p. 325.

28. Ibid., no. 428, p. 328.

29. Parks, 'The Parma Letters', p. 317.

30. Scarisbrick, J., 'Henry VIII, Stinking Sadist' in *Catholic Herald* (4 February 2016), online.

31. Wabuda, p. 100.

32. MacCulloch, D., *Tudor Church Militant, Edward IV and the Protestant Reformation* (London, 1999), p. 6.

33. Hutchinson, *Henry VIII*, p. 251.

34. Ibid., p. 253, Wabuda, p. 157.

35. MacCulloch, *Tudor Church Militant*, p. 5.

36. Starkey, *The Reign*, p. 5; MacCulloch, *Tudor Church Militant*, p. 5.

37. MacCulloch, *Tudor Church Militant*, p. 7.

38. Mayer, *Prince and Prophet*, pp. 169–70.

39. Whitelock, p. 132.

40. Wabuda, pp. 194, 196.

41. Ibid., p. 201.

42. Stoyle, M., *A Murderous Midsummer, The Western Rising of 1549* (New Haven and London, 2022), p. 175.

43. CRP 2, no. 601, pp. 102–118, note no. 34; Marshall, p. 335.

8 Mary Tudor and 'my good cousin' Reginald Pole

1. AAV, Segr. Stato, Inghilterra 3, fo. 141v.

2. Edwards, J., *Mary I, England's Catholic Queen* (New Haven and London, 2011), p. 6.

3. Clifford, H., *The Life of Jane Dormer, Duchess of Feria* (London, 1887), p. 80.

4. Porter, pp. 15–16.

5. Titler, R., *The Reign of Mary I* (London, 1983), p. 3.

6. Clifford, p. 82.

7. Edwards, *Mary I*, p. 69.

8. Ridley, J., *Bloody Mary's Martyrs* (London 2001), p. 31.

9. Fenlon, Heresy and Obedience, p. 233.

10. Edwards, *Archbishop*, p. 120 gives June, but letters were sent from Maguzzano in May of that year: CRP 2, no. 610, p. 124. See Overell, 'Pole and the spirituali', p. 54 for this alternative view of his absence.

11. AAV, Segr. Stato, Inghilterra 3, fos 39r: 'una cosi importante e manifesta vittoria della divina sua bontà contra la militia de gli homini, battendo a terra in un momento tutti I loro longhi disegni per mezzo di una donna, la quale contra ogni giustitia ha patito tanti anni si grave oppressione'. Also in Tellechea Idigoras, J. I., *La Legaciòn del Cardenal R. Pole (1553–54), Cuando Inglaterra volvió a ser catolica* (Salamanca, 2002), p. 65.

12. Ibid., 41r '... felice e veramente miracoloso successo'; Tellechea Idigora, p. 66.

13. AAV, Segr. Stato, Inghilterra 3, fo. 39r 'essendo io di quella patria, et havendo altre volte havuto carico di questo negocio'; Tellechea Idigoras, p. 66.

14. CRP 2, no. 619, p. 129.

15. Ibid., no. 620, pp. 129–31.

16. Ibid., no. 649, pp. 161–3.

17. Ibid., no. 721, p. 210 and no. 746, pp. 222–3.

18. Beccadelli, p. 92; AAV, Segr. Stato, Inghilterra 3, fo. 55 v: 'Quanto più io vo innanzi nel lo caminio verso Inghilterra tanto piu chiaramente vedo in che mare et quanto tempestoso io mi mitto'; Tellechea Idigoras, p. 77.

19. Soberton, S. B., *Rival Sisters, Mary and Elizabeth Tudor* (published by author, 2019), p. 101.

20. Kelsey, H., *Philip of Spain, King of England, The Forgotten Sovereign* (London, 2012), p. 174, note no. 20.

21. Schenk, p. 126.

22. Hutchings, p. 21. The Simancas letter is dismissed by Pastor, XIII, p. 257.

23. Mangano, S., 'Mantenere l'Inghilterra nella Respublica Christiana, Il cardinal legato Reginald Pole e il suo messaggio ai sovrani d'Europa (1537–9)', in *Eurostudium* 2016, pp. 3–60, pp. 14–15.

24. Dodds, II, p. 337.

25. Marshall, p. 274.

26. Edwards, *Mary I*, p. 149; Pastor, XIII, p. 259, note no.2.

27. Pastor, XIII, p. 262.

28. Ibid., p. 261.

29. Ibid., p. 262.

30. Ibid.

31. Ibid., pp. 268–9; Edwards, *Archbishop*, p. 133; CRP 2, no. 743, pp. 220–1; ibid. no. 775, pp. 241–2.

32. G. Russell, *The Palace. From the Tudors to the Windsors, 500 years of History at Hampton Court* (London, 2023), p. 127.

33. Porter, pp. 300, 312.

34. AAV, Segr. Stato, Inghilterra 3, fo. 73r: '… la particular protettione che ha di quella Regina et di quell Regno'; Tellechea Idigoras, p. 86.

35. Hughes, p. 59; AAV, Segr. Stato, Inghilterra 3, fo. 73v.

36. Richards, J. M., *Mary Tudor*, Abingdon 2008, p. 170.

37. Pastor, XIII, pp. 276, 280.

38. Edwards, *Mary I*, p. 215.

39. Whitelock, p. 247 and AAV, Segr. Stato, Inghilterra 3, fo. 138r: 'debbano et per sé, et per gli altri trovar et proponer qualche modo, che sia di commune satisfattione a tutti'.

40. AAV, Segr. Stato, Inghilterra 3, 142r. '… essere venuto il tempo maturo di chiamarmi dopo cosi lunga dimora, et di trattare, et conclude in questo parlamento il ritorno di quel regno all'unione et obedientia della chiesa'.

41. Ibid. fos 139r, 142v; AAV, Segr. Stato, Inghilterra 3, fo. 131v.

42. Whitelock, p. 247; Loades, D., *The Reign of Mary Tudor, Politics, Government and religion in England 1553–8* (second edition, London, 1991), p. 266, Hughes, p. 64; Titler, p. 31.

43. AAV, Segr. Stato, Inghilterra 3, fo. 152r: 'il qual mostrava molta divotione et allegrazza della vista di S.S. R[everendissi]ma dimandando la beneditione'.

44. Ibid., fo. 156r: 'Io ero privo della patria, privo delli beni, et privo della nobilta, ne havevo modo da riveder li miei consaguinei, et m'era interedetto fin'il poterli parlare in loco alcuno.'

45. Whitelock, p. 251; Titler, p. 31.

46. CRP 2, no. 618, p. 128.

47. Schenk, p. 132; Loades, *Reign of Mary Tudor*, p. 269, Edwards, *Archbishop*, p. 218.

9 'I am come not to destroy, but to build; to reconcile, not to condemn'

1. Marshall, p. 390.

2. Velasco Berenguer, G., *Politics and Religion in Habsburg England in the reign of Philip I (1554–8)* (Leiden, 2022), p. 163. See also Pogson, R., 'The Legacy of the Schism, Confusion, Continuity and Change in the Marian Clergy' in *The Mid-Tudor Polity c. 1540–60* (eds J. Loach & R. Titler, London, 1980), p. 132.

3. AAV, Segr. Stato, Inghilterra 3, fo. 152v: 'Questo si e' risoluto, che posdimane tutti I Vescovi venghino qui da S. S. R[everendissi]ma per conferire con lei dei bisogni delle loro diocesi.'

4. Edwards, *Archbishop*, p. 170.

5. For example see Loades, D., *The Oxford Martyrs* (London, 1970), esp. pp. 234 ff.

6. Pole, R., *The Reform of England by the Decrees of Cardinal Pole, Legate of the Apostolic See promulgated in the year of Grace 1556*

(trans. & ed. by H. Raikes, Chester, 1830), pp.5, 6, 7, 9, 10, 12, 21, 23, 28, 32, 33, 36, 39, 44, 45, 49, 51, 52.

7. Edwards, *Mary I*, pp. 239–40.

8. Loach. J, 'Mary Tudor and the Re-Catholicisation of England' in *History Today Volume 44* (1994) online.

9. Duffy, E., *Fires of Faith, Catholic England under Mary Tudor* (New Haven and London, 2009), pp. 22, 25. See also Pogson, 'The Legacy', pp. 128–130.

10. Pogson, 'The Legacy', p. 123.

11. Velasco Berenguer, p. 191.

12. Ibid., p. 126.

13. Loach, 'Mary Tudor'.

14. See Russell, *The Palace*, pp. 136–7 for the possible explanations for these 'pregnancies'.

15. Hutchings, p. 57.

16. CRP 3, no. 1194, p. 92: 'grandissima consolation, et allegrezza per la cognition et esperienza che io ho della bontà, dottrina, et delle altre sue rare, et ottime qualità'.

17. Edwards, *Archbishop*, p. 43; Parks, G. B., 'Italian Tributes to Cardinal Pole' in *Studies in the Continental Background of Renaissance English Literature: Essays presented to John L. Lievsay* (eds D. B. J. Randall & G, W. Williams, Durham N.C., 1977) pp. 43–55, p. 47: 'vir sanctissimus, & doctissimus'.

18. Simoncelli, P., *Il caso Reginald Pole, l'eresia e santità nelle polemiche religiose del Cinquecento* (Rome, 1977), p. 82, citing a letter from Gheri to Beccadelli of 29 April 1553.

19. CRP 2, no. 636, pp. 154, 158: 'ut haec quasi cicatrix ex nostra amicitia tollitur'.

20. CRP 3, no. 1260, p. 116 and Edwards, *Archbishop*, p. 203.

21. Murphy, p. 191.

22. CRP 3, no. 1783, p. 340; ibid., no. 1874, p. 375.

23. Loades, *Reign*, p. 297.
24. Whitelock, p. 295.
25. CRP 3, no. 2155, p. 497.
26. Fenlon, *Heresy and Obedience*, 271; Edwards, *Archbishop*, p. 228.
27. CRP 3, no. 2011, p. 436.
28. Ibid., no. 2010/11, pp. 433–6; ibid., no. 2048, pp. 450–1; Fenlon, *Heresy and Obedience*, p. 271; Edwards, *Archbishop*, p. 210.
29. Simoncelli, p. 166, citing a report of the Venetian ambassador.
30. Edwards, *Archbishop*, p. 226; Smith, *Transnational Catholicism*, p. 195.
31. CRP 3, no. 2076, pp. 462–9, p. 463.
32. Ibid., passim and Edwards, *Archbishop*, pp. 301, 3, 11.
33. Ryrie, p. 29.
34. Hutchings, M., 'The Reign of Mary Tudor – A Reassessment' in *History Today Issue 33*, March 1999, online.
35. Ibid.
36. AAV, Segr Stato Inghilterra 3, fo. 144r: 'Temeva tanto questi heretici, che sono persone desperate.'
37. Porter, pp. 237–8.
38. Ridley, *Bloody Mary*, p. 1.
39. Duffy, *Fires*, p. 7.
40. AAV, Segr. Stato, Inghilterra 3, fos 172r-v: '... I quali mostreranno segno di riconoscersi, et pentirsi del loro errore ... siano rimesse tutte le pene canoniche.'
41. Ridley, *Bloody Mary*, p. 3.
42. Ibid., p. 58.
43. Duffy, *Fires*, pp. 94–5, 149–50; CRP 3, no. 1418, p. 186.
44. CRP 3, no. 1459, p. 210; Duffy, *Fires*, pp. 149, 131.
45. Ibid., pp. 147, 149.
46. Ridley, *Bloody Mary*, p. 166.
47. Foxe, J., *Foxe's Book of Martyrs* (e-book, from the 1848 edition), pp. 511–2.

48. CRP 3, no. 2040, p. 447, note no. 104: 'più volte quanto si opera da qui contra di lei, qual li ha risposto, che se vorrano attender l'operation che fa nel Regno d'Inghilterra, et come perseguita li heretici, se potranno chiarir se e lutherano, o non'.

49. Duffy, *Fires*, p. 132.

50. Freeman, T. F., 'Burning Zeal: Mary Tudor and the Marian Persecution' in *Mary Tudor, Old and New Perspectives* (eds S. Doran & T. S. Freeman, Basingstoke 2011) pp.171–205, p. 177; Duffy, Fires, p. 93.

51. Edwards, *Archbishop*, p. 163.

52. Fenlon, *Heresy and Obedience*, p. 223.

53. Foxe, p. 443.

54. CRP 3, no. 2076, p. 467.

55. Richards, p. 200.

56. Edwards, *Mary I*, p. 265.

57. Smith, *Transnational Catholicism*, p. 190.

58. Pole, *The Reform of England*, p. 10.

59. For the Spanish theologians and their views, see Velasco Berenguer, pp.183 and 187.

60. Foxe, p. 539.

61. Smith, *Transnational Catholicism*, p. 196.

62. Duffy, E., *Reformation Divided, Catholics, Protestants and the Conversion of England* (London, 2017), p.100, Loades, *Reign*, p. 372.

63. Schenk, p. 167.

64. CRP 1, no. 290, p. 243; CRP 3, no. 1104, p. 52, Mayer, *Prince and Prophet*, pp. 272–3.

65. Russell, p. 132.

66. *Archdeacon Harpsfield's Visitation, 1557* two volumes (ed. Rev. L. E. Whatmore, London, 1950), I, see for example pp. 22, 34, 39, 53, 125, 133, 169, 193.

67. Velasco Berenguer, p. 231 and see also p. 195.

68. Duffy, *Fires*, p. 186.

69. Ibid. p. 187.

10 *Reginald Pole and Thomas Cranmer: Poles Apart?*

1. Ridley, J., *Thomas Cranmer* (Oxford, 1962), p. 13.
2. Ibid.
3. MacCulloch, D., *Thomas Cranmer* (London, 1996), pp. 45–6.
4. Schenk, p. 16, citing Richard Morison, *An Exhortation to Stir all English Men to the Defence of Their Country* (London, 1539), fol. D.
5. Ridley, *Thomas Cranmer*, p. 30.
6. MacCulloch, *Thomas Cranmer*, p. 53.
7. Ridley, *Thomas Cranmer*, p. 36.
8. Ibid.
9. MacCulloch, *Thomas Cranmer*, p. 88; Ridley, *Thomas Cranmer*, p. 51.
10. MacCulloch, *Thomas Cranmer*, p. 89.
11. Ridley, *Thomas Cranmer*, p. 64.
12. Ibid., pp. 102, 104.
13. MacCulloch, *Thomas Cranmer*, p. 270.
14. Duffy, E., *Saints, Sacrilege and Sedition, Religion and Conflict in the Tudor Reformation* (London, 2012), p. 185.
15. Ibid., p. 186.
16. MacCulloch, *Thomas Cranmer*, p. 365.
17. Ibid. p. 383.
18. Ridley, *Thomas Cranmer*, pp. 272, 275, 311.
19. Ibid., p. 295.
20. Edwards, *Mary I*, p. 258 and see also MacCulloch, *Thomas Cranmer*, pp. 475–6.
21. Ibid., p. 476.
22. Skidmore, C., *Edward VI, The Lost King of England* (London, 2007), p. 251.
23. Ibid., p. 252.
24. Ridley, *Thomas Cranmer*, pp. 356–9.
25. MacCulloch, *Thomas Cranmer*, pp. 575–6.
26. *Writings of the Rev. Dr. Thomas Cranmer Archbishop of Canterbury and Martyr 1556* (Philadelphia, 1842), p. 272.

27. Ibid., p. 273.

28. CRP 3, no. 1411, p. 181.

29. Ibid., pp. 188–190.

30. Ibid., pp. 188, 189, 190.

31. Ibid., pp. 282–3; MacCulloch, *Thomas Cranmer*, p. 581 believes that the other part of the Pope's anatomy was his bottom, but it could equally be his hand.

32. See MacCulloch, *Thomas Cranmer*, pp. 589–95.

33. Ibid., p. 597.

34. Ibid., p. 600.

35. Ibid., p. 603.

36. Ridley, *Bloody Mary*, p. 139.

37. Duffy, *Saints, Sacrilege and Sedition*, p. 187.

38. MacCulloch, *Thomas Cranmer*, p. 597.

39. Edwards, *Mary I*, p. 264.

40. Ibid., p. 233.

41. Ridley, *Thomas Cranmer*, p. 77.

42. CRP 3, no. 1104, p. 52.

43. Ibid., no. 1458, pp. 209, 210; MacCulloch, *Thomas Cranmer*, p. 588.

44. Edwards, *Mary I*, p. 242.

45. 'Translations of some letters relating to Cardinal Pole' in *Report to the Master of the Rolls on Documents in the Archives of Venice* (London, 1866), pp. 50–69, British History Online http://www.british-history.ac.uk/no.series/master-of-rolls-report, pp. 50–69, accessed 28 February 2024.

46. Duffy, *Saints, Sinners and Sacrilege*, p. 191.

47. Ridley, *Thomas Cranmer*, p. 156.

48. Mayer, *Prince & Prophet*, p. 277.

49. Duffy, *Saints, Sinners and Sacrilege*, p. 192.

50. MacCulloch, *Thomas Cranmer*, p. 252.

51. Ibid., p. 631.

11 *Philip I of England and Cardinal Pole: Another King and Another Conflict?*

1. Kelsey, p. 52.
2. Sansom, A., *Mary and Philip, The Marriage of Tudor England and Habsburg Spain* (Manchester, 2020), p. 24.
3. Kelsey, p. 53.
4. Parker, G., *Imprudent King, A New Life of Philip II* (New Haven, 2014), p. 43.
5. Velasco Berenguer, p. 17.
6. Kelsey, pp. 59, 65; Sansom, p. 67; Parker, p. 44.
7. Kelsey, p. 54.
8. Parker, p. 44.
9. Ibid., p. 45.
10. Velasco Berenguer, p. 37.
11. Sansom, p. 173.
12. Velasco Berenguer, pp. 54, 111; Parker, p. 47.
13. Kelsey, p. 57; see Velasco Berenguer pp. 118–20 and Sansom, p. 110 for the fact that Philip was never crowned and the problems of precedence with Mary which were gradually resolved during her reign.
14. Sansom, p. 16.
15. CRP 2, no. 796, p. 256.
16. Ibid., no. 887, p. 318.
17. Ibid., no. 938, p. 337.
18. Velasco Berenguer, p. 169.
19. Ibid., p. 170.
20. Loades, *Reign,* pp. 166, 167.
21. Mayer, *Prince and Prophet*, p. 220; Loades, *Reign*, p. 167.
22. AAV, Segr. Stato, Inghilterra 3, fo. 148v: 'accolto con ogni amorevolezza dalla Maestà del Re'.
23. Velasco Berenguer, p. 177.
24. Ibid., p. 178.

25. Vermeir, R & De Meulenaere, V, '"To bring good agreement and concord to Christendom", The Conference of Marck (1555) and English neutrality, 1553–1557' in *Revue du Nord (2013/1 no. 400–1)*, pp. 681–95, p. 686.

26. Ibid., p. 687.

27. CRP 3, no. 1031, p. 20.

28. Mayer, *Prince and Prophet*, p. 227; Vermeir & De Meuelnaere, p. 688.

29. Ibid.

30. Ibid., p. 692; Mayer, *Prince and Prophet*, p. 228; Sansom, p. 150.

31. Loades, *Reign*, p. 178.

32. Ibid., p. 295.

33. Ibid., p. 179.

34. See Velasco Berenguer, pp. 153–5.

35. Ibid. p. 156 and for the members of the council.

36. Sansom, p. 174.

37. Velasco Berenguer, pp. 157–8.

38. CRP 3, no. 1362, pp. 159–60.

39. Ibid., no. 1378, pp. 165–6; no. 1396, pp. 175–6.

40. Ibid., no. 1414, p. 183.

41. Mayer, *Prince and Prophet*, p. 230.

42. CRP 3, no. 1680, p. 299.

43. Mayer, *Prince and Prophet*, p. 232.

44. Sansom, p. 150.

45. Velasco Berenguer, pp. 179–80.

46. Mayer, *Prince and Prophet*, p. 230.

47. CRP 3, no. 1345, pp.152–3: 'Feci con ogni istanza.'

48. Ibid., no. 139, pp. 158–9; no. 1430, pp. 193–4 'rex pacificus'; ibid., no. 1480, p. 221.

49. Ibid., no. 1589, p. 269.

50. Kelsey, p. 126.

51. Ibid., pp. 126–7.

52. CRP 3, no. 1615, p. 278.

53. Parker, p. 53.

54. CRP 3, no. 1778, pp. 336–7.

55. Ibid., no. 1783, pp. 339–40; ibid., no. 1789, p. 342.

56. Ibid., no. 1938, pp. 404–5.

57. Ibid., no. 2146, pp. 492–4.

58. Parker, p. 40.

59. Sansom, p. 4.

60. Kamen, H., *Philip of Spain* (New Haven & London, 1997), p. 41.

61. Ibid., p. 62.

62. Sansom, p. 146.

63. Kelsey, p. 62.

64. Velasco Berenguer, p. 187.

65. Sansom, p. 147.

66. Parker, p. 49.

67. Loades, *Reign*, p. 294.

68. Ibid., p. 368.

69. CRP 3, no. 2282, pp. 556–7: 'Questi pochi della famiglia mia che io condussi d'Italia, i quali io non ho avuto modo di poter cosi accomodare del mio come volentieri haverei fatto, essendo stato da loro sempre con molta fede et amore servitor…'

12 *Cardinal Pole and the Women in His Life*

1. Beccadelli, pp. 71–2, 74.

2. Pennington, A., https://adammu.podbean.com/e/ursula-pole-baroness-stafford-the-forgotten-plantagenet-daughter/

3. Pierce, *Margaret Pole*, p. 53.

4. Pierce, 'Pole, Margaret'; Harris, p. 56.

5. Davies, 'Stafford, Henry'.

6. Pennington, A., https://adammu.podbean.com/e/ursula-pole-baroness-stafford-the-forgotten-plantagenet-daughter/

7. Pierce, *Margaret Pole*, p. 180.

8. Routledge, F. J., 'Six letters of Cardinal Pole to the Countess of Huntingdon' in *The English Historical Review (Volume 28)*, July 1913, pp. 527–531, p. 528.

9. Pierce, *Margaret Pole*, p. 65.

10. Cross, C., *The Puritan Earl, the life of Henry Hastings Third Earl of Huntingdon* (London, 1966), pp. 65–6; Cross, C., 'Hastings, Francis, second earl of Huntingdon (1513/14–1560)' in *O.D.N.B.*

11. Cross, 'Hastings, Francis'.

12. Ibid.

13. Ibid.

14. Cross, *The Puritan Earl*, p. 8.

15. Cross, 'Hastings, Francis'.

16. Cross, *The Puritan Earl*, p. 15.

17. Routledge, p. 528.

18. Ibid.

19. Ibid., p. 529 and CRP 3, no. 1273, p. 121. Mayer, in note no. 14 gives this as Jeronimo Osorio, *De nobilitate civili libri II. Eiusdem De nobilitate Christiana libri III* (Florence, Torrentino, 1552), but Henry Hastings' translation was never published.

20. CRP 3, no. 1437, p. 199.

21. Routledge, p. 530.

22. Ibid., p. 531.

23. Ibid.

24. CRP 3, no. 1605, p. 275.

25. Cross, *The Puritan Earl*, p. 17.

26. Routledge, p. 528.

27. Bennett Connolly, S., *Heroines of the Tudor World* (Stroud, 2024), p. 151.

28. CSP Spain, volume 4 (2), 1161 cited in Higginbotham, p. 78.

29. Pierce, *Margaret Pole*, p. 39.

30. TNA, SP 1/138, fos 132r-v.

31. Pierce, *Margaret Pole*, p. 35.

32. Ibid., p. 92.

33. Ibid., pp. 99–102.

34. TNA SP/1, 105, f. 66 r.

35. Pierce, *Margaret Pole*, pp. 123–4.

36. Ibid., p. 69.

37. Mayer, *Prince and Prophet*, p. 112.

38. CRP 1, no. 258, p. 222.

39. Ibid., no. 290, p. 243.

40. CRP 2, no. 765, p. 236.

41. Bennett Connolly, p. 151.

42. Targoff, *Renaissance Woman*, p. 60.

43. *Vittoria Colonna. Selected Letters, 1523–45. A bilingual edition* (eds A. Brundin and V. Copello (New York-Toronto, 2022), p. 5.

44. Garcés Avalos, G., 'Un soneto de Vittoria Colonna a Reginald Pole (1546). Traduccion y comentario' in *Lemir: Revista de literatura Española medioeval y del rinacimento*, 20 2016, pp. 547–560, p. 552.

45. Targoff, *Renaissance Woman*, p. 103; Brundin and Copello eds, p. 105.

46. Brundin, A., 'A "more than maternal love": Pole and Vittoria Colonna' in *Reformation Cardinal, Reginald Pole in Sixteenth-Century Italy and England* (ed. J. Willoughby, Oxford, 2023), pp. 57–63, p. 60.

47. See Garcés Avalos, p. 556.

48. CRP 1, no. 325, p. 267; Targoff, *Renaissance Woman*, p. 243.

49. Forcellino, A., *L'ultimo Michelangelo, dal Giudizio Universale alla Cappella Paolina* (Città di Castello, 2024), p. 45.

50. CRP 1, no. 459, p. 342; ibid., no. 412, p. 315; Targoff, *Renaissance Woman*, p. 249.

51. Garcés Avalos, p. 554.

52. CRP I, no. 407, pp. 310–11, my translation.

53. Brundin, 'A "more than maternal love"', p. 59.

54. Brundin and Copello (eds), p. 129 and see also CRP 1, no. 409, pp. 312–13 and no. 459, p. 342.

55. CRP 1, no. 500, p. 362.

56. Brundin and Copello (eds), p. 134; Targoff, *Renaissance Woman*, p. 251 and ibid., 'Late Love: Vittoria Colonna and Reginald Pole' in *Vittoria Colonna. Poetry, Religion, Art, Impact* (eds V. Cox & S. McHugh, Amsterdam 2021), pp. 55–72, p. 55.

57. Pagano, S. and Ranieri, C., *Nuovi documenti su Vittoria Colonna e Reginald Pole, Collectanea Archivi Vaticani* 24, Vatican City 1989, p. 77 and see also Cali, M., *Da Michelangelo all'Escorial* (Turin, 1980), p. 123.

58. Brundin, '"A more than maternal love"', pp. 62–3.

59. Ibid., p. 63.

60. Dall'Olio, G., 'Gonzaga, Giulia' in *D.B.I.*

61. Firpo, M., *Juan de Valdés e la Riforma nell'Italia del Cinquecento* (Rome, 2017), p. 50.

62. Ibid., pp. 57, 60.

63. Dall'Olio, 'Gonzaga, Giulia'.

64. Russell, p. 64.

65. Dall'Olio, 'Gonzaga, Giulia'.

66. Ibid.

67. *Vittoria Colonna Marchesa di Pescara, Carteggio* (eds E. Ferrero & G. Muller, second edition Turin, 1892), p. 237: '… a mandare tante et si buone cose al signor Cardinale et a quelli altri signori … ha preso le cose della S.V. con grandissimo piacere, vedendo tanta affettione et charita' and ibid., p. 239 '… che e' occupatissimo'.

68. Ibid., p. 240.

69. Russell, pp. 96–97.

70. Ibid., p. 117.

71. Pastore, A., *Marcantonio Flamino Fortune e sfortune di un chierico nell'Italia del Cinquecento* (Milan, 1981), p. 109: 'Molte persone

mormoravano che lo tenesse in casa, perche si diceva che era allievo del Valdesio e di frate Bernardino da Siena.'

72. Maddison, p. 110.

73. Russell, p. 146.

74. Ibid., p. 193; Simoncelli, pp. 204–5: '… l'ardente desiderio … si per Gloria di Dio principalmente, si anchora per poter anche lui godere la parte sua di tanto bene'; and see also Peyronel Rambaldi, S., *Giulia Gonzaga tra reti familiari e relazioni eterodosse* (Rome, 2012), p. 252.

13 *Cardinal Pole as Governor and Patron of Town and Household*

1. CRP 2, no. 875, pp. 297–302, p. 297: 'unius et in cute'; 'io piglio volentiere ogni occasion di retirarmi dai negotii et retornar alla vita privata'; 'noi seguendo il voler suo non manchiamo a le occasioni che li manda'; my translation, given that Mayer abbreviates Pole's Italian.

2. Ibid., pp. 297–8: 'io ho sempre tenuto di retirarmi spesso ali studii non mi ingerendo nelle actioni, ne mostrando desiderio alcuno di quei gradi che portano maggior occupatione di negotii, potria facilmente dare ad un tale occasione di pensare o che io sia molto ignavo, o che io stimi i miei private studii piu che ogni sorte d'actione'.

3. Ibid., p. 298: 'sempre inclinato a servire a chi trovandosi in tale grado quel sappia e voglia bene commandare … servire al honore di Dio et procurare il bene di altri'.

4. Edwards, *Archbishop*, p. 244.

5. Cipriani, G., *Reginald Pole, Cardinale governatore di Bagnoregio dal 1547al 1558, Biografia essenziale e ricostruzione dell'azione di governo a Bagnoregio* (Grotte di Castro, 2020), p. 91.

6. CRP 1, no. 332, pp. 273–4.

7. CRP 2, no. 512 and 513, pp. 8–9.

8. Cipriani, p. 92: 'de informarlo pienamente de tutto quello che conosciarete necessario esser di bisogn, che noi no mancheremo alla giornata di provvedere a quanto occurrera in benefitio commune di essa città et particular di voi tutti'.

9. Ibid., p. 93. Mayer, *Prince and Prophet*, p. 165, believes that problems occurred again in the future.

10. Targoff, *Renaissance Woman*, pp. 269–70; CRP 2, no. 585, pp. 92–3.

11. Cipriani, pp. 95, 97 and CRP 2, no. 520, p. 12.

12. Cipriani, p. 99.

13. Ibid., pp. 100–2.

14. CRP 2, nos 572, 573, pp. 77–88.

15. Cipriani, p. 105.

16. Pastor XIII, p. 159.

17. Cipriani, p. 105. For a detailed discussion of what a *valcheria* did, see ibid., p. 113.

18. Ibid., p. 114.

19. Ibid., p. 115: 'causam et origine multorum malorum'.

20. Ibid. and p. 116.

21. Ibid., p. 106.

22. Ibid., p. 108.

23. Ibid., pp. 108–9.

24. CRP 2, no. 739, p. 218.

25. Mayer, *Prince and Prophet*, p. 166, believes that Pole merely converted one of the loans into his gift, but I have been unable to find proof of this.

26. Ibid., p. 165. His interpretation of the financing of the *valcheria* is incomplete.

27. CRP 2, no. 875, p. 299: 'la minima actione che io potessi fare in beneficio di la più baza persona del mondo'.

28. Cortesi, P., *De Cardinalatu* (Rome, 1510), fos 56v–57r, cited in Chambers, D. S., 'The economic predicament of Renaissance

cardinals' in *Studies in medieval and Renaissance history* (ed. W. M. Bowsky, Lincoln, Nebraska, 1966 pp. 289–313), p. 293.

29. Hollingsworth, M., *The cardinal's hat: money, ambition and housekeeping in a Renaissance court* (London, 2004), p. 188.

30. CRP 1, no. 287, p. 241.

31. Beccadelli, p. 133.

32. Mayer, T. F., 'When Maecenas was broke: Cardinal Pole's 'spiritual patronage' in *Cardinal Pole in European Context* (ed. T. F. Mayer, Aldershot, 2000), XIV pp. 419–35, p. 419.

33. Beccadelli, p. 139.

34. Mayer, 'When Maecenas', pp. 420 and 422.

35. Ibid., p. 423.

36. McClung Hallman, B., *Italian cardinals, reform and the Church as property* (London, 1985), p. 100. For a specific example of a cardinal's household, see Hyde, pp. 75–88 *passim*.

37. Chambers, D. S., *A Renaissance cardinal and his worldly goods: the will and inventory of Francesco Gonzaga (1444–1483)* (London, 1992), p. 14; D'Amico, J. F., *Renaissance Humanism in Rome* (Baltimore-London, 1983), p. 52.

38. Edwards, *Archbishop*, p. 263.

39. Priscianese, F., *Del governo della corte d'un signore in Roma* (second edition, Città di Castello, 1883), p. 45.

40. CRP 1, pp. 24–5.

41. Ibid.; no. 246, p. 213; no. 251, p. 216; no. 257, pp. 220–1; no. 263, pp. 224–5.

42. Ibid., no. 280, pp. 235–6, p. 236; no. 284, p. 239.

43. Ibid., no. 286, pp. 240–1.

44. CRP 2., nos 610, 626, 631, 638, 642, 684 and pp. 124, 136, 137, 158 and 159, 165.

45. Ibid. no. 651, p. 165.

46. CRP 1, no. 257, p. 221: 'persona di bono intelletto et pratica in queste corti'. My translation varies from Mayer's; CRP 2, no. 723, p. 211.

47. CRP 3, no. 1032, p. 20; no. 1243, p. 109; no. 1465, pp. 213–4.

48. Ibid., no. 1556, p. 254; no. 1674, p. 296; no. 1456, p. 209 and no. 1508, p. 236.

49. Ibid., no. 1204, pp. 95–6: 'instrumento sincero'.

50. Schenk, p. 35; Woolfson, *Padua*, p. 251; Mayer, T. F., 'Lily, George' in *O.D.N.B.*

51. Mayer, T. F., 'Reginald Pole in Paolo Giovio's Descriptio: a strategy for reconversion' in *Cardinal Pole in European Context* (ed. T. F. Mayer, Aldershot 2000), pp. 431–450, esp. pp. 439, 446 and 450.

52. Mayer, 'Lily, George'.

53. Ibid.

54. CRP 1, no. 500, p. 362.

55. Mayer, 'Lily, George'; CRP 3, no. 2195, pp. 515–6.

56. Woolfson, J., 'Morison, Sir Richard' in *O.D.N.B.*

57. Sowerby, pp. 20, 23.

58. Ibid., p. 28.

59. Woolfson, 'Morison'.

60. Sowerby, pp. 28–30.

61. Ibid., p. 31. I have used modern English when quoting from Morison.

62. Woolfson, 'Morison'.

63. CRP 1, no. 116, p. 113.

64. 'Henry VIII: July 1536, 21–25', in *Letters and Papers, Foreign and Domestic, Henry VIII, Volume 11*, July-December 1536, ed. James Gairdner (London, 1888), British History Online https://www.british-history.ac.uk/letters-papers-hen8/vol11/pp54–73 [accessed 21 October 2024].

65. Sowerby, p. 109.

66. Ibid., p. 94.

67. Ibid., pp. 95–6.

68. Ibid., p. 99.

69. Edwards, *Archbishop*, p. 83.

70. CRP 1, no. 243, p. 208.

71. Sowerby, p. 102.

72. Ibid., p. 103.

73. Brigden, *Thomas Wyatt*, p. 237 citing from *An Invective*.

74. Sowerby, p. 119.

75. See Woolfson, 'Morison'.

14 *Cardinal Pole's Artistic Patronage*

1. Lampsonius, D., *The Life of Lambert Lombard (1565) and Effigies of Several Famous Painters from the Low Countries (1572)* (ed. and trans. Edward H Wouk, Los Angeles 2021), p. 4.

2. CRP 1, no. 184, pp. 165–7.

3. Helbig, J., *Lambert Lombard. Peintre et Architecte* (Brussels 1893), p. 21.

4. Dehaene, G., *Lambert Lombard. Renaissance et Humanisme à Liège* (Antwerp, 1990), p. 16.

5. Ibid. p. 74.

6. Lampsonius, p. 78.

7. Ibid. p. 96, note no. 22.

8. Wouk, E. H., 'Michelangelo, Lambert Lombard, and the inalienable gift of drawing' in *Zeitschrift fur Kunstgeschichte Vol. 86* (2023), pp. 15–59, p. 23.

9. Dillon, A., 'Martyrdom and Michelangelo' in *Reformation Cardinal, Reginald Pole in Sixteenth-Century Italy and England* (ed. J. Willoughby, Oxford, 2023), pp. 65–84, p. 68. For the architecture of the building and the earlier sources which confirm that there was no existing building on the site, see Bacciolo, A., ''Belonging to our English nation'. The Oratory of Domine Quo Vadis, Reginald Pole, and the English Hospice in Rome', *R.I.H.A. Journal, 0238, 30 March 2020* online.

10. Dillon, 'Martyrdom', pp. 69–70.

Notes

11. Chapman, H., *Michelangelo drawings: closer to the master* (London, 2005), p. 254 and see also Wouk, 'Michelangelo', passim; Forcellino, M., *Michelangelo, Vittoria Colonna e gli 'spirituali'. Religiosita e vita artistica a Roma, negli anni Quaranta* (Rome, 2009), p. 64.

12. Hirst, M., *Michelangelo and his drawings* (London 1988), p. 106.

13. See also Nagel, A., *Michelangelo and the Reform of Art* (Cambridge 2000), p. 146.

14. Wouk, 'Michelangelo', p. 25.

15. Chapman, pp. 256–7

16. Condivi, A., The Life of Michelangelo (trans. Alice Sedgwick Wohl, Oxford 1976), p. 103.

17. *Vittoria Colonna, Carteggio*, Vittoria Colonna to Michelangelo, CXXIII, p. 238. (my translation).

18. Wouk, 'Michelangelo', p. 19.

19. Ibid., p. 35.

20. De la Verpillière, L., '"God is in the details": visual culture of closeness in the circle of Cardinal Reginald Pole' in *Renaissance Studies Vol. 30* (2016) pp. 752–72, p. 752.

21. Targoff, *Renaissance Woman*, p. 179.

22. Pagano & Ranieri, p. 31.

23. Condivi, p. 102.

24. Chapman, pp. 252–3.

25. Forcellino, M., *Michelangelo,* pp. 35, 39.

26. See also ibid., pp. 43, 73.

27. Ibid., p. 86: '... egli ne ha uno propria del detto, che volentieri glielo manderebbe; ma in forma di Pietà, pure se gli vede tutto il corpo. Dice che questo non sarebbe un privarsene, perciochè dalla marchesa di Pescara ne può avere un altro.'

28. Forcellino, M., 'Un nuovo disegno copia della Pietà di Michelangelo per Vittoria Colonna e Reginald Pole' in *Arte Lombarda (new series 1–2, 2017),* pp. 49–57, p. 51; Forcellino, A., *L'ultimo Michelangelo,* p. 109.

29. Forcellino, M., *Michelangelo*, p. 88. '… quando mi possiate far haver quello *quadro* (my italics) della immagine di Christo del Re.mo Polo solo ch'io possa far copiar…' and 'Quando prima v s mi manderà il *quadro* del R[everendissi]mo Polo…'

30. Forcellino, A., *The Lost Michelangelos* (trans. L. Byatt, Cambridge 2011), p. 18.

31. Forcellino, M., 'The Pietà by Michelangelo, for Vittoria Colonna: sources, documentation and art-historical literature' in eds Bussagli, M., Mora, C. & D'Alessandro, L. M. G. *The Ragusa Pietà, history and restoration* (Rome, 2014), pp. 87–97, p. 90.

32. Jerrold, M. F., *Vittoria Colonna with some account of her friends and her times* (New York, 1906), p. 132: 'Perché la mente vostra, ornate e cinta/ D'eterno lume, servi la sembianza/Del gran motor nella piur interna stanza/Over albergar non puote immagin finta;/ Forse da quella ardent voglia spinta/Che mai non s'empie, anzi ad ognor s'avanza,/ Com'esser suol de' veri amanti usanza/Aggradir la potrebbe anco dipinta/Cio pensando, signor, la vostra umile/Nova madre ed ancella ora v'invia/L'opra, ch'in voi miglior maestro scolpio…'

33. Forcellino, M., 'The Pietà by Michelangelo', p. 90.

34. Forcellino, A., *L'ultimo Michelangelo*, p. 168.

35. Forcellino, A., *The Lost Michelangelos*, p. 18 and passim, esp. pp. 91–101 and Forcellino, 'Un nuovo disegno', p. 51: 'da riconoscersi quasi certamente nella cosidetta Pietà di Ragusa, in collezione private americana'.

36. Mercalli, M. & Mora, C., 'Methodological considerations in the restoration of the Ragusa Pietà' in *The Ragusa Pietà, history and restoration* (eds M. Bussagli, C. Mora, & L. M. G., D'Alessandro, Rome, 2014), pp. 15–19, pp. 17–18.

37. Forcellino, A., *The lost Michelangelos*, p. 18. For further discussion of the British Museum Christ on the Cross drawing and the Pietà in the Isabella Stuart Gardener Museum in Boston for Vittoria, see Vowles, 'Vittoria Colonna', pp. 89–100.

38. Dillon, A. *Michelangelo and the English Martyrs* (Farnham, 2012), pp. 117–36 and Dillon, 'Martyrdom', pp.75–9.

39. Strinati, C., 'Sebastiano del Piombo e il Rinascimento a Roma' in *Sebastiano del Piombo 1485–1547*, ed. C. Strinati, Rome 2008) pp. 15–21, p. 17.

40. Hyde, *passim*.

41. Wivel, M., 'A meeting of minds. The extraordinary artistic partnership of Michelangelo and Sebastiano', in *Michelangelo & Sebastiano* (ed. M. Wivel, London 2017), pp. 15–51, p. 24.

42. Libina, M., *Sebastiano del Piombo and the Sacred Image* (Turnhout, 2022), p. 14.

43. Letter from Soranzo to Pietro Bembo 8 June 1530, cited in Cali, 136.

44. See Peyronel Rambaldi, pp. 81–85. I am grateful to Dr. Piers Baker-Bates for his help with Sebastiano and Giulia Gonzaga and also the Hermitage portrait. My conclusions on the latter are entirely my own.

45. Hyde, p. 58.

46. See Lucco, M., 'Catalogo delle opere' in Volpe, C., & Lucco, M., *L'opera complete di Sebastiano del Piombo* (Milan, 1980), pp. 90–144, p. 133 for the history of attributions (although Lucco believes it is not by Sebastiano) and more recently Bacchi, A., 'Il rinnovamento evangelico degli "spirituali"' in *L'Eterno e il Tempo tra Michelangelo e Caravaggio* (eds A. Paolucci, A. Bacchi, D. Benati, P. Refice, & U. Tramonti, Cinisello Balsamo, 2018), pp. 196–7; Balzarotti, V., '38. Ritratto del cardinal Reginald Pole' in *L'Eterno e il Tempo tra Michelangelo e Caravaggio op. cit.*, pp. 364–5 and Agosti, B., & Balzarotti, V., 'Nuove ipotesi per la Cappella del Santissimo Sacramento nella Basilica di San Pietro in Vaticano' in *Bollettino d'Arte 30* (2016, pp. 71–84).

47. See Hyde, pp. 121–2; Balzarotti, 'Ritratto', p. 365 for the hands and the Titian portrait.

48. Hirst, *Sebastiano*, p. 120, note no. 129.

49. Ibid., p. 121.

50. Pastore, *Marcantonio Flaminio*, p. 154, citing Vasari, who knew the artist.

51. See De la Verpillière, pp. 768–70.

15 *The Death of Cardinal Pole, His Legacy and His Reputation*

1. CRP 3, no. 2282, p. 556.

2. TNA, 31/9/5, fo. 243r. See also CRP 3, no. 2315, pp. 588–90.

3. Ibid.

4. Ibid. 243v–4r: 'come in tutta la vita sua di nessuna cosa haveva ricevuto maggiore piacere e content che di considerare … la providenza di Dio … e che in tutto il progresso della vita della Regina e della sua havendo veduto una gran conformità, essendo stato cosi lei come per lui la medesima causa per tanti anni travagliati, e di poi piacque a Dio, che la regina fosse assunta al Regno'. '… congiuntione del sangue gran conformita d'animo'.

5. Mayer, 'Pole, Reginald' in *O.D.N.B.*; TNA SP 11/24, 1r.

6. TNA, SP 11/14, 1r: 'meum intimum amicum et familiarem cuius summam in deum pietate et singularem erga me fidem et amorem viginti cinque … annis'; TNA, SP 12/1, 10r.

7. Duffy, *Fires*, p. 192.

8. Duffy, *Saints*, p. 208.

9. CRP 1, no. 77, pp. 81–2.

10. Parks, 'Italian Tributes', pp. 43–55, 44, citing Beccadellli.

11. Hutchings, p. 5.

12. Parks, 'Italian Tributes', p. 46.

13. Cross, The Puritan Earl, p. 16, citing CSP Spain 1554–8.

14. Cipriani, p. 61: 'un santo, di ottimo giuditio nello [*sic*] cose del mondo, di dottrina grandissima'.

15. *Pasquinate*, p. 172: 'Qui giace il cardinal d'Inghilterra/dotto, da ben, catolico e divino/ e chi li volse ben fui io, Pasquino/cosa nova e non mai veduta in terra.'

16. Ross Williamson, p. 92; Fenlon, *Heresy*, p. 116.

17. Fenlon, *Heresy and Obedience*, p. 283.

18. Edwards, *Archbishop*, p. 269.

19. Ibid., p. 111.

20. Parks, 'Italian Tributes', p. 60.

21. Overell, 'Pole's Piety', p. 459; Fenlon, 'Pietro Carnesecchi and Cardinal Pole', p. 530.

22. *Original Letters*, II, p. 68.

23. Russell, p. 149, note no. 72.

24. Parks, 'Italian Tributes', pp. 61–2.

25. Mayer, *Prince and Prophet*, p. 347.

26. Beccadelli, pp. 172–3.

27. Dillon, 'Martyrdom', p. 66.

28. Edwards, *Archbishop*, p. 258.

29. Parker, M., *De Antiquitate Britannicae Ecclesiae*, np 1572, fos 345, 6, 8, 350, 1, 3.

30. Ibid., fo. 357.

31. Mayer, *Prince and Prophet*, pp. 443–7.

32. Ibid., p. 445.

33. Edwards, *Archbishop*, p. 267.

34. Ibid.

35. Duffy, E., 'Hampton Court, Henry VIII and Cardinal Pole' in *Henry VIII and the Court: art, politics and performance* (eds T. Betteridge, & S. Lipscomb, Farnham 2013), pp. 197–214, p. 208.

36. Fenlon, *Heresy and Obedience*, p. 284.

CHRONOLOGY

1486		Henry VII and Elizabeth of York marry
		Birth of Prince Arthur
	(2 Jul.)	Thomas Cranmer is born
1491		Birth of Henry VIII
1499		Proxy marriage of Prince Arthur and Katharine of Aragon
		Warwick is executed
1500	(Mar.)	Birth of Reginald Pole
1501		Prince Arthur and Katharine of Aragon are married
1502		Death of Prince Arthur and Henry becomes heir to the throne
1504		Death of Richard Pole
1509	(21 Apr.)	Death of Henry VII. His son ascends the throne as Henry VIII the following day
1512		Margaret Pole is created Countess of Salisbury
1514		Henry Pole becomes Lord Montagu
1516		Mary Tudor, later Mary I, is born

1521	Reginald Pole leaves England for Padua
	Duke of Buckingham is executed
1522	First recorded appearance of Anne Boleyn at court
1525	Reginald briefly visits Rome
1526	Reginald leaves Italy and returns to England
1527	Sack of Rome by Imperial troops
1529	Reginald goes to Paris. The Treaty of Barcelona is signed
1530	Reginald returns from Paris
1531	Reginald sends his first (lost) book to Henry
1532	Reginald leaves England
	Act in Conditional Restraint of Annates
	Submission of the clergy
1533	Thomas Cranmer is consecrated Archbishop of Canterbury
	Marriage of Henry and Katharine is annulled and the marriage of Henry and Anne Boleyn declared valid
	Birth of Elizabeth Tudor (later Elizabeth I)
1534	Act of Succession and oath to be taken
	John Fisher and Thomas More are sent to the Tower
	Act of Supremacy and Act of High Treason
	Death of Clement VII and election of Paul III as Pope
1534–5	Reginald is in Venice and meets other reformers
1535	Juan de Valdés arrives in Naples
	Thomas Starkey writes to Reginald to solicit his views on the divorce and the supreme headship
	Reginald replies to Starkey saying he would make the king happy
1536	John Fisher and Thomas More are executed
	Dissolution of the monasteries begins
(7 Jan.)	Death of Katharine of Aragon
(19 May)	Execution of Anne Boleyn

	(30 May)	Marriage of Henry and Jane Seymour
	(May)	Michael Throckmorton takes *De Unitate* to England
		Act Extinguishing the Authority of the Bishop of Rome
	(22 Jun.)	Mary Tudor takes the oath
	(19 Jul.)	Reginald is summoned to Rome by the Pope
	(Oct.)	Pilgrimage of Grace begins
	(Nov.)	Reginald arrives in Rome
		Consilium delectorum to review reform within the Church
	(22 Dec.)	Pole is made a cardinal
1537		Cardinal Pole is chosen to help reform the Datary
	(18 Feb.)	Pole leaves on his first legation
	(12 Oct.)	Birth of Prince Edward
	(19 Oct.)	Pole renounces his legation in consistory
1538	(Jan.)	Pole is chosen to help prepare for a General Council
		Pole and other cardinals accompany the Pope to Nice
	(29 Aug.)	Geoffrey Pole is arrested
	(26 Oct.)	Geoffrey Pole starts to talk
	(Nov.)	Members of the 'Exeter Conspiracy' are arrested
	(9 Dec.)	Montagu, Exeter and Neville are executed
	(17 Dec.)	Paul III finally promulgated excommunication of Henry VIII
	(27 Dec.)	Pole leaves on his second legation
1539		Fortification programme in England
		Margaret Pole is questioned
	(Jan.)	Treaty of Toledo
	(Feb.)	Pole arrives in Toledo
	(May)	Attainder against Pole, Margaret and members of the conspiracy
1540		Pole is in Rome and has a papal bodyguard

1541	(29 May)	Margaret Pole is executed
	(Aug.)	Pole is appointed to the Patrimony of St. Peter
	(Oct.)	Flaminio arrives in Viterbo
1542	(Aug.)	Death of Cardinal Contarini
		Vermigli and Occhino flee Italy
1543		Publication of the *Beneficio di Cristo*
		Act for the Advancement of True Religion, and for the Abolishment of the Contrary
		King's Book
1545		Dall'Armi appears in Italy
		Vittoria Colonna sends a *Pietà* by Michelangelo to Pole
	(Apr.)	Pole leaves for Trent
	(Dec.)	The Council of Trent assembles
1546	(7 Jan.)	Pole's opening address to the Council is read by Massarelli
		Pole is ill
	(21 Jun.)	Pole's last speech to the Council
	(28 Jun.)	Pole leaves Trent
		Pietro Carnesecchi is summoned by the Inquisition to Rome
1547		Dall'Armi dies
	(Jan.)	Pole is appointed governor of Bagnoregio
	(28 Jan.)	Death of Henry VIII. He is succeeded by his nine-year-old son, Edward VI
1549		Death of Paul III
		Prayer Book Rebellion
	(Nov.)	Conclave to elect a new Pope begins
	(Dec.)	Carafa attacks Pole in the conclave for his 'heresy'
1550		Death of Marc'antonio Flaminio
	(8 Feb.)	The conclave ends with the election of Julius III as Pope
	(Nov.)	The *valcheria* is set up in Bagnoregio

1551		Pole is active in other commissions
1551/52		Pole lends money to Bagnoregio
1552		Second Book of Common Prayer
1553		The Forty-two Articles
	(May)	Pole moves to the quiet of Maguzzano
	(6 Jul.)	Edward VI dies
	(Aug.)	Dudley is executed
	(1 Oct.)	Coronation of Mary I
	(17 Nov.)	Parliament challenges Mary on her choice of husband
1554	(14 Jan.)	Marriage treaty signed
		Wyatt's Rebellion
	(25 Jul.)	Mary and Philip of Spain marry
	(3 Nov.)	Council agrees to let Cardinal Pole enter the country
	(24 Nov.)	Pole arrives in London
	(30 Nov.)	England is reconciled to Rome
1555	(16 Jan.)	See of Rome Act (Second Statute of Repeal) receives royal assent
	(23 Mar.)	Death of Julius III
	(Feb.)	Burning of Protestants begins in England
	(1 May)	Marcellus II dies
		Peace conference
	(23 May)	Gian Pietro Carafa become Pope as Paul IV
	(summer)	Philip I leaves England
	(12 Sep.)	The trial of Thomas Cranmer opens
	(Dec.)	Pole is made a cardinal priest
1556	(5 Feb.)	Treaty of Vaucelles between Charles V and Henri II
	(8 Feb.)	Publication of decrees from Synod
	(21 Mar.)	Cranmer is burnt
	(22 Mar.)	Pole becomes Archbishop of Canterbury
	(Sep.)	War between Philip and the papacy

1557		Charges are drawn up in Rome accusing Pole of heresy
		Pole sends a gift of 100 ducats to Bagnoregio
	(**Mar.**)	Philip I returns to England
	(**Apr.**)	Stafford conspiracy
	(**Apr.**)	Pole's legations revoked
	(**May**)	Cardinal Morone is arrested
	(**7 Jun.**)	England declares war on France
	(**14 Jun.**)	William Peto is made cardinal and papal legate to England
	(**Sep.**)	Paul IV surrenders
1558		Calais is lost
	(**17 Nov.**)	Cardinal Pole and Mary I die
	(**15 Dec.**)	Cardinal Pole is buried in Canterbury Cathedral

BIBLIOGRAPHY

Archival Sources

AAV, Arch Concist Acta Vice Canc. 5

AAV, Arch Concist Acta Camerarii 3

AAV, Segr Stato, Inghilterra 3

AAV, Arch. Consist. 10

TNA, SP 1/105

TNA, SP 1/138

TNA, SP 1/139

TNA, SP 11/14

TNA, SP 12/1

TNA, 31/9/5

Published and Online Primary Sources

Archdeacon Harpsfield's Visitation, 1557 (two volumes, ed. Rev. L. E. Whatmore (London, 1950)

Beccadelli, L., *The Life of Cardinal Reginald Pole, written originally in Italian by Lodovico Beccatelli, Archbishop of Ragusa* (trans. & ed. B. Pye, London, 1766)

Chronicle of King Henry VIII, of England: Being a Contemporary Record of Some of the Principal Events of the Reigns of Henry VIII, and Edward VI (trans. & ed. M. A. S. Hume, London, 1889)

Condivi, A., *The Life of Michelangelo* (trans. Alice Sedgewick Wohl, Oxford, 1976)

Correspondance Politique de MM. de Castillon et de Marillac Ambassadeurs de France en Angleterre (1537–1542) (ed. J. Kaulek, Paris, 1885)

Ellis, H. (ed.), *Hall's Chronicle* (London, 1809)

Ferrero, E. and Muller, G. (eds), *Vittoria Colonna Marchesa di Pescara, Carteggio*, second edition (Turin, 1892)

Flaminio, M. A., *Lettere* (ed. A. Pastore, Rome, 1978)

Foxe, J., *Foxe's Book of Martyrs* (e-book, from the 1848 edition)

Henry VIII: July 1536, 21–25, in *Letters and Papers, Foreign and Domestic, Henry VIII, Volume 11, July-December 1536*, ed. James Gairdner (London, 1888), *British History Online* https://www.british-history.ac.uk/letters-papers-hen8/vol11/pp54–73 [accessed 21 October 2024].

Lampsonius, D., *The Life of Lambert Lombard (1565) and Effigies of Several Famous Painters from the Low Countries (1572)* (ed. & trans. E. H. Wouk, Los Angeles, 2021)

Original Letters, Illustrative of English History; including numerous royal letters: from autographs in the British Museum and one or two other collections Volume II (ed. H. Ellis, second series, London, 1827)

Pagano, S. and Ranieri, C., *Nuovi Documenti su Vittoria Colonna e Reginald Pole.* (*Collectanea Archivi Vaticani*, 24, Vatican City 1989)

Parker, M., *De Antiquitate Britanniae Ecclesiae* (n.p., 1572)

Pasquinate del Cinque e Seicento (ed. V. Marucci, Rome 1988)

Pole, R., *Causes of Christian Disunion, Cardinal Pole's Legatine Address at the opening of the Council of Trent, 7 January 1546* (ed. & trans. V. McNabb O. P., London, 1936)

Pole, R., *De Concilio liber Reginaldis Polis cardinalis* (Rome, 1562)

Pole, R., *Pole's Defense of the Unity of the Church* (trans. and with introduction by J. G. Dwyer, Westminster, Maryland, 1965)

Pole, R., *The Reform of England by the Decrees of Cardinal Pole, Legate of the Apostolic See promulgated in the year of Grace 1556* (trans. & ed. H. Raikes, Chester, 1830)

Priscianese, F., *Del governo della corte d'un signore in Rome* (second edition, Città di Castello, 1883)

Report to the Master of the Rolls on Documents in the Archives of Venice (London, 1866), pp. 50–69, *British History Online http://www.british-history.ac.uk/no.series/master-of-rolls-report*, pp. 50–69, accessed 28 February 2024

Sanuto, M., *I diarii di Marin Sanuto* (fifty-nine volumes, Venice, 1879–1903)

Tellechea Idigoras, J. I., *La Legación del Cardenal R. Pole (1553–54), Cuando Inglaterra volvio a ser catolica* (Salamanca, 2002)

The Correspondence of Reginald Pole: A Calendar (three volumes, ed. T. F. Mayer, Aldershot, 2000–4)

'Translations of some letters relating to Cardinal Pole' in *Report to the Master of the Rolls on Documents in the Archives of Venice* (London, 1866), pp. 50–69, *British History Online http://www.british-history.ac.uk/no.series/master-of-rolls-report*, pp. 50–69, accessed 28 February 2024.

Vittoria Colonna, Marchesa di Pescara. Carteggio (eds E. Ferrero and G. Muller, second edition, Turin, 1882)

Vittoria Colonna. Selected Letters, 1523–45. A bilingual edition (eds A. Brundin and V. Copello, New York-Toronto, 2022)

Writings of the Rev. Dr. Thomas Cranmer Archbishop of Canterbury and Martyr 1556 (Philadelphia, 1842)

Published Secondary Sources

Agosti, B., & Balzarotti, V., 'Nuove ipotesi per la Cappella del Santissimo Sacramento nella Basilica di San Pietro in Vaticano' in *Bollettino d'Arte 30* (2016, pp. 71–84)

Amin, N., *Henry VII and the Tudor Pretenders, Simnel, Warbeck and Warwick* (Stroud, 2020)

Antony, C. M., *The Angelical Cardinal: Reginald Pole* (London, 1909)

Bacchi, A., 'Il rinnovamento evangelico degli "spirituali"' in *L'Eterno e il Tempo tra Michelangelo e Caravaggio* (eds A. Paolucci, A. Bacchi, D. Benati, P. Refice & U. Tramonti, Cinisello Balsamo, 2018), pp. 196–7

Bacciolo, A., "Belonging of right to our English nation', The Oratory of Domine Quo Vadis, Reginald Pole and the English Hospice in Rome' in *RIHA 238* (March 2020)

Balzarotti, V., '38. Ritratto del cardinal Reginald Pole' in *L'Eterno e il Tempo tra Michelangelo e Caravaggio tra Michelangelo e Caravaggio* (eds A. Paolucci, A. Bacchi, D. Benati, P. Refice & U. Tramonti, Cinisello Balsamo, 2018), pp. 364–5

Barrington, R., 'Two Houses both alike in dignity: Reginald Pole and Edmund Harvell' in *The Historical Journal Vol. 39* (1996), pp. 895–913

Bennett Connolly, S., *Heroines of the Tudor World* (Stroud, 2024)

Bernard, G. W., *Anne Boleyn, Fatal Attractions* (Yale and London, 2010)

Borman, T., *Henry VIII and the Men Who Made Him* (London, 2019)

Brigden, S., 'Bryan, Sir Francis [called Vicar of Hell]' in *O.D.N.B.*

Brigden, S., 'The Early Life of Reginald Pole' in *Reformation Cardinal, Reginald Pole in Sixteenth Century Italy and England* (ed. J. Willoughby, Oxford, 2023)

Brigden, S., *Thomas Wyatt, The Heart's Forest* (London, 2012)

Brundin, A., 'A "more than maternal love": Pole and Vittoria Colonna' in *Reformation Cardinal, Reginald Pole in Sixteenth-Century Italy and England* (ed. J. Willoughby, Oxford, 2023)

Calí, M., *Da Michelangelo all'Escorial* (Turin, 1980)

Chambers, D. S., *A Renaissance cardinal and his worldly goods: the will and inventory of Francesco Gonzaga (1444–1483)* (London, 1992)

Chambers, D. S, 'The economic predicament of Renaissance cardinals' in *Studies in medieval and Renaissance history* (ed. W. M. Bowsky, Lincoln, Nebraska, 1966 pp. 289–313)

Chapman, H., *Michelangelo drawings: closer to the master* (London, 2005)

Clifford, H., *The Life of Jane Dormer, Duchess of Feria* (London, 1887)

Cipriani, G., *Reginald Pole, Cardinale governatore di Bagnoregio dal 1547al 1558, Biografia essenziale e ricostruzione dell'azione di governo a Bagnoregio* (Grotte di Castro, 2020)

Cross, C., 'Hastings, Francis, second earl of Huntingdon (1513/14–1560)' in *O.D.N.B.*

Cross, C., *The Puritan Earl, the life of Henry Hastings Third Earl of Huntingdon* (London, 1966)

Cunningham, S., *Prince Arthur, The Tudor King Who Never Was* (Stroud, 2016)

Dall'Olio, G., 'Gonzaga, Giulia' in *D.B.I.*

D'Amico, J. F., *Renaissance Humanism in Rome* (Baltimore-London, 1983)

Davies, C. S. L., 'Stafford, Edward, third Duke of Buckingham (1478–1521)' in *O.D.N.B.*

Dehaene, G., *Lambert Lombard, Renaissance et Humanisme a Liege* (Antwerp, 1990)

De la Verpillière, L., 'God is in the details': visual culture of closeness in the circle of Cardinal Reginald Pole' in *Renaissance Studies Vol. 30* (2016) pp. 752–72

Dillon, A., 'Martyrdom and Michelangelo' in *Reformation Cardinal, Reginald Pole in Sixteenth-Century Italy and England* (ed. J. Willoughby, Oxford, 2023)

Dillon, A., *Michelangelo and the English Martyrs* (Farnham, 2012)

Dodds, M. H. & Dodds, R., *The Pilgrimage of Grace 1536–7 and the Exeter Conspiracy 1538* (2 vols, London, 1971)

Duffy, E., *Fires of Faith, CatholicEngland under Mary Tudor* (New Haven and London, 2009)

Duffy, E., 'Hampton Court, Henry VIII and Cardinal Pole' in *Henry VIII and the Court: art, politics and performance* (eds T. Betteridge & S. Lipscomb, Farnham 2013), pp. 197–214

Duffy, E., *Reformation Divided, Catholics, Protestants and the Conversion of England* (London, 2017)

Duffy, E., *Saints, Sacrilege and Sedition, Religion and Conflict in the Tudor Reformations* (London, 2012)

Edwards. J., *Archbishop Pole* (Abingdon, 2021)

Edwards, J., *Mary I, England's Catholic Queen* (New Haven and London, 2011)

Emmerson, O., & McCaffrey, K., *Becoming Anne, Connections, Culture, Court* (Norwich, 2022)

Eubel, C., & Van Gulik, G. (eds), *Hierarchia catholica medii et recentioris aevi sive summorum Pontificum, SRE cardinalium, ecclesiarum antistitum series* (second edition, Munster 1913–200.

Fenlon, D., *Heresy and Obedience in Tridentine Italy, Cardinal Pole and the Counter Reformation* (Cambridge, 1972)

Fenlon, D., 'Pietro Carnesecchi and Cardinal Pole: New Perspectives' in *Journal of Ecclesiastical History Volume 56, no. 3* (July, 2005) pp. 529–533

Firpo, M., *Juan de Valdés e la Riforma nell'Italia del Cinquecento* (Rome, 2017)

Fletcher, C., *The Divorce of Henry VIII, The Untold Story* (London, 2013)

Forcellino, A., *L'ultimo Michelangelo, dal Giudizio Universale alla Cappella Paolina* (Citta di Castello, 2024)

Forcellino, A., *The Lost Michelangelos* (trans. L. Byatt, Cambridge, 2011)

Forcellino, M., *Michelangelo, Vittoria Colonna e gli "spirituali", Religiosità e vita artistica Roma, negli anni Quaranta* (Rome, 2009)

Forcellino, M., 'Un nuovo disegno copia della Pietà di Michelangelo per Vittoria Colona e Reginald Pole' in *Arte Lombarda new series 1–2* (2017), pp.49–57

Forcellino, M., 'The Pietà by Michelangelo, for Vittoria Colonna: sources, documentation and art-historical literature' in *The Ragusa*

Pietà, history and restoration (eds M. Bussagli, C. Mora, & L. M. G. D'Alessandro, Rome, 2014), pp. 87–97

Fowler, T., *The History of Corpus Christi College with its list of members* (Oxford, 1893)

Freeman, T. F., 'Burning Zeal: Mary Tudor and the Marian Persecution' in *Mary Tudor, Old and New Perspectives* (eds S. Doran & T. S. Freeman, Basingstoke 2011) pp.171–205

Garcés Avalos, G., 'Un soneto de Vittoria Colonna a Reginald Pole (1546), Traducion y comentario' in *Lemir, Revista de Literatura Espanola medioeval y del rinacimento, Volume* 20 (2016, pp. 547–60)

Gasquet, F. A. Cardinal, *Cardinal Pole and His Early Friends* (London, 1927)

Gasquet, F. A. Cardinal, *Henry VIII and the English Monasteries* (two volumes, third edition, London, 1888)

Gee, J. A., *The Life and Works of Thomas Lupset with a critical text of the Original Treatises and the Letters* (London, 1928)

Guy, J., *The Children of Henry VIII* (Oxford, 2013)

Guy, J., *Thomas More, A very brief history* (London, 2017)

Guy, J., & Foxe, J., *Hunting the Falcon, Henry VIII, Anne Boleyn and the Marriage that shook Europe* (London, 2023)

Gwyn, P., *The King's Cardinal, The Rise and Fall of Thomas Wolsey* (London, 1990)

Haile, M., *The Life of Reginald Pole* (second edition, London, 1911)

Harris, B. J., *Edward Stafford Third Duke of Buckingham* 1478–1521 (Stanford, 1986)

Harrison, E., 'Henry the Eighth's Gangster: the affair of Ludovico da l'Armi' in *Journal of Modern History Volume* 15 (1943) pp. 265–74

Helbig, J., *Lambert Lombard, Peintre et Architecte* (Brussels, 1893)

Higginbotham, S., *Margaret Pole, The Countess in the Tower* (Stroud, 2016)

Hirst, M., *Michelangelo and his drawings* (London, 1988)

Hollingsworth, M., *The cardinal's hat: money, ambition and housekeeping in a Renaissance court* (London, 2004)

Hughes, P., *Rome and the Counter-Reformation in England* (Birmingham, 1941)

Hutchings, M., *Reginald Cardinal Pole 1500–1558, the last Archbishop of Canterbury* (Chippenham, 2008)

Hutchings, M., 'The Reign of Mary Tudor – A Reassessment' in *History Today Issue 33, March 1999*, accessed online 3 March 2024.

Hutchinson, R., *Henry VIII, The Decline and Fall of a Tyrant* (London, 2019)

Hutchinson, R., *Young Henry, The Rise of Henry VIII* (London, 2012)

Hyde, H., *Cardinal Bendinello Sauli and Church Patronage in Sixteenth Century Italy* (Woodbridge, 2009)

Ives, E., *The Life and Death of Anne Boleyn* (first edition, Oxford, 2004)

Jerrold, M. F., *Vittoria Colonna with some account of her friends and her times* (New York, 1906)

Kamen, H., *Philip of Spain* (New Haven & London, 1997)

Kelsey, H., *Philip of Spain, King of England, The Forgotten Sovereign* (London, 2012)

Langley, P., *The Princes in the Tower, Solving History's Greatest Cold Case* (Cheltenham, 2023)

Libina, M., *Sebastiano del Piombo and the Sacred Image* (Turnhout, 2022)

Lipscomb, S., *1536, The Year That Changed Henry VIII* (Oxford, 2009)

Loach, J., 'Mary Tudor and the Re-Catholicisation of England' in *History Today Volume 44* (1994) and accessed online 3 March 2024.

Loades, D., *Henry VIII* (Stroud, 2013)

Loades, D., *The Oxford Martyrs* (London, 1970)

Loades, D., *The Reign of Mary Tudor, Politics, Government and religion in England 1553–58* (second edition, London, 1991)

Loughlin, S., *Insurrection, Henry VIII, Thomas Cromwell and the Pilgrimage of Grace* (Stroud, 2016)

Lucco, M., 'Catalogo delle opere' in Volpe, C., & Lucco, M., *L'opera complete di Sebastiano del Piombo* (Milan, 1980), pp. 90–144

MacCulloch, D., *Thomas Cranmer* (London, 1996)

MacCulloch, D., *Thomas Cromwell, A Life* (London, 2019)

MacCulloch, D., *Tudor Church Militant, Edward IV and the Protestant Reformation* (London, 1999)

Maddison, C., *Marcantonio Flaminio, Poet, Humanist and Reformer* (London, 1965)

Mangano, S., 'Mantenere l'Inghilterra nella Respublica Christiana, Il cardinal legato Reginald Pole e il suo messaggio ai sovrani d'Europa (1537–9)', in *Eurostudium* 2016, pp. 3–60

Marshall, P., *Heretics and Believers, A History of the English Reformation* (New Haven and London, 2017)

Mayer, T. F., 'A Fate Worse than Death, Reginald Pole and the Paris Theologians' in *English Historical Review Vol. 103* (1988, pp. 870–91)

Mayer, T. F., 'Lily, George' in *O.D.N.B.*

Mayer, T. F., 'Lupset, Thomas (*c.* 1495–1530)' in *O.D.N.B.*

Mayer, T. F., 'Pole, Reginald (1500–1558)' in *O.D.N.B.*

Mayer, T. F., 'Reginald Pole in Paolo Giovio's *Descriptio*: a strategy for reconversion' in *Cardinal Pole in European Context* (ed. T. F. Mayer, Aldershot 2000), pp. 431–450

Mayer, T. F., *Reginald Pole, Prince & Prophet* (Cambridge, 2000)

Mayer, T. F., 'Starkey, Thomas (c. 1498–1538), humanist & royal servant' in *O.D.N.B.*

Mayer, T. F., 'The Success of Cardinal Pole's Final Legation' in *The Church of Mary Tudor* (eds E. Duffy & D. Loades, Aldershot 2006)

Mayer, T. F., 'The War of the Two Saints, the Conclave of Julius III and Cardinal Pole' in *Cardinal Pole in European Context* (ed. T. F. Mayer, Aldershot, 2000) IV, pp. 2–21

Mayer, T. F., 'When Maecenas was broke: Cardinal Pole's 'spiritual patronage' in *Cardinal Pole in European Context* (ed. T. F. Mayer, Aldershot, 2000), XIV pp. 419–435

Mayer, T. F. & Starenko, P. E., 'An unknown diary of Julius III's conclave by Bartolomeo Stella, a servant of Cardinal Pole' in *Cardinal Pole in European Context* (ed. T. F. Mayer, Aldershot, 2000) pp. 345–75

McClung Hallman, B., *Italian cardinals, reform and the Church as property* (London, 1985)

McNair, P., *Peter Martyr in Italy, An Anatomy of Apostasy* (Oxford, 1967)

Mercalli, M. & Mora, C., 'Methodological considerations in the restoration of the Ragusa Pietà' in *The Ragusa Pietà, history and restoration* (eds M. Bussagli, C. Mora, & L. M. G. D'Alessandro, Rome, 2014), pp. 15–19

Merriman, R. B., *Life and Letters of Thomas Cromwell* (two volumes, Oxford, 1902)

Murphy, B. A., *Bastard Prince, Henry VIII's lost son* (Stroud, 2001)

Murphy, J., 'Cardinal Reginald Pole: Questions of Self-Justification and of Faith' in *Royal Studies Journal Vol. 4* (2017), pp. 177–195.

Nagel, A., *Michelangelo and the Reform of Art* (Cambridge, 2000)

Ogier, D. M., 'Mewtas [Mewtis], Sir Peter (d.1562) soldier & courtier', in *O.D.N.B.*

Olin, J. C., *Catholic Reform from Cardinal Ximenes to the Council of Trent 1495–1563* (New York, 1990)

Olin, J. C., *The Catholic Reformation, Savonarola to Ignatius Loyola* (New York, 1992)

Overell, M. A., 'An English Friendship and Italian Reform, Richard Morison and Michael Throckmorton, 1532–1538' in *Journal of Ecclesiastical History Vol. 57* (2006, pp, 478–493)

Overell, M. A., 'Pole and the Spirituali' in *Reformation Cardinal, Reginald Pole in Sixteenth-Century Italy and England* (ed. J. Willoughby, Oxford, 2023)

Parker, G., *Imprudent King, A New Life of Philip II* (New Haven, 2014)

Parks, G. B., 'Did Pole write the 'Vita Longolii'?' in *Renaissance Quarterly Vol. 26* (1973, pp.274–85)

Parks, G. B., 'Italian Tributes to Cardinal Pole' in *Studies in the Continental Background of Renaissance English Literature: Essays presented to John L. Lievsay* (eds D. B. J. Randall & G. W. Williams, Durham N.C., 1977), pp. 43–55

Parks, G. B., *The English Traveller to Italy* (two volumes, Rome, 1954)

Parks, G. B., 'The Parma Letters and the Dangers to Cardinal Pole' in *The Catholic Historical Review Vol.* 46 (1960), pp. 299–317

Pastor, L. F. von., *The History of the Popes, From the Close of the Middle Ages* (ed. R. F. Kerr, volumes XI–XIII, London, 1912–51)

Pastore, A., *Marcantonio Flamino Fortune e sfortune di un chierico nell'Italia del Cinquecento* (Milan, 1981)

Paul, J., *Catherine of Aragon and her Friends* (New York, 1966)

Pennington, A., https://adammu.podbean.com/e/ursula-pole-baroness-stafford-the-forgotten-plantagenet-daughter/

Peyronel Rambaldi, S., *Giulia Gonzaga tra reti familiari e relazioni eterodosse* (Rome, 2012)

Pierce, H., *Margaret Pole, Countess of Salisbury, 1473–1541, Loyalty, Lineage and Leadership* (Cardiff, 2003)

Pierce, H. 'Pole, Margaret, suo jure countess of Salisbury', in *O.D.N.B.* online

Pogson, R. H., 'The Legacy of the Schism, Confusion, Continuity and Change in the Marian Clergy' in *The Mid-Tudor Polity c. 1540–60* (eds, J. Loach & R. Tittler, London, 1980)

Porter, L., *Mary Tudor, The First Queen* (London, 2009)

Prosperi, A., *Tra Evangelismo e Controriforma. G.M. Giberti (1495–1543)* (Rome, 1969)

Rex, R., *Henry VIII* (Stroud, 2009)

Richards, J., *Mary Tudor* (Abingdon, 2008)

Ridley, J., *Bloody Mary's Martyrs* (London, 2001)

Ridley, J., *Thomas Cranmer* (Oxford, 1962)

Ross Williamson, H., 'Cardinal Pole in Italy' in *History Today Vol.* 20 (1970, pp. 20–27)

Routledge, F. J., 'Six letters of Cardinal Pole to the Countess of Huntingdon' in *The English Historical Review (Volume 28)*, July 1913, pp. 527–531

Russell, C., *Giulia Gonzaga and the religious controversies of sixteenth century Italy* (Turnhout, 2006)

Russell, G., *The Palace, From the Tudors to the Windsors. 500 years of History at Hampton Court* (London, 2023)

Ryrie, A., *The English Reformation, A Very Brief History* (London, 2020)

Sansom, A., *Mary and Philip, The Marriage of Tudor England and Habsburg Spain* (Manchester 2020)

Scarisbrick, J., *Henry VIII* (London, 1988)

Scarisbrick, J., 'Henry VIII, Stinking Sadist' in *Catholic Herald* (4 February 2016)

Scarisbrick, J., 'The Plot to Depose Henry VIII' in *Catholic Herald (20 December 2018)*

Schenk, W., *Reginald Pole, Cardinal of England* (London, 1950)

Simar, Th., *Christophe de Longueil, humaniste (1488–1522)* (Paris, 1911)

Simoncelli, P., *Il caso Reginald Pole, Eresia e Santità nelle Polemiche Religiose del Cinquecento* (Rome, 1977)

Skidmore, C., *Edward VI, The Lost King of England* (London, 2007)

Smith, F. E., 'From Royal Servant to Arch Traitor, Pole, Henry VIII and "De Unitate"' in *Reformation Cardinal, Reginald Pole in Sixteenth-Century Italy and England* (ed. J. Willoughby, Oxford, 2023)

Smith, F. E., *Transnational Catholicism in Tudor England, Mobility, Exile and Counter-Reformation, 1530–1580* (Oxford, 2022)

Soberton, S. B., *Rival Sisters, Mary and Elizabeth Tudor* (Published by author, 2019)

Soberton, S. B., *The Forgotten Tudor Women: Gertrude Courtenay: Wife and Mother of the Last Plantagenets* (Published by author, 2021)

Sowerby, T., *Renaissance and Reform in Tudor England, The Careers of Sir Richard Morison* (Oxford, 2010)

Starkey, D., *Henry, Virtuous Prince* (London, 2008)

Starkey, D., *Six Wives, The Queens of Henry VIII* (London, 2003)

Starkey, D., *The Reign of Henry VIII, Personalities and Politics* (second edition, London, 2002)

Stoyle, M., *A Murderous Midsummer, The Western Rising of 1549* (New Haven and London, 2022)

Strinati, C., 'Sebastiano del Piombo e il Rinascimento a Roma' in *Sebastiano del Piombo 1485–1547* (ed. C. Strinati, Rome, 2008)

Targoff, R., 'Late Love: Vittoria Colonna and Reginald Pole' in *Vittoria Colonna, Poetry, Religion, Art, Impact* (eds V. Cox & S. McHugh, Amsterdam, 2021), pp. 55–72

Targoff, R., *Renaissance Woman, The Life of Vittoria Colonna* (New York, 2018)

The Genius of Venice, exhibition catalogue (eds Martineau, J. & Hope, C., London, 1983)

Titler, R., *The Reign of Mary I* (London, 1983)

Velasco Berenguer, G., *Habsburg England, Politics and Religion in the Reign of Philip I (1554–8)* (Leiden, 2022)

Vermeir, R & De Meulenaere, V, '"To bring good agreement and concord to Christendom", The Conference of Marck (1555) and English neutrality, 1553–1557' in *Revue du Nord (2013/1 no. 400–1)*, pp. 681–95

Vowles, S, 'Vittoria Colonna' in *Michelangelo. The last decades* (eds Vowles, S. & Lewis, G., London 2024), pp. 77–110

Vos, A., 'The 'Vita Longolii', Additional Considerations about Reginald Pole's Authorship' in *Renaissance Quarterly Vol. 3* (1977), pp. 324–33

Wade, T., 'Reginald Pole and Humanism in Padua' in *Reformation Cardinal, Reginald Pole in Sixteenth Century Italy and England* (ed. J. Willoughby, Oxford, 2023)

Wabuda, S., *Thomas Cranmer* (Oxford and New York, 2017)

Walsh, G. G., 'Cardinal Pole and the Problem of Christian Unity' in *The Catholic Historical Review Vol. 15* (1930) pp. 389–407.

Whitelock, A., *Mary Tudor, England's First Queen* (London, 2010)

Williams, P., *Katharine of Aragon* (Stroud, 2013)

Wivel, M., 'A meeting of minds, The extraordinary artistic partnership of Michelangelo and Sebastiano' in *Michelangelo & Sebastiano* (ed. M. Wivel, London, 2017)

Woolfson, J., 'John Claymond, Pliny the Elder and the Early History of Corpus Christi College, Oxford' in *English Historical Review Vol. 112* (1997), pp. 882–903

Woolfson, J., 'Morison, Sir Richard' in *O.D.N.B.*

Woolfson, J., *Padua and the Tudors, English students in Italy 1485–1603* (London, 2020)

Wouk, E. H., 'Michelangelo, Lambert Lombard and the inalienable gift of drawing' in *Zeitschrift fur Kunstgeschichte Vol. 86* (2023), pp. 15–59

Wroe, A., *Perkin, A Story of Deception* (London, 2004)

INDEX

Aragon, Ferdinand of   17, 33–34
Aragon, Katharine of
  attitude towards divorce   37–38,
    40
  betrothal to Henry, Prince of
    Wales   18
  coronation   18
  marriage of Mary to Pole   46,
    101–103
  marriage to Henry VIII   33
  marriage to Prince Arthur   17, 38,
    52
  miscarriages and still births   20,
    33–34, 35
  Pole's opinion of her   52–53
  relations with Margaret Pole   17,
    18, 20–22, 96, 165
  tensions with Anne Boleyn   43–45
  treatment under Henry VII   17, 18
Armi, Ludovico dall'   89–90
Arthur, Prince of Wales   13,
    15–17–18, 38, 52, 95

Bagnoregio   174, 176–81, 184, 193
Bartoli, Bernardo de   80
Bembo, Cardinal Pietro   25, 28, 29,
    75, 171, 200, 209
Beaufort, Margaret   13, 14, 15, 18,
    21, 41
Beneficio di Cristo, il   78, 115
Bergavenny, Lord   20, 22, 63
Bertano, Pietro Bishop of
    Fano   201
Bianchello, Gabriele   178
Boleyn, Anne   43, 45, 47, 53, 96
  accompanies Henry to France   44
  appears at court   36
  birth   35
  courted by Henry VIII   36
  execution   53, 55
  Marchioness of Pembroke   19
  marries Henry   44
  sent to French court   36
  sent to Mechelen   36
  Pole's opinion of her   52

Boleyn, Thomas Earl of
    Wiltshire   35, 40, 126, 127
Bonner, Edmund   119
Botolph, Gregory   88, 89
Botonti, Giovanni   204
Brandon, Charles Duke of
    Suffolk   20, 38, 131
Bryan, Sir Francis   59, 60, 86
Buckingham, Duke of   16, 21
  at court   21
  claim to the throne   21
  closeness to the Poles   22
  criticism of Henry VIII   22
  indictment and execution   22
  marriage of son to Ursula
    Pole   21
  royal ward   21
Buonamico, Lazaro   30

Campeggi, Cardinal
    Alessandro   181
Campeggio, Cardinal Lorenzo   38
Carafa, Cardinal Carlo   114, 152,
    154
Carafa, Cardinal Gian Pietro (later
    pope Paul IV)   73, 82, 85, 113,
    148
  accuses Pole of heresy in
    conclave   83, 112, 211
  co-founder of Theatines   47
  draws up charges against
    Pole   115
  early relations with Pole   112
  early relations with Philip I   113,
    151
  elevation to cardinal   74
  elevation to pope   112
  hatred of Flaminio   112
  hatred of Spain   113, 151
  nominates Bernardino Scotti   152
  part of the Inquisition   181

  recalls Pole to Rome   113–4
  reconciliation with Pole   112
  religious views   47, 83, 112
  revokes Pole's legation   113
  threatens Philip I with
    excommunication   153
  view of heretics   85
  view of Pole after becoming
    pope   113
  war between papacy and
    Spain   152–3
Carew, Sir Nicholas   64
Carnesecchi, Pietro   75, 77, 78,
    82, 170, 175, 178, 204
  arrests   81, 82, 211
  execution   82
  follower of Valdés   75, 173
  joins Pole at Viterbo   77
  relations with Giulia
    Gonzaga   173, 174, 175
Carpi, Cardinal Ridolfo da
    Pio   60, 206
Carranza, Bartolomé   109, 111,
    121, 123, 136, 146, 155
Castillon, Louis de Perreau Sieur de
    Castillon   64
Castro, Alfonso de   155
Catholicism in England   109
  success of restoration   111
  survival of   116
Catholic Reform movement   30
Chapuys, Eustace   42, 46, 48, 50,
    57, 64, 102, 165, 167
Cervini, Cardinal Marcello (later
    pope Marcellus II)   77, 79, 88,
    90, 111, 179
Charles V   36, 59, 66, 99, 102,
    106, 127, 141, 143, 145, 148,
    152, 155, 209, 212
  audience with Pole in
    Toldedo   69

becomes Holy Roman
Emperor   34
betrothal to Isabella of
Portugal   35
betrothal to Princess Mary   35,
36
fails to support Pole as legate   58
meeting with Henry VIII at
Canterbury   22
meets Pole at Nice   62
obstructs Pole's return to
England   99
offers Mary protection under
Edward VI   97
Pole writes to the emperor in
1535   48
promotes Philip as husband for
Mary   101, 103, 141
Sack of Rome   37
reaction to Wyatt's rebellion   105
supports Pole in 1549
conclave   82
Treaty of Toledo   62
urged to action by Pole in *De
Unitate*   52
Church property, alienation
of   105, 106, 107, 110, 146,
147
Clement, John   26, 30, 50
Clement VII, pope   30, 31, 39, 47,
204
death   48
decisions on divorce   38, 44, 45
personality   38
Sack of Rome   37
Colonna, Vittoria   177, 204
bequest to Pole   172, 178
drawings by Michelangelo   197,
198, 206
fasting   170
follower of Valdés   75

hostility of Pole's *famiglia*   76
Pole's second mother   170, 175,
202
relations with Occhino   76, 77,
169
relations with Pole   156, 169–
172, 187
relations with
Michelangelo   199, 200
Rime Spirituali 202
sends Pole a *Pietà*   200–3
youth and marriage   169
Commendone, Gian
Francesco   103
Contarini, Cardinal Gaspare   47,
48, 51, 67, 70, 73, 75, 76, 77,
112, 122, 182, 184, 185, 206,
209, 210
Corner, Cardinal Alvise   180, 181
Courtenay, Edward   65, 67
earldom of Devon   101
imprisonment   63, 65, 67
involvement in Wyatt's
Rebellion   104
suggested as husband to
Mary I   65, 101
Cortese, Cardinal Gregorio   72,
73, 76
Courtenay, Gertrude   63, 64, 65,
101
Courtenay, Henry Marquess of
Exeter   62, 63, 64, 64, 101,
191
Cranmer, Thomas   8
acceptance of *Six Articles*   128
ambassador to Charles V   127
argues for the divorce   39, 125
arrest and imprisonment   132
attainder and writes to
Mary   132, 133, 134-5
belief in royal absolutism   129

birth 124
Book of Common Prayer 93
burnings under Edward VI 131
condemned as heretic 133
consultation of the
  universities 125
contact with German
  evangelicals 126
death 136
declares marriage of Henry and
  Katharine invalid 45
defends Anne Boleyn and
  Cromwell 129
destruction of images 130
devotion to Henry 128, 129
disputation at Oxford 133
education 124–5
excommunication and
  deprivation 137
Forty-Two Articles 93
intervention for Mary with
  Henry VIII 137
intimate with the Boleyns 126
marriages 125, 127
nomination and consecration as
  Archbishop of Canterbury 44,
  127
opinions of Pole 42, 127, 130
protests against oath to the
  papacy 127–8
recantations and refutation 135
refuses papal jurisdiction 127–
  8, 133, 134
religious changes under
  Edward VI 130
support for Lady Jane
  Grey 131–2
theologians sent to convert
  him 135
trials 132, 133
visits Rome 126

watches burning of Ridley 134
Cromwell, Thomas 20, 44, 46,
  49, 51, 56, 61, 62, 64, 65, 67,
  103, 129, 138, 139, 165, 189,
  190, 192

De emendanda ecclesia,
  council 74
De Unitate *see* Pole, Cardinal
  Reginald
Dormer, Jane 96, 97
Dudley, John Duke of
  Northumberland 97, 98, 100,
  133
Duke of Northumberland *see*
  Dudley, John

Elizabeth I 96, 101, 123, 131,
  162, 164, 186
  birth 46
  implicated in Wyatt's
    rebellion 104
  Pole's opinion of her 52
  queen of England 111, 208, 209
Edward VI, king of England 94,
  100, 118, 133, 141, 160, 161,
  162, 212, 231
  accedes to throne 90
  evangelical beliefs and acts 90,
    108, 116, 130
  his 'Devise' 131–2
English Hospice 8, 187, 196
Erasmus, Desiderius 25, 29
Exeter conspiracy 62–6, 101,
  160, 165, 191

Farnese, Cardinal Alessandro 82
Feria, Count of 121, 122
Fisher, Cardinal John 47, 48, 51,
  52, 56, 135, 210, 215
  accused of *praemunire* 41

arrested   45, 46
awarded cardinalate   50
defender of Katharine of
    Aragon   41, 46
execution   50
Fitzroy, Henry   35
Flaminio, Marc'antonio   30, 78,
    84
  death   112
  follower of Valdés   75
  friendship with Longolio   29
  joins Pole at Viterbo   76, 77
  mss of Valdés   174
  relations with Carafa   112
  relations with Giulia
      Gonzaga   173, 174
Fox, Richard   27
Foxe, Edward   40, 125, 160
Francis I, king of France   28, 36,
    44, 59, 66, 87, 88, 184
  accedes to throne   34
  fails to support Pole as
      legate   38, 60
  refuses to see Pole in 1538   69
  Treaty of Toledo   62
Friar, John   71

Gardiner, Stephen   51, 60, 121,
    125, 127, 147
George, Duke of Clarence   14, 15,
    165
Giberti, Antonio   119
Giberti, Gian Matteo   29, 31, 47,
    54, 55, 70, 72, 73, 209
Gonzaga, Cardinal Ercole   78,
    173, 201, 202, 209
Gonzaga, Giulia, Countess of
    Fondi   171, 204
  early marriage   172
  follower of Valdés   76, 173
  publication of Pole's works   175

publishes Valdés   173, 174
relations with Flaminio   174
sends mss of Valdés to
    Viterbo   173, 174
Grey, Lady Jane   98, 104, 131,
    132, 133, 162
Grimani, Cardinal Domenico   181
Harpsfield, Nicholas   84, 122
Harvel, Edmund   189
Hastings, Francis Lord
  active at court   161-2
  dines with Princess Mary   45
  eldest son   162
  ill health   161
  imprisonment   162
  Knight of the Bath   45, 161
  marries Catherine Pole   161
Henri II, king of France   99, 142,
    148, 152
Henry VII, king of England   13,
    14, 15, 17, 18, 19, 21, 22
Henry VIII, king of England   7,
    8, 13, 14, 15, 16, 22, 30, 34,
    88, 93, 95, 103, 105, 125, 128,
    131, 134, 138, 139, 140, 158,
    159, 165, 181, 187, 189, 206,
    211, 214
  Act for the Advancement of
      True Religion and for the
      Abolition of the Advancement
      of the   Contrary   91
  Act of Succession   46, 47, 53
  anticlerical measures   41, 43
  ascends throne   18
  asks for Pole's opinion on
      divorce   41, 42, 49
  approves Pole leaving
      England   24, 42
  betrothal to Katharine of
      Aragon   18
  death   90

Defender of the Faith 35
divorce from Katharine 32, 35,
    36, 37
executions of Fisher and
    More 50
excommunication 69
execution of Anne Boleyn 55
falls in love with Anne
    Boleyn 35, 36
finances Dall'Armi 89, 90
initial reaction to *De Unitate* 54
involves Wolsey in divorce 37
justification for divorce 37
King's Book 91
legal disputes with Margaret
    Pole 166
Legatine Court 58
marriage to Katharine of
    Aragon 20, 34, 100
marries Anne Boleyn 44
marries Jane Seymour 53
offers Pole archbishopric of
    York 41
opinion of Margaret Pole 167
papal dispensation 18, 38, 39
Pilgrimage of Grace 56, 57,
    101, 103, 160, 195
plots against Pole 53, 60, 69,
    86, 87, 89, 90, 195, 215
Pole's benefices 23, 42, 49, 61
praemunire against priests 41,
    54
Prince of Wales 18
relations with Cranmer 139
religious beliefs 91–2
resists innovations of
    Cranmer 91
restores Margaret Pole 18
Six Articles 66, 91
Supreme Head of Church of
    England 52

views Pole as traitor 58, 60
writes treatise defending
    papacy 34
Holland, Hugh 60, 62, 168

Inquisition 77, 78, 81, 82, 85, 93,
    98, 119, 121, 156, 170, 171, 174

Julius III, pope (previously
    Cardinal Giovanni Maria
    Ciocchi del Monte) 85, 98,
    102, 104, 105
death 111
delight at accession of Mary 98
election as pope 84
support for Pole's return to
    England 98, 99, 105

Lampson, Dominic 196, 208
Leo X, pope 29, 35
Leoni, Battista 27
Leonico, Nicoló Tomeo *see*
    Tomeo, Nicoló Leonico
Linacre, Thomas 26, 28, 29
Latimer, Hugh 133, 134, 135
Latimer, William 26, 29
Lily, George 172, 186–8, 189,
    193, 212
Lisle, Viscount 88, 89
Lombard, Lambert 194–9, *figs
    16 & 17*
Longolio, Cristoforo 28–9, 210
Longueil, Christophe de *see*
    Longolio, Cristoforo
Louis XII, king of France 19, 34
Lupset, Thomas 26, 40
    relations with Erasmus 29
    relations with Pole 28, 29
    relations with Wolsey 27
    tutor to Thomas Winter 27

Marck, Cardinal Érard de la   60,
    86, 195, 197
Marcellus II, pope   *see* Cervini,
    Cardinal Marcello
Marck, Conference of   148, 156
Marillac, Charles de   66, 68
Martyr, Peter   76, 77, 78, 93, 119
Mary I, queen of England   8, 32,
    45, 56, 98, 101, 131, 133, 134,
    137, 141, 145, 153, 154, 155,
    156, 157, 158, 160, 161, 162,
    165, 167, 180, 211, 214
  accedes to throne   98
  accepts advice of Charles V on
    marriage   103
  Act of Succession   46, 53, 54
  betrothal to Charles V   35, 36
  birth   20
  blocks Pole's return   100
  christening   20
  considers fleeing England   93, 97
  coronation   100
  death   207
  declares war on France   114
  devoted Catholic   93, 97
  final illness   207
  Guildhall speech   104
  hatred of Cranmer   133, 136
  ignores Pole's letters   99
  joins household of Elizabeth   46
  loss of Calais   114
  Margaret Pole as governess   21,
    22
  marriage to Philip   103, 141,
    142, 144, 150–1
  mediator in wars   148, 154
  opens Parliament   100
  persecution of Protestants   95,
    115-22
  possible marriage to Pole   46, 63,
    67, 101–3, 213
  pregnancies   111
  promotion of Pole as pope   149
  rejects marriage to Edward
    Courtenay   101
  refuses to allow Pole to return to
    Rome   114, 154
  refuses to allow Pole to see papal
    documents   114
  relations with Edward VI   97–8
  relations with Margaret Pole   21,
    22, 96, 165
  relaxation of terms of marriage
    contract   143, 144
  repeals religious legislation of
    Edward VI   100
  replies to Pole's letters   99–100
  responsibility for
    persecutions   118, 120–1, 154
  restores Catherine and Winifred
    Pole   162
  saying of Mass under
    Edward VI   97
  Supreme Headship of English
    Church   99
  Wyatt's Rebellion   104–5
Mason, John   26
Merenda, Apollonio   76, 82, 174
Mewtas, Sir Peter   59, 60, 86
Michelangelo
  drawings for Vittoria
    Colonna   197
  influence on Lambert
    Lombard   197–8
  Pietà for Cardinal Pole   199–
    203, *fig. 18*
  relations with Sebastiano del
    Piombo   203
  relations with the *spirituali*   200,
    203
  relations with Vittoria
    Colonna   199, 200

Montagu, Lord   *see* Pole, Henry
Monte, Cardinal Giovanni Maria
    Ciocchi del   *see* Julius III pope
More, Sir Thomas   26, 30, 50
  execution   50
  relations with Pole   50
  resignation as Chancellor   44
  sent to Tower of London   47
Morison, Richard   212
  *An invective against the great and
    detectable vice, treason*   65,
    190, 193
  career   188–9
  relations with Cromwell   189
  relations with Pole   30, 188–9
Morone, Cardinal Giovanni   76,
    79, 81, 90, 115, 122, 137, 145,
    151, 153, 171, 172, 174, 176,
    179, 181, 200
Neville, Sir Edward   62, 63, 64
Neville, Jane   20, 161
Ochino, Bernardino   76, 77, 78,
    169, 173, 174
Pace, Richard   30
Packenham, Constance   20, 28,
    29
Padua   24, 25, 26, 27, 30, 34, 46,
    50, 71, 80, 186, 188
Parker, Matthew   213
Parpaglia, Vincenzo   180, 184–6,
    193
Patronage   7, 20, 24, 26–7, 28,
    31, 51, 65, 157, 166, 181, 182,
    183, 188, 189, 190, 193, 194–
    206, 212, 214
Paul III, pope   54, 73, 112, 122,
    126, 170, 204, 205, 211
  death   82
  election   48
  elevates Pole to cardinalate   56,
    58, 64, 102

  excommunication of
    Henry VIII   64
  legation of 1537   57–8
  plots against dall'Armi   89
  promotion of Pole as new
    pope   82
  summons Pole to Rome   54
Paul IV, pope   *see* Carafa,
    Cardinal Gian Pietro
Pecorino, Girolamo   177, 178
Penning, Henry   116
Peto, William   76, 115
Philip I of England and IV of
    Spain   8, 101, 103, 104, 106,
    107, 140–57
  affection for Mary   105, 150–1
  asks for English support against
    pope   152–3
  birth   140
  early relations with
    Paul IV   151, 152
  first marriage   141
  Church Property   146–7
  King of Naples   144
  lack of enthusiasm for
    marriage   141–2, 144
  fails to support Pole's candidacy
    as pope   149
  helps reconcile England to
    Rome   145–6
  nomination of Bernardino
    Scotti   152, 155, 156
  obedience to father   141–2
  persecution of English
    Protestants   154–5
  proposed by his father as
    husband to Mary   103, 141
  reasons for marrying Mary   101,
    141
  relations with Pole   140–57
  Select Council   149–50

shows respect for Pole   147
terms of marriage contract and
    relaxation   143–5
war against papacy   113, 114,
    147, 152–3
Pickering, Jane   20, 168
Pilgrimage of Grace   56, 57, 102,
    103, 160, 195
Piombo, Sebastiano del   203–6
Pole, Arthur   19, 20, 32, 159, 168
Pole, Cardinal Reginald
  absolves England of schism   99
  adherence to canon law   115,
      117, 122
  Admonitio ad Patres   79–80
  affection for Walter Pole   163–4
  Apologia   115, 120
  apostolic protonotary   56
  appointment as Archbishop of
      Canterbury   111, 113, 119,
      120, 123, 124, 130, 136, 137,
      138, 150, 160, 196, 213
  attainder   67, 94, 106, 107, 147
  attitude to becoming pope   84–5
  avoids contention   210
  benefices received in
      England   23, 42, 49, 61
  birth   13
  cardinal deacon   56, 63, 102
  Christ on the Cross   197–9, *fig.*
      17
  Church property   105, 106, 107,
      110, 146, 147
  claim to the throne   15, 48, 54,
      62
  commission to supervise
      Inquisition   82
  conclave of 1549   82–4
  Council of Trent   73, 74, 79, 80,
      81, 85, 90, 109, 110, 183, 200,
      210, 211
  criticism of Henry   *see Pro*
      ecclesiasticae
  death and burial   207–8, *fig.* 20
  De Concilio liber Reginaldi
      Poli   79
  De iustificatione annotation   81
  Discorso di Pace   148
  doubts about his religious
      beliefs   80, 81, 112, 211
  early relations with Carafa   112
  education   23
  efforts to establish peace   99,
      100, 113, 138, 145, 146, 148–
      9, 152, 153, 154
  elevation to cardinalate   56
  English Hospice   8, 187, 196
  execution of Fisher and
      More   51, 52
  execution of Margaret Pole   68,
      168–9, 170
  favours received from
      Henry VIII   23, 25, 39, 40
  fails to support Contarini   75
  governorship of
      Bagnoregio   177–81
  graduates from Oxford   23
  gratitude to Henry   51
  hagiography   212–3
  homosexuality   214
  ill health   80, 81, 148, 179, 209
  imprisonment of Margaret
      Pole   67
  influence of his nobility   24, 25,
      99, 214
  intervenes with pope for
      Carnesecchi   82
  involvement in divorce in
      Paris   39–40
  involvement in English affairs
      under Mary   108–11, 116–23,
      145–6, 149–51

lack of enthusiasm for Spanish
    marriage 104
leaves England 1532 42, 43
leaves for Padua 1521 24
legate to England and for
    Peace 58, 97–8
legate to Patrimony of St
    Peter 75
letters to Catherine Pole 162–4
lost book on the divorce 42, 49,
    126–7
loyalty to Paul IV 115
loyalty to pope and the
    Church 51, 52, 55, 61, 72,
    80, 81, 87, 99, 105, 113, 153,
    156, 158, 210–11, 212, 215
meets Catholic Reformers 47,
    72, 73
Matthew Parker 213
meets Charles V in Toledo 69
meets Henry about
    divorce 41–2
Nice peace conference 62
objects to becoming a
    cardinal 57
opinion of Anne Boleyn 52
oratory of the English Hospice in
    Rome 196–7, *fig. 15*
personality 28, 82, 122, 175,
    209–11
papal legate 1537 58, 97–8
papal legate 1538 69
papal pension 56
patronage of household 25,
    27–8, 30, 181–9
patronage of Lambert
    Lombard 194–9
persecution of Protestants 116–
    22, 123
Pietro Bembo 25, 28, 29, 75,
    171

plan to rescue Margaret Pole 89
plots against England 48, 87–9
political naivety 52, 92, 94, 148
Portrait by Sebastiano del
    Piombo 205, *fig. 19*
possible marriage to Mary 46,
    63, 67, 101–3 213
praised in his lifetime 151,
    209–10
*Pro ecclesiasticae Unitatis
    Defensione (De
    Unitate)* 51–3, 54, 55, 56, 59,
    61, 71, 73, 83, 94, 128, 160,
    166, 167, 189, 210, 211, 212,
    213, 215
Ragusa Pietà 199–203, *fig. 18*
reaction to elevation of
    Marcellus II 112
reaction to Mary ascending
    throne 98
reconciles England to
    Rome 107
reconciliation of 1553 with
    Carafa 112–13
reform of the Vatican 73, 74,
    81
relation of king 28, 40, 124
relations with Cranmer 124–39
relations with Edward VI 92,
    94
relations with Giulia
    Gonzaga 173–5
relations with Margaret
    Pole 166–9
relations with
    Michelangelo 197, 199–200
relations with More 50, 52
relations with Paul IV 112–16,
    151–4
relations with Philip I 145–54,
    156–7

relations with Richard
    Morison   188–93
relations with Vittoria
    Colonna   156, 169–72, 187
relations with Wolsey   27
restoration of monasteries   122–3
returns from Paris   40
returns to England 1526   31
returns to England from
    exile   106–7
revocation of legations   113, 154
seminaries   110
S Maria in Cosmedin   57, 187,
    fig. 7
SS Nereo ed Achilleo   56, *fig. 8*
SS Vito e Modesto   57, *fig. 9*
Select Council   149, 155, 156
summoned to Rome by
    Paul III   54
synod of English bishops   109–
    11, 121, 147, 155
Tabula Cebetis (Tablet of
    Cebes)   196–7, 199, *fig. 14*
urges Charles V to action in *De*
    Unitate   52
viewed as a traitor   54, 59–61,
    67, 167, 192
visitation of churches   110, 119
writes to Mary without
    success   99
Venice   25, 26, 30, 43, 50, 72, 189
visit to Rome 1525   30
Pole, Catherine, Countess of
    Huntingdon   96
letters and gifts to
    Reginald   162–4
marries Francis, Lord
    Hastings   161
restored to estates   162
Pole, Geoffrey   16, 20, 45, 48, 60,
    61, 64, 66
arrest and imprisonment   62
dines with Princess Mary   45
marriage to Constance
    Packenham   20
release   64
sends messenger to Pole   60, 168
Pole, Henry Lord Montagu   17,
    18, 45, 46, 62, 64, 65, 161,
    162, 167, 168, 191
arrest after Buckingham
    conspiracy   22
arrest and execution for Exeter
    Conspiracy   62, 63, 64
birth   16
created baron   42
dines with Princess Mary   45
Field of Cloth of Gold   19
gifts from Henry VIII   18
knighthood   19
marriage to Jane Neville   20
relations with Duke of
    Buckingham   22
return to royal favour   22
royal ward   17
signs petition to pope   45
sympathy for More   50
writes to Reginald   55
Pole, Henry son of Lord
    Montague   62, 65, 67, 68–9
Pole, Margaret   14, 32, 125, 159,
    161, 162, 164
annuities to court figures   20
arrest and imprisonment   67
attainder   67
beatification   169
childhood   15
children   16
claim to the throne   15
Countess of Salisbury   18
dedicates Reginald to the
    Church   23, 166

denounces Reginald   54, 55
embroidered tunic   67, 103
execution   170
favours from Henry VIII   18, 22
legal dispute with Henry VIII   166
married to Richard Pole   15
relations with Cardinal
    Wolsey   20
relations with Katharine of
    Aragon   17, 18, 20–22, 95, 96,
    165
relations with Jane Pickering   168
relations with Mary I   20. 96
relations with Reginald   166–9
religious beliefs   23, 165–6
Pole, Richard   15–16
Pole, Ursula   16, 20, 21, 22, 67,
    114, 159–60, 161, 163
Pole, Walter   163–4
Pole, Winifred   161, 162
Prayer Book Rebellion   93, 130
*Pro ecclesiasticae Unitatis
    Defensione (De Unitate)*   *see*
    Pole, Cardinal Reginald
Priuli, Alvise   81, 171, 175, 185,
    187, 196, 200, 208, 214
Pucci, Cardinal Antonio   177
Ragland, Jerome   63
Ragusa Pietà   10, 200–03, *fig. 18*
Reformation Parliament   40
  Act in Conditional Restraint of
      Annates   43
  Act Extinguishing the Authority
      of the Bishop of Rome   53
  Act in Restraint of Appeals   44
  Act of Succession   46, 47, 53
  Act of Supremacy   47, 128
  High Treasons Act   47
  Submission of the Clergy   44, 46
Renard, Simon   103, 146, 155
Ridley, Nicholas   133, 134, 135

Rochester, bishop of   *see* Fisher,
    John
Sack of Rome   37, 204
Sadoleto, Cardinal Jacopo   29,
    43, 47, 54, 69, 72, 73, 74, 84,
    172, 209
Sampson, Richard   51
Sauli, Cardinal Bendinello   9, 28,
    204
Sauli, Stefano   28, 29, 30, 205
Scotti, Bernardino   152
Select Council   149, 155, 156
Seripando, Girolamo   81, 210
Seymour, Edward Duke of
    Somerset   92, 98, 130
Seymour, Jane   53, 55, 62, 161
Simnel, Lambert   15, 16
Soto, Pedro de   135, 155
Soranzo, Vittorio   82, 204
Spirituali, the   75, 76, 77, 78,
    112, 121, 171, 183, 196, 197,
    198, 199, 200, 203, 204, 206
Stafford, Edward   *see* Duke of
    Buckingham
Stafford, Henry
  marriage to Ursula Pole   20
  under Edward VI   160
  under Mary Tudor   160
Stafford, Thomas   114, 153, 161
Stella, Bartolomeo   184, 196, 200
Starkey, Thomas   71
  accompanies Pole to Paris   40
  chaplain to Margaret Pole   49
  Padua   30, 188
  reaction to *De Unitate*   53, 55,
      57, 190
  requests opinion on divorce   42,
      49
  royal chaplain   49
  secretary to Pole   48
Synod of English bishops   109–11

Ten Articles 56
Throckmorton, Michael 53, 54,
    61, 92, 188
Tomeo, Nicolò Leonico 26, 27,
    29, 30, 50
*Trattato utilissimo del beneficio
    di Gesu Cristo crocifisso verso
    i Cristiani* *see Beneficio di
    Cristo, Il*
Treaty of Barcelona 39
Treaty of Toledo 62, 66
Tremelli, Emanuele 77
Trent, Council of 55, 61, 73, 74,
    79, 80, 81, 85, 109, 110, 210,
    201, 211
Tunstall, Cuthbert 54, 57, 62, 190

Valdés, Juan de 74, 76, 78, 172,
    173, 174
Vaughan, William 61
Vermigli, Pietro Martire *see*
    Martyr, Peter

Vaga, Perino del 205

Warbeck, Perkin 16
Warham, William Archbishop of
    Canterbury 44
Warwick, Edward of
  birth 14
  claim to the throne 14
  execution 16, 17, 18, 19
  imprisonment 15
  reversal of attainder 96
Winter, Thomas 27, 188, 189
Wolsey, Cardinal Thomas 20, 27,
    32, 36, 37, 38, 39, 40, 41, 44,
    72, 188
Wyatt's Rebellion 104–5, 133, 162
Wyatt, Sir Thomas 60, 62, 65, 69,
    87
Wyatt, Thomas the younger 104

Zelanti, the 75, 82
Zormosa, Martin de 48